The person charging this material is responsible for its return to the library from which it was withdrawn on or before the **Latest Date** stamped below.

Theft, mutilation, and underlining of books are reasons for disciplinary action and may result in dismissal from the University.

UNIVERSITY OF ILLINOIS LIBRARY AT URBANA-CHAMPAIGN

L161—O-1096

EDUCATION FOR AN OPEN SOCIETY

Prepared by the ASCD
1974 Yearbook Committee

Delmo Della-Dora and James E. House
Co-Chairpersons and Co-Editors

Association for Supervision and Curriculum Development
Suite 1100, 1701 K Street, N.W., Washington, D.C. 20006

CONTENTS

FOREWORD

THE ASCD TRADITION of publishing distinguished yearbooks retains and increases its luster in *Education for an Open Society*. In the perspective of the past quarter century, the volume emerges as a capstone in the structure of social change and more humane interpersonal relationships which our Association has striven to design since its inception in the mid-1940's.

Readers will discover that our "open society" yearbook performs two functions. It is both a statement of belief and a specific policy guide. Part One, in crisply measured prose, reviews some of the progress made toward an open society during the past two decades. It clearly delineates the exasperatingly slow but important gains that have been registered since the Supreme Court decision of 1954 initiated progress toward a desegregated education for children and youth in the United States.

Part Two deals with some of the basic problems and concepts with which ASCD has striven to cope since—at the very least—the late 1950's and early 1960's. The four chapters strongly suggest our potential ability as a professional group to deal with racism, the problem of creating better media, the improvement of teacher education, and the remaking of faulty curriculum practices. At the same time the authors leave us in no doubt as to the need to retain our discontent with the status of "things as they are" in 1974.

The use of power in an open society, the focal point for the third section of the yearbook, faces squarely the implications of developments in the 1960's and early 1970's: the problems and paradoxes of "power" and its important emerging components. While the readers are led to recognize the dangers of centrifugal forces in the culture as they read Part Three, they also are sensitized to the "centripetal potential": the potential for a more solidly and meaningfully united society.

Unlike some concluding sections, the chapter which concludes the yearbook really *does* serve as a "wind up" section in the sense that a well-coiled spring powers a clock. It is less a concluding statement than a manifesto suggesting desirable alternative routes that lead to more open social living in tomorrow's world.

In fine, to express appreciation and to offer congratulations to the yearbook team on behalf of the ASCD membership and Washington staff is almost to risk trivializing the first-rate piece of work produced under the leadership of the co-editors and the authors. Simply let me say that in my opinion we again have a portentous and useful yearbook developed in the ASCD tradition of editorial craftsmanship by both the authors and Robert R. Leeper and his associates: Teola T. Jones, Nancy Olson, Mary Albert O'Neill, and Lana Pipes.

Indiana University   HAROLD G. SHANE, *President 1973-74*
January 1974   Association for Supervision and
                                        Curriculum Development

PREFACE

IN THE SPRING of 1971, Norman Drachler, Chairman of the ASCD Commission on Ethnic Bias in Instructional Materials, presented an outline for a proposed ASCD Yearbook which would discuss the consequences of the U.S. Supreme Court decision of 1954. Such a book was to have a working title of *Brown v. Topeka: Twenty Years Later.* It would deal with our country's progress toward the ideal of racially integrated public schools.

The ASCD Executive Council gave tentative approval to this concept for the 1974 Yearbook but raised some questions about the scope of the proposed book. The Council appointed us to be co-chairpersons of the 1974 Yearbook Committee and asked us to submit a revised outline with a broader outlook. We did so and also recommended appointment of other members to the Yearbook Committee who would represent various regions of the U.S.A. and who, in composite, represented a wide range of experiences at all levels in working with multiethnic issues.

These were James Banks (Seattle), Dan Dodson (Georgetown, Texas), Lucia James (College Park, Maryland), and Clare Broadhead (San Rafael, California). (All members of the committee became contributors to this volume.) In addition, we invited others to be authors also: Samuel Ethridge and Boyd Bosma (NEA's Human Relations Division), LaMar Miller (Director of New York University's Institute for Afro-American Affairs), R. Bruce Irons (University of North Carolina at Charlotte), Barbara Sizemore (formerly Associate Secretary of AASA, now Superintendent, Washington, D.C. schools), Leon Met (Project Coordinator, Student Leadership Center in Cincinnati), David Selden (President, AFT), Charles Billings (Professor of Politics, New York University), and Deborah Partridge Wolfe (Professor of Education, Queens College, New York). It has been a capable and stimulating group of authors, to whom we extend our heartfelt thanks at this time. We would also like to thank William C. Miller, Deputy Superintendent, Wayne County Intermediate School District, Michigan, for assisting with the final editing.

The final outline approved for the Yearbook (and which we have followed in its writing) broadened the major issue to the one of opening the society for *all* people—but particularly for those who have not been properly represented heretofore. This, of course, refers to all racial and ethnic minorities, women, poor people, young people; and others as well. The questions we have tried to address in this volume are:

• What has been happening during the past 20 years? How open is our society to all its members?

• What has been going on within the education establishment to promote or inhibit the growth of an open society?

• How can *power* be exercised in a society to maintain or create openness?

• What can we look forward to and what can we suggest to help those who are interested in seeing to it that the U.S.A. becomes a truly open society?

Much of the material in Chapters 1-12 was first drafted one or two years ago. Rapid changes in our social order have necessitated updating of material until the moment of this writing. For example, Watergate is just unfolding in the public media as we write the final chapter and complete our editing activities. We have a feeling that a looseleaf notebook, rather than a hardbound book, might have been more appropriate to keep it up to date with the current social scene.

We are very much caught up in the changes we write about, and it is difficult to maintain a long-term perspective as a result. The forces at work for an open society *and* for a closed society are powerful. The issues are volatile. This is an exciting period in the history of our country and editing such a volume has been both *exciting*—and *disturbing*—to us. We hope that the book will be as valuable to those who read it as it has been to all of us who helped produce it.

DELMO DELLA-DORA *and* JAMES E. HOUSE
Co-Chairpersons and Co-Editors
ASCD 1974 Yearbook Committee

PART 1

MOVEMENT TOWARD AN OPEN SOCIETY, 1954-1974

AN OPEN SOCIETY "lets people come from wherever they are" and gives everyone equal opportunity for access to what they want from that society. It prizes differences and diversities. During the past 20 years, we have seen some evidence of movement toward an open society, but the gains have been slow and the pace uneven. There is always resistance to change and a sincere desire to maintain our institutions in a stable condition. However, we cannot deny that obvious changes have been made in areas such as sexism and greater freedom of expression in all types of media. Still there is much to be done in improving the quality of man's relationship to man. The initial chapter sets the stage for this Yearbook as it presents a general review of the gains and setbacks in moving toward an open society.

The authors of Chapter 2 (Bosma, Ethridge) then examine one dimension of an open society, integration of the schools, during the period 1954-1973. Unfortunately, the dual school systems are still a part of the American scene, but they need not be. Some people believe that the present furore about busing will seriously delay the elimination of dual school systems. They may be right. It has been 20 years since the landmark Supreme Court decision sounded the clarion on unequal education opportunity. The 1954 *Brown* v. *Board of Education of Topeka* decision declared that a "separate but equal" education for black and white students was unacceptable. The writers of Chapter 2 give a vivid and candid description of the impact of the 1954 decision on the schools and society. Even though fewer black and white students attend school together now than in 1954, there is evidence of significant gains. A look at the 1954 court decision 20 years later should cause each of us to ask, "What would going to school and participating in society be like today if we had resolutely implemented the Supreme Court decision?"

CHAPTER 1: EDUCATION FOR AN OPEN SOCIETY

DELMO DELLA-DORA and JAMES E. HOUSE

TWENTY YEARS HAVE passed since the *Brown* v. *Topeka* decision ordering schools to integrate with all deliberate speed. A large number of Americans are still hostile to that idea, and the dream of an integrated society has faded. That dream has been replaced by the bleak reality, highlighted by the Kerner Commission report, that our nation's racial polarization is growing more widespread and intense.

What Is an Open Society?

The whole concept of an "integrated society" was based on at least one spurious assumption, however, even among those who wanted racial justice. It was the "melting pot" concept that aimed at mixing all the exotic ingredients of races and ethnic backgrounds represented among the people of America into one bland homogeneous mass. This concept of an "integrated" society would, in effect, not only strip all people from the ties of their cultural background, but substitute for it the value systems and life styles of white middle class Americans.

The viewpoint of this yearbook is that the schools should help our nation become an "open society" in which a variety of cultures, value systems, and life styles not only coexist but are nurtured. The concern in such a society would not be on the numbers of blacks and whites in each school, for example, but on the nature and quality of their relationships, whatever the percentages. The major concern of the society at large, and of the schools in particular, would be for full participation of all human beings with rights which are not dependent on race, ethnicity, sex, or social class. Individual and group differences would be prized, not merely accepted or grudgingly tolerated, and every person would have equal access to what they want from and can give to the society. Societal institutions (including the schools) would establish or reinforce an ethos that differences in perception, diversity of values, and variety of life styles are valuable and rewarding.

Where Are We Now?

The kind of open society described here does not exist now, except perhaps among small circles of friends in various places around the world. However, we believe that an open society *can* come into being in this country and *must* come into being as an alternative to the accelerating drift toward a police state which we have been experiencing for a number of years.

Not *all* movement has been to the right in recent years. At the moment we are enjoying relatively great freedom of expression in movies, dress, hair style, writing, sexual relationships, and marriage. The role of women in our society is receiving greater attention and the beginnings of some positive changes for women in regard to jobs and other life relationships are becoming evident. There is a minor outbreak of "alternative schools" and "alternative programs," most of which are just new organizational forms with no substance, but some of which foster open society concepts. There is also, at least for this moment, a healthy amount of civil disobedience which has not been completely repressed.

Some of the major blocks to achievement of an open society are manifested by racism, sexism, social class barriers, concentration of economic power, and the whole concept of a hierarchy of human worth. The "hierarchy" concept is an overarching theme within our own society currently and in most (if not all) societies of the world. It seems to have been part of the history of all humankind. In the language of some psychologists it is a "pecking order" syndrome. In the language of liberals, it is "lack of equal opportunity" and in the language of the revolutionaries it is "the oppressor and the oppressed." Whatever the language, the result is the same. That is, some arbitrary basis is used to sort and classify humans into more worthy and less worthy categories.

The bases for so doing have most often been sex, race, ethnicity, education, family background, wealth, religion, or occupation. Stereotypes are established for the categories and everyone in that category is "guilty" of fitting the stereotypic model or at least "guilty" until proven "innocent." The need to dominate as an outlet for sexual aggression is postulated as the basis for one of these phenomena, namely racism and racial prejudice in our country. White psychiatrist Joel Kovel sets forth this viewpoint in his book, *White Racism: A Psychohistory*. [1] The same general thesis was developed earlier in somewhat different terms by black historian Winthrop Jordan in his award-winning *White Over Black*. [2] Whatever the reasons, institutional racism, accompanied by racial prejudice and discrimination, is with us and still growing.

Some of the other factors which stand as obstacles to achieving an open society seem to be growing in strength also. For example, the concentration of economic power into the hands of fewer people in the U.S.A., and in the world, has been well-documented by conservatives as well as liberals many times in recent years. Women are still under-employed, paid less than males for comparable work, treated as mentally and/or emotionally inferior by most males, and are barely represented in state or national government in the legislative, executive, or judicial branches.

The number of newspapers and magazines in circulation, particularly the larger ones, has dropped sharply in recent years, and with proposed increases in postal rates we can expect the decline to continue. Most of those that remain attempt to be noncontroversial, at best, or to reflect the viewpoints of those in positions of power, with some notable exceptions.

Recent appointees to the U.S. Supreme Court and those who will be appointed through 1976 are likely to be narrow "constructionists" in interpreting the U.S. Constitution, and this majority will be with us for the next 15-20 years.

The interrelationship of big business and the military becomes closer as larger numbers of military men "retire" to big business—which in turn does a bigger dollar volume of business with the military every year. The advent of a volunteer army does nothing to assuage anxiety about militaristic influences, for we now face the spectre of our first large standing army of professionals instead of a small professional corps which is bolstered by a citizens' army in times of emergency.

Attacks by the executive branch on the press and television and the growth in the power of the Presidency have reached new heights. This does not seem to augur well in fostering a climate for diversity of viewpoints.

The 1972 national election provided the spectacle of Big Labor and Big Business supporting the same ends in ways not as evident as

[1] Joel Kovel. *White Racism: A Psychohistory.* New York: Pantheon Books Inc., 1970.

[2] Winthrop Jordan. *White Over Black.* Chapel Hill: University of North Carolina Press, 1968.

in past years. The top officials of the labor movement are affluent and are behaving more and more like their counterparts in business. The many major factors working *against* an open society have been reviewed here, and so have the few factors which seem to be working *toward* such a society.

There are other forces which could go either way. Among these are the various power blocs which have emerged since the 1930's, such as organized labor (particularly teachers organizations), black power groups, community control advocates, student rights groups, and women's liberation forces. The initial thrust of all power blocs is to win rights for their adherents, sometimes at the expense of other groups. This kind of "zero-net-sum competition" is the old-fashioned "dog-eat-dog" idea that if someone wins, someone else must lose. Quite often, however, the power has been used to help many others gain their rights as well, as exemplified by the NAACP and the United Auto Workers. What needs to be done with power and authority in this country in the future? Can and will such power and authority be used to create a more open society? The questions and some answers are provided in Chapters 7 through 12 by Dan Dodson, Barbara Sizemore, Charles Billings, David Selden, Leon Met, and Deborah P. Wolfe.

The judiciary has been a major, perhaps the single most powerful, force in recent years in freeing up the society. What will happen now with changes in the U.S. Supreme Court composition? News analysts predict a movement away from individual rights, and there seems to be ample reason to believe this may happen. There is, however, some hope that this may not occur if we examine what happened to men like Justice Hugo Black after his appointment. There is also some hope in knowing that the men who serve are often responsive to the social and political climate of the day.

The interpretations of *Brown* v. *Topeka* have not all been to the benefit of black people or other minority groups, as Bosma and Ethridge point out in Chapter 2. Court orders are still preoccupied with integration on a *quantitative* (percentage of whites and blacks) basis and ignore the *qualitative* bases in terms of relationships among students, among staff, among parents, and also among all these groups. The nine men at the top and all the other men and women in the federal judiciary will continue to influence the openness of our society in major ways. There is no way of really predicting what those ways will be, but the election of a U.S. President who is committed to an open society would obviously increase the number of judges and justices of a similar disposition.

The largest major power potential is in the "grass-roots democracy" movements like those inspired, or led, by some college students, Rosa Parks, Martin Luther King, Jr., Saul Alinsky, and hundreds of lawyers in federally sponsored community action programs. Many of the activist college students of the 1960's are now safely back in their middle class niches. Rosa Parks lives quietly in Detroit. Dr. King and Saul Alinsky are dead. Federal funds for grass-roots community action programs are gone. Somewhere the power is still out there, waiting to be tapped, and not just by John Gardner's uncommon "Common Cause." There are thousands of people who really do want to work for and live in a liberated society. It may all come together for enough people to make the grass-roots forces our major vehicle for change. Or maybe we watched too many Frank Capra movies as we were growing up. For example, the ones in which Jimmy Stewart is an innocent boob elected to political office, discovers he is being used by the political bosses and *their* bosses, then tells THE PEOPLE and they turn the rascals out. It is a good script. We need to use it in real life.

How Do We Move Toward an Open Society?

What do we do about all this? Given a desired direction for the society and some notions about the forces working for and against such movement, who does what to make it all happen? Specifically what do we do as professional educators? Obviously some changes are in order in teacher education along the lines proposed by Irons (Chapter 6). In addition, those already on the job need to work on changes in the curriculum (Banks, Chapter 4) and instructional materials (Miller, Chapter 5).

Most of all, however, we need to rediscover that educational systems are not neutral in the movements that determine what the U.S.A. will look like in the near future. Scientists once considered their work to be of the highest intellectual order—amoral, objective, pure, untainted by political considerations or other base human behaviors. That was before Hiroshima and Nagasaki. Scientists then discovered that human values determine human endeavors. So it must be with us as educators.

An open society is more likely to come into being if teachers and administrators want it to and also if we work for it. Those who believe that the schools are not to be involved in social change and that educators must keep out of the arena of social action are really arguing that education and educators should preserve all the oppressive forces which currently exist. For example, all the teachers who use the biased textbooks are helping instill racist and sexist concepts. They share this responsibility with the administrators and supervisors who help select the texts and with the authors and publishers. Typically, we say, "What can we do about it when all those political and economic powers are at work?" Consider the answer of Rosa Parks who decided she was too tired to stand in the back of the bus and therefore sat in front. How long would those textbooks continue to be published and purchased if just a few teachers in each school said, "I refuse to use tainted textbooks! Give me a proper text and I'll use it"?

As a group, the Association for Supervision and Curriculum Development is the only major national education organization which is function oriented rather than job oriented. Implicit in our operation is the belief that "leadership" roles do not necessarily relate to job titles. Teachers can be curriculum leaders and so can supervisors, administrators, students, and parents. All of us can act singly on our beliefs to help liberate ourselves and each other. We can also do some things together through state units and at the national level. The most effective actions, however, may be those in which each of us does what can be done in matters which we control or directly influence. Establishing and carrying out affirmative action policies in hiring, firing, and promotion is something that every person who reads this can affect in some way, to cite just one example.

Sidney Simon and associates have done some work in values clarification which offers a model for action by every member of ASCD. It comes to this:

• *Find out for yourself what you believe in.* Is the kind of open society described in this book one you want to live in?

• *Affirm your beliefs publicly.* Say what you believe in every situation regardless of whether it is likely to be popular and even if it is very unpopular.

• *Act positively on your beliefs so that your beliefs and behavior are consistent with each other as often as possible.*

• *Help others to clarify their own values, affirm them, and act on them.*

There are, and continue to be, problems with people who hold values that are at odds with each other. Acting on mine may deprive you of acting on yours or vice-versa. The challenge of a truly open society will be to find ways of having differing value systems coexist. The dynamics of such a society will be frustrating to most, impossible to cope with for others. What higher order can we hope for than one in which men and women are working as hard to provide maximum freedom for others as for themselves? It combines the best elements of selfishness and selflessness. It used to be called "enlightened self-interest." Call it what you will. Working for and living in an open society is to make of each of us what we are capable of being—exciting, stimulating, thinking, feeling, wholly alive beings, living to the full limits of our potential.

We feel, as does Margaret Mead, that "Our future is not determined for us already. We can determine it for ourselves—from the small details of social evolution to the large details of cosmic evolution." [3]

We can have social order without building *a* social order. Who says we cannot have *several* political and social systems that exist simultaneously with great diversity? Do you? Shed that cynicism and fear. It's past time to be doing what has never been done before. Let's not calculate odds for success before venturing. A bookmaker's mentality will not produce an open society. Commitment to the values of an open society and living those values *will* do so.

[3] Quoted by David Perlman in June 19, 1973, article in the *San Francisco Chronicle*.

CHAPTER 2:
BROWN V. TOPEKA: TWENTY YEARS LATER
TWO PERSPECTIVES

1. BOYD BOSMA

Perspective 1.

CERTAINLY FEW PERSONS expected the change to take place overnight. Yet how easy it might have been by comparison had federal and state authorities been willing to move more promptly to bring into reality the constitutional ideals of *Brown* v. *Topeka*, that "separate but equal" education for black and white students was unacceptable.

By any reasonable standards black schools in the South were inferior in 1954, at least in the sense of physical condition, economic resources, and support from the existing power structures. The few improvements made during the period of the early 1950's (the general facelifting, the consolidations, the token improvements, the new buildings often several miles out in the country) were usually little more than reflexive actions to delay change and to maintain the pretense of "separate but equal" in the face of the burgeoning legal battles.

Desegregation then appeared to be a viable alternative, perhaps the only one, that might offer long-range solutions to the drastic inequality in distribution of educational and material resources. The objective of obtaining a bigger piece of the educational pie for black students was thoroughly understandable, and for many it was a time for optimism.

The Intermediate Effects of the 1954 Decision

In retrospect, later events must be judged in light of the failure of enforcement of the 1955 "all deliberate speed" order intended to implement the *Brown* decision. That order, well-intentioned though it was, represented a compromise at best and left open a number of issues which still plague the nation's schools today. It failed to require immediate action at all levels of the dual school systems, and also failed to provide penalties for noncompliance. The 1955 decision resulted in laying the base for the massive resistance movement, in the development of guidelines requiring an absolute minimum of compliance, in the protracted delay of enforcement efforts and litigation, and ultimately in the spread of Northern patterns of segregated housing and neighborhood schools in many Southern communities for the first time.

Perhaps the most important failure of the post-1954 legal efforts was found in the adoption of federal standards which defined desegregation and inequality primarily as a "Negro" problem and ignored the effects of racial isolation and discrimination on white youngsters in schools which continued to tolerate injustice. Where white parents failed to identify their own self-interest in educational reform and the movement toward equality in distribution of educational resources, they became prey for the haters and fearmongers and exploiters who so successfully helped to divide the nation around the question of school desegregation and "busing."

Even today the federal reports emphasize the proportions of black students in either majority-black or majority-white schools. This gives unwonted credence to the false assumption that majority-black schools are of necessity inferior and permits those who really control the schools to escape accountability by pretending the problem is that of the victims, and not one of misfeasance, malfeasance, or nonfeasance by those in authority. This approach suggests that "if a school is white, it's all right," and minority students are automatically placed in the undesirable position of being intruders as well as being outnumbered.

In the absence of programs which dealt effectively with the consequences of racial isolation of white as well as of black students, desegregation came to mean many things inconsistent with the hopes engendered in 1954: one-way busing of black students; the closing of black schools; the elimination of black symbols, trophies, awards, pictures, and heroes; demotion and dismissal of black authority figures, including principals, teachers, coaches, band instructors, counselors, and others; and a widespread range of retaliatory actions against black students and educators alike as white reaction crystallized and as the few progressive educators who had sought change either ran for cover or lost their jobs. In too many communities the forces of reaction sought to exclude blacks from the schools rather than to encourage their participation in building better communities.

Virtually any action involving fundamental social change, especially one of such magnitude as school desegregation, sets off a range of reactions affecting related issues. When leaders failed to foresee the consequences of the single-minded efforts to put black and white students together in classrooms without providing necessary sanctions to protect their rights and without preparing students, educators, and the communities for the changes to come, the field remained free for the forces of reaction to shift from one defensive—or offensive—posture to another in turning aside the mandate for change.

How much simpler might it have been had the definition of a unitary school meant one in which we could look beyond the numbers and percentages to the removal of the last vestiges of the dual system of segregation and to the provision of educational programs which could fairly and adequately meet the educational needs of every student! What if the authorities had earlier recognized the unconstitutionality of actions which placed the "burden" of change on only one segment of the community? What might the schools be like today had we had the courage to recognize the fantastic opportunity to begin to move toward genuine educational reform throughout the nation? What if it had been possible to focus the debate, rather than on the misleading code word "busing," on the alternative means for bringing real equality of educational opportunity and the most favorable possible educational conditions in schools where integrated education could mean a quality of openness and opportunity for all?

While the results are not yet in on the numbers of black teachers, principals, coaches, and others who lost their positions as the schools began to desegregate, we do know that such displacement became physically visible as desegregation moved across the South, and that it continues today, although in less obvious forms. The first large impact after 1954 was seen in the border states, and when the pace was stepped up with the adoption of the HEW guidelines for desegregation in 1964, the trickle of dismissals became a stream, with the torrent yet to come as the states of the Deep South (Louisiana, Mississippi, Georgia, Alabama, North Carolina, and South Carolina) found themselves under increasing federal pressure, largely from the courts, after 1968.

Displacement of Black Educators

The initial educator displacements usually occurred in small rural communities where inefficient, often decrepit one- and two-room schools were closed, with pupils transferred and teachers dismissed. At first, national attention focused on the beginning attempts to desegregate the city school systems of the border states, later turning to the more dramatic confrontations, including "massive resistance" and "blocking the schoolhouse door." Few outside those most directly involved were able to perceive the extreme educational, social, and economic hardships as black teachers and principals were eliminated in those communities where they represented the mainstay of black educational achievement, community leadership, and professional aspiration.

So long as there remained a shortage of teachers nationally and a continued demand for black teachers in the segregated schools of the South, the problems were less immediately obvious. When the public schools of Prince Edward County, Virginia, for example, were closed from 1959 through 1964 to avoid desegregation, almost forgotten were the 63 black teachers who lost their jobs and were forced either to give up their teaching careers or to move elsewhere, sacrificing friends, homes, and property.

Acquisition of accurate data on educator displacement has been difficult for a variety of reasons. Racial data were simply not collected between 1954 and 1964. Most displaced, dismissed, or demoted educators, for a variety of reasons, did not attract the attention of authorities and agencies who might have helped. Among these reasons were fear of harassment, intimidation, or retaliation; the hope that somehow "things would work out"; unmerited reliance on white authorities for assistance; the hope of obtaining other employment without being blacklisted as a troublemaker or receiving a negative recommendation from the former employer. There was also fear of transfer to other positions, sometimes with higher pay and more impressive titles but with less real authority, less contact with students. There was also a common lack of awareness of or confidence in available sources of assistance.

At least 5,000 classroom teachers had been dismissed by 1970.[1] In fact, through such factors as nonreplacement of teachers who resigned or retired, through hiring practices which favored whites through transfer of regularly certified teachers to federally-supported programs, the actual displacement was much higher. Samuel B. Ethridge and Donald Shire conducted a study of such displacement, using the number of pupils and the average teacher-pupil ratio for 1970 to project the number of black teachers who would have been employed had school boards continued to hire at a rate which reflected the number of black

---

[1] Testimony of Samuel B. Ethridge before the Senate Select Committee on Equal Educational Opportunity, June 23, 1970.

pupils. They reported a projected loss of 31,584 teaching positions for the 17 states with former dual school systems.[2]

Patterns of misassignment, loss of status and salary, inability to relocate, infringement on civil and human rights, unethical and discriminatory practices, new and unfair evaluation procedures, and arbitrary terminations of employment have been the costs paid by individual black teachers and principals. The ultimate costs for black communities and for the society as a whole will be felt for generations to come.

The failure to monitor and enforce federal program guidelines has been a major factor in actions leading to dismissal of or loss of security for thousands of educators. When Title I of the Elementary and Secondary Education Act of 1965 provided massive funds for compensatory education, many black educators were reassigned as "Title I," "project," or "ESEA" teachers, with contract provisions calling for dismissal when federal funds were terminated. The search for "objective" guidelines for selecting teachers to be dismissed when staff was "reduced" after desegregation led to the massive adoption of cutoff requirements on the National Teacher Examination across the South, resulting in unfair and arbitrary dismissals of hundreds of successful teachers. When legal challenges began to cut in on the mass dismissals, school boards in many cases went through the motions of due process as the dismissals continued.

Part of the answer to these problems may come when the courts and federal agencies require the maintenance of fair employment standards, elimination of discriminatory tests such as the NTE, and assignment of effective responsibility for monitoring and enforcement to state authorities who can be held accountable. In the long term, the abilities of black teachers themselves to organize both for their own protection and toward the achievement of professional objectives will be of utmost importance—along with identifying and acting on their common interests with students, parents, and communities in seeking educational reform.

Problems Related to Busing and Its Effect on Black Students

The national controversy over busing offered untold occasions for opportunism among politicians willing to stem the broad progressive changes which have come about since 1954. As a device for rallying public opposition to expenditures for public education as well as to

[2] Samuel B. Ethridge, in a statement before the NAACP Legal Defense Fund Law Institute, New York, May 19, 1972.

integration, the busing issue has had no peers. No matter that busing is the safest way to travel to school, no matter that it is often the best and most convenient means to achieve legal desegregation, no matter that students may now move to better schools and opportunities; the cities of the nation have been held in bondage as the debate has raged on. As of this writing, the final verdicts in many of the city cases are not yet in, but the damage that has been done must be seen as a factor in the success of attacks on poverty and social welfare programs of all types, in reducing the flow of funds for educational opportunities for the most needy children, and in moving the nation away from the lofty ideals and aspirations typifying the civil rights movement of the 1960's.

Of first concern must be the effects of desegregation on students themselves, those who offer the hope for our future. Their interests and needs have often been ignored as adults have carried on their own battles.

Having seen their teachers so often dismissed or placed in subordinate positions, many black youngsters no longer look to careers in education as a means either for social advancement or for making their career contributions to achievement of a better society. Students have been bused across town to attend largely segregated classes, made that way because of discriminatory testing, tracking, and assignment to "remedial" programs. Many now wonder if it was worth the trouble as they observe the loss of social activities, cheerleaders, proms, symbols, trophies, and their identification with their former schools.

In predominantly black parts of the South, and in many of the cities now being desegregated, black students have observed the furore over busing and have noted the numbers of white children moving to private segregated academies, parochial schools, and more traditional private schools. They observe the resegregation of the cities, and they move toward patterns of resistance—militancy, hostility, apathy, disobedience, conflict, dropping out.

Students become painfully aware that much-ballyhooed programs often have results exactly the opposite of their stated purposes. They distrust compensatory programs, vocational education, and career education, for example, because the opportunities for resegregation and for further controlling the life opportunities of both black and white students are becoming increasingly apparent.

The serious problem of displacement of black and other minority students from schools across the nation as a corollary to school desegregation has gone largely unnoticed. Continuing reports of massive suspensions, expulsions, and "force-outs" are leading national organizations to renew their interest and efforts in behalf of those whom the desegregation movement was supposed to have helped.

Violence and school conflict, boycotts, demonstrations, protests, and arrests occasionally make the headlines. Yet few notice those districts where the boycotts have continued for months, even for years, inadequately reported because of local news blackouts and indifference or hostility of public officials, community leaders, and others. There is no way we can accurately measure the number of black, Chicano, Puerto Rican, Indian, or white students who daily are suspended, expelled, or driven out of the schools because of arbitrary, discriminatory actions of school authorities. Who can measure the educational results in the face of the problems associated with school desegregation? The general absence of mechanisms for effective student involvement and for resolution of grievances across the nation is an important measure of the difficulties faced by students in getting a handle on the problems. While educators have often done an outstanding job in identifying desirable curriculum reforms, patterns of school organization, and technological advances, the promise of education for an open society, for improving the opportunities of all in the system, will remain as hostage until we can ensure that the consequences of the changes will not continue to force people out of the system.

In reality, there is substantial hope even yet. If we can provide enforcement and monitoring, if school officials can concentrate on expansion of educational opportunities and curriculum reform, if teachers can utilize their newfound organizational strength for progress, we may yet have a chance to bring about real integration, where there is respect for the rights of each person and where cultural values and contributions within a multicultural, pluralistic society are respected and honored. The *Brown* decision in 1954 offered the first real chance for this nation to move to save its own soul. The struggles and temptations have been difficult, but to turn our eyes away from the objectives of equality and opportunity for all would be to deny any chance for the future. And that we cannot afford.

2. SAMUEL B. ETHRIDGE

Perspective 2.

ONE REASON WE have failed to understand American history is that many early textbooks act as if nothing happened here prior to 1492. Likewise, I think we miss the impact of the *Brown* decision if we look at it from the narrow perspective of 1954. A greater appreciation might be assured by starting with 1944 or even 1934.

In 1934, I can remember getting up at 4:30 to walk a mile to catch the 5:30 a.m. school bus for the 30-mile ride to Southern Normal, a private school supported by the Dutch Reform Church. Even so, we considered ourselves lucky to live close enough to be bused. Children in the surrounding counties lived so far away that they had to leave home and family to live in the dormitory.

This is not to imply that there were no public schools in our community and the other Alabama communities to which I alluded. As a matter of fact there were a number of one-room (grades 1-6) schools available. And these could hardly be called "public" when the only thing supplied by the county was a very inadequate teacher's salary. More often than not, the building and the school land were donated by the community. Supplies and books were furnished by the parents. Upkeep, fuel, and janitorial services were the responsibility of the children and the teacher.

Pupil-teacher ratio in the public schools was one teacher and all the children in walking distance, minus those few who could afford the $1.50 a month tuition and transportation to the private schools, where they would find a library, science and home economics laboratories, brick buildings with spacious, well-manicured lawns, athletic fields, basketball and badminton courts, and teachers with degrees from Hampton, Tuskegee, and New York University.

In 1934, not more than a dozen of Alabama's 115 public school systems offered public education to black children beyond the tenth grade. Outside the metropolitan area, those black students wishing to complete high school had to go to a church-supported academy or to a college laboratory high school. Those who could not afford the board and tuition, and who did not happen to reside in a town near one of the academies or college-sponsored laboratory schools, simply had to go North or get a job. Nobody spoke about dropouts in those days. They were the rule, not the exception.

By 1944 at least five significant things had occurred or were under way which helped to influence the changes in education.

1. The draft had taken a higher proportion of whites to fill the monthly quotas because so many of the blacks were illiterate. The failure of the rural South to provide even a modicum of education came home to roost in an ironic and cruel way. Thus, mothers of white soldiers became advocates of teaching blacks at least to read and write.

2. The NAACP had placed before the courts a series of cases in higher education which held that equal education had to be provided at state expense; that it had to be provided within the state; that, where equal courses were not provided in the separate black college, black students had to be admitted to the formerly white university; and finally that equal education had to be provided *now*, not when separate facilities could be built. The NAACP then began to file a series of suits at the elementary and secondary school level which touched off panic among Southern school officials. Afraid that the courts would rule that districts with unequal schools would have to admit black students, these officials embarked on a building program from 1944 to 1954 that has been un-equaled in this century. Furthermore, the state boards set up a require-ment that black teachers must have bachelor's degrees, and many encouraged black teachers to acquire master's degrees. The states paid for out-of-state education at Columbia and Northwestern and other Northern and Eastern colleges and added graduate courses at the separate black colleges rather than admit blacks to Southern white universities.

3. The NAACP and the black teachers associations won a series of suits which brought equal pay, at least for beginning teachers, and some equity for even the more experienced black teachers and admin-istrators.

4. The Southern Association of Colleges and Secondary Schools began to apply a single standard to the accreditation of secondary schools and colleges and to undertake a long-range plan to merge the separate accreditation associations.

5. The GI Bill permitted large numbers of males to receive an

education and enter the teaching profession. These male students were independent both spiritually and financially, and unwilling to accept the paternalistic, domineering treatment which students on scholarship and work opportunity programs had to accept in order to remain in college. The GI's could take their trade elsewhere and they knew it. They opened the campuses to intellectual inquiry not only for themselves but also for the younger students, both male and female, who would join them as teachers in improving college education for the ever-increasing post-war baby boom.

Prior to this, male students from most black families had to help take care of the family and help finance the women students through school. Many of these veterans had been stationed in the U.S.A. outside the South and others had served with dignity and pride in many lands around the world.

The *Brown* decision thus came at a time of great ferment in many black communities in a period when education in the urban South was beginning to show some signs of quality. A higher percentage of black students were going to college, and many more scholarships and honors were being won. Parents and students were beginning to take pride in their teams, their bands, the modern physical plants, and in their dedicated corps of experienced teachers who were working hand in hand with the new young breed of tough-minded veterans and semi-liberated women teachers.

In many poor areas and rural areas, the delivery of public educational service was (and still is) inexcusably poor. Yet in many progressive rural communities, school consolidation had been under way for more than a decade. School consolidation in this context meant closing one- and two-room white schools and busing those children to a larger school in the white community, and closing the one- and two-room black schools and busing children from all over the county to the one county training school. In those days busing was a way of life. As a matter of fact, many communities with a sparse black population bused their black children across county lines and paid tuition to another district to educate their black students. Where distances were prohibitive, the districts often paid for black students to go to boarding school.

In 1954 black parents hailed the *Brown* decision because they thought this would stop their children's being bused past schools in their neighborhoods to more distant all-black schools. They thought that white children who were being bused out of the neighborhood would come to the predominantly black neighborhood school. They felt that the presence of whites in their schools would cause the central office to deal more fairly with these schools. The irony is that 20 years later, nothing has changed! Black children are being bused from their neighborhoods, but for different reasons. Black parents whose children have to ride excessive distances to white schools in white neighborhoods secretly (and some overtly) applaud the "liberal" whites and conservative whites who have taken up the black fight against the "yellow chariot." In some communities the bus is called the "pumpkin" which takes their "Cinderellas" to the palace by day but returns them to the chimney "ghetto" at the stroke of 3 p.m.

Because so many black parents had to walk long distances along unpaved dusty or muddy streets while being splashed by mud or choked by dust from buses reserved for their white neighbors, they tend to think of having a bus to ride as an improvement over walking in the rain and traffic. They tend to be more interested in what happens at the end of the bus ride rather than whether or not there is busing except where black children have an unfair and disproportionate share of the busing.

Early Desegregation Efforts

While in the preceding section, I pointed out that 1934 or 1944 would be a better time frame for looking at the effects of the *Brown* decision, 1964 could well be the time frame for most of the states. The doctrine of "massive resistance" coupled with the "freedom of choice" movement effectively prevented desegregation in most of the 11 deep-South states until after the passage of the Civil Rights Act of 1964.

In my opinion the greatest error of the 20 year period was made in 1955, when the court explained the 1954 decision using the phrase "all deliberate speed." Most school administrators thought the court had intended the immediate end to the dual system. Anticipating a strong order, some administrators had secretly redrawn school lines in a way that would create a unitary school system with children attending the nearest school based on capacity. As a matter of fact, many school systems had for five years prior to 1954 set out on a plant equalization program for blacks that would meet the standards of white parents in the zone and reduce the tendency of black parents to transfer their children to the predominantly white school.

Because the housing patterns of most Southern communities at that time were much more integrated than in communities of the North, rezoning in 1954 would have offered adequate desegregation of schools in all but a few neighborhoods.

The era of all deliberate speed and free choice allowed Southern city residents ample time to move from predominantly black communities, time to remove some black communities via the interstate freeway, also called urban renewal, commonly referred to by blacks as "Negro removal." Now most large Southern cities have sufficiently copied their Northern sisters to plead for the more dignified de facto status.

If the courts had asked for ending the dual system forthwith in 1954, white people would not have had time to move, free choice might not have been invented, and massive resistance would not have had time to gain strength. This is not to say that there would not have been some difficult situations. But in my opinion the courts misjudged the willingness of parents to accept, as well as the ability of school officials to carry out, their mandate. HEW repeated this mistake in 1964 and 1965.

Many school superintendents welcomed the opportunity to be relieved of the necessity to attend two principals' meetings, two faculty meetings, two book selection committees, two PTA councils, two curriculum committees, two in-service committees, two teachers associations, two accreditation associations, two athletic associations, etc. In their less guarded moments, they would admit being glad to be relieved of the extra work. They looked forward to spending some time with their families instead of countless hours in needless duplication. But when the politicians stepped in with massive resistance, the secret maps for immediate integration disappeared. The superintendents became scared hired hands, embittered by their disappointment that the courts had left many of them "out on a limb." Superintendents who fought desegregation survived. Those who did what was right had their careers wrecked or shortened.

In many communities, the so-called "free choice" was not free at all. Exercising that option could bring economic or physical disaster. In one small community all the black parents decided to transfer their children under free choice. Employers were notified of their action. The transfer forms were recalled and new transfer forms were passed out. Only one student, the son of a local undertaker, signed up on the second go-round. Moreover, in those communities where a few students did volunteer to enter the previously "all-white" schools without overt intimidation from the white community, the volunteer students were intimidated by the black community. "They want to be white." "They think they are better than us." "Don't come down here to our school dances; go back to the integrated school." Thus, the black students found themselves unwelcome at the white school and ostracized in their own communities. This phenomenon tended to discourage if not halt the progress toward a unitary school system.

Another deterrent to "free choice" was teacher displacement. Whenever 30 black students exercised the "free choice" option to select an integrated school, one black teacher was displaced. If 300 students transferred, 10 teachers were displaced. Failure to transfer teachers tended to mobilize the black teachers and the black community against desegregation under "free choice." Black parents in some small towns refused to send their children to the former white school unless the judge ordered the black teachers transferred along with the children. They said that they were afraid for their children's safety among strangers. Thus, the absence of black teachers in white schools may have had another chilling effect on desegregation of pupils under "free choice."

Title VI of Civil Rights Act

If Title VI of the 1964 Civil Rights Act did nothing else, it effectively destroyed the so-called "free choice" myth and helped set standards which the judges copied and then surpassed. As accomplishments of the Civil Rights Act in areas other than education are examined with regard to the speed with which these other sectors responded, serious questions arise about the schools and their ability to lead.

Two weeks after the passage of the Act, hotels, lunchroom counters, and buses were doing business as if these doors had always been open. With all their faults, big business and the federal government began to seek out and hire minorities in positions of leadership. The schools responded by demoting black principals and firing black teachers.

Despite all the difficulties, the voting rights section of the Civil Rights Act was clearly operational within two years after its passage. Millions of people have already voted and hundreds of new officials serve in state houses, county courts houses, and city halls; while ten years later, most school districts still have not accepted the mandate of the Congress. Based on recent amendments for various education bills, the Congress tends to negate its own Act.

I am not being a Monday morning quarterback when I talk about mistakes which I feel the Office of Education made and other mistakes which were made by Congress and the school administrators. I said these same things in 1964, 1965, and 1966 that I say here.

I think the greatest mistake in the school arena was made by the Congress itself when it provided for cutting off funds to black kids, who need them most, when their all-white school boards (who could care less) refuse to obey the law of the land. It would have been better to "cut off" the school board by providing fines and jail sentences for failing to carry out their duty under the U.S. Constitution. Since the federal share of the public school budget was so small at that time (pre-ESEA 1965), cutting of federal funds was really a big joke.

The second big mistake in my opinion was made by the schoolmen themselves when they asked the Office of Education to draw up a set of guidelines to tell them how little they could do in order to get federal funds.

During the first year of Title VI, there were no guidelines. School systems were asked simply to submit a plan which satisfied the Commissioner of Education. It was ironic to hear people who had been able to maintain a 100 percent dual system crying and wringing their hands pretending they did not know how to dismantle it. Even then, many of us pleaded with USOE officials not to give them guidelines.

The Office of Education fell into the trap and set forth some guidelines and were immediately pounced upon by both sides. Civil rights groups criticized the guidelines for being too weak. School boards and politicians in the South criticized the guidelines for being too harsh.

But the Office of Education had already, in my opinion, made two big errors, long before it issued its guidelines. First, it started off the enforcement of Title VI with dual standards. School districts outside the 17 states covered by the *Brown* decision were permitted to file a form which said, "We do not discriminate." Within the 17 states, those districts under a court order and those districts having no black population were permitted to file a similar document. All other districts had to file a plan which satisfied the Commissioner that they would end the dual system within two years. I argued that the Act applied to all 50 states and that all systems should be required to prove nondiscrimination.

I know the reason for this decision. But I still disagree with it. The HEW staff had some serious doubts about the legality of the Act as it applies to schools, especially as it relates to schools which are de facto segregated. I thought the Office of Education should have done as the Commerce Department did: it should have taken the law to the courts immediately after passage and asked for a ruling. As a matter of fact, it was Jack Greenberg, Director of the NAACP Legal Defense Fund, who two years later took the Office of Education's Revised Guidelines of 1966 into the Fifth Circuit Court of Appeals and asked that these be used as minimum standards for all districts. Thanks to the NAACP Legal Defense Fund, the U.S. Office of Education finally found out that its guidelines were legal and enforceable.

A second action which I consider wrong, but which may not have been a bad strategy, was a deliberate decision by the Office of Education to make it easy for school systems to sign up and qualify for Title I and Title II ESEA funds. This was a deliberate gamble based on the assumption that a system which had never had a million dollars in federal funds would never miss having it cut off. On the other hand, it was felt that a system which had tasted what a million dollars would buy would be more likely to want to keep it and would more willingly meet tougher guidelines later.

When I met with the advisory committees which helped to shape the HEW Revised Guidelines of 1966, I had great concerns about requirement for certain percentages of students in each school. But since I had another agenda (seeing that a strong nondiscrimination in hiring clause was inserted), I did not vigorously argue my views on student desegregation.

I think that it is fair to point out that the Title VI people were sincere, dedicated, and anxious to carry out the law. They thought that they had a weak law; and they had very little staff to cover 50 states. The ones who tried hardest to carry out the law often found themselves transferred under pressure exerted by individual congressmen. Some of the more forceful ones were even summarily fired or forced to resign. Many of us would have followed a different course than the Title VI administrators did. For example, instead of spending a lot of time and energy on a few helpless little hard-core districts, many people think they should have taken on DeKalb and Atlanta, Houston and Dallas. With those victories behind them, the little districts would have been a bit more willing to obey the law and would have known that HEW's position was backed by the courts.

Despite the various political statements to the contrary, it appears that the Title VI operation has had some effect and that most school systems have, at least on paper, dismantled the dual system. Cutting off funds works with the "good guys" who want to do the right things. But it is totally inadequate for the "bad guys" who are more interested in maintaining the status quo than in securing adequate funds to provide quality education for children.

Beginning in 1971, enforcement under Title VI came to a standstill for all practical purposes. The Department of Health, Education, and Welfare, which is charged with enforcing the law, found itself on the other side when the NAACP Legal Defense Fund in *Adams* v. *Richardson* asked the court to require HEW to carry out the law of the land.

With the presence of four new Justices, appointed by President Richard Nixon, the Supreme Court is somewhat unpredictable. My guess is the Court will direct HEW to carry out the law of the land by requiring affirmative action on the part of the state departments of education. Based on the fine print in the Charlotte case, I have concluded that courts will relinquish jurisdiction of school cases in the very near future. This will probably be done by a simple declaration that the dual system of education has ended as of a specific date in those systems meeting criteria established by HEW. Systems not meeting those criteria will be put into receivership by the state. The U.S. district judges who for 20 years have been serving as super-superintendents will once again return to their pre-1954 pursuits.

Brown and the Open Society

Before 1954, when where one lived had very little to do with where one went to school, black and white and brown and white lived side by side in the South. But during the 10 years of massive resistance to the *Brown* decision, the white Southerner, taking a lesson from the book of his Northern brother, fled to the suburbs. Inasmuch as the housing patterns of 1972 were much more segregated than in 1952, the courts are blamed for that. Since 1954 careers for black professionals as secondary principals and head coaches have been practically eliminated and opportunities for black administrators in elementary and junior high schools have been reduced by more than 50 percent.

Opportunities for black students to participate in honor societies, cheering squads, proms; to reign as the Queen of May or as Homecoming Queen have been eliminated or seriously curtailed. Physical danger in hostile neighborhoods where blacks are bused has increased. Black parents feel left out or turned off by school administrators and many white parents. Fewer blacks receive athletic and academic scholarships, and smaller percentages of blacks graduate from the integrated schools. Black schools have been downgraded, closed, or renamed. Black students are expected to enjoy carrying the rebel flag and singing "Dixie." The struggle for integration has run head-on into the search for self-identity and pride in race and the struggle for political liberation.

From a narrow perspective of 10 years or even 20 years, one might have some second thoughts about the *Brown* decision. As a matter of fact, Roy Innis, president of the Congress on Racial Equality (CORE), is leading a movement to set up separate school districts with blacks as the majority and in control of the Board of Education. According to Innis, integration of schools has failed because the same people are in charge of the integrated systems as were in charge of the dual systems.

From a 40-year perspective, there can be no question about the effect of the 1954 decision on the quality of education and also on the quality of life in the South by virtue of a chain of events which it set off.

In 1934, a black child born in 95 percent of the counties in Alabama could not receive a public education beyond the tenth grade in any school, white or black. Now, in spite of the difficulties and odds against him, a black child in any county in the United States can expect 12 years of public schooling, even if the whites withdraw in protest of his coming. In 1934, in many counties only the whites enjoyed the luxury of a school bus at public expense. Now, black students are riding buses away from the neighborhood schools they originally tried to enter. If the various anti-busing amendments pass outlawing the school bus, black and white may be forced to walk together.

But the *Brown* decision was not really about schools. It was about the rights of first class citizens. It marked the beginning of a series of decisions about rights: (a) the right to equal educational opportunity; (b) the right to sit at a public lunch counter and be served; (c) the right to ride in the front as well as the back of a bus; (d) the right to be treated at a hospital; (e) the right to swim and play in a public park; (f) the right to sleep in a public inn; (g) the right to vote and have that vote counted; (h) the right to equality in employment practices; (i) the right to run for and to hold public office.

The South has not overcome many of its shortcomings, but it has without a doubt made a 180-degree turn since 1954. A person who moved from the South in 1954 and never returned until 1974 will experience cultural shock in every aspect of life from the moment of arrival to time of departure.

Viewed from the 40-year perspective, 20 years before *Brown* and 20 years after, the Supreme Court decision has had significant impact in improving the quality of life in the South and in the nation, not just for blacks but also for Chicanos, Asians, First Americans, Puerto Ricans, and women.

PART 2

THE EDUCATION ESTABLISHMENT
AND THE OPEN SOCIETY

IF THERE IS to be movement toward an open society, all of our major institutions must work in concert with each other. No phase of American life must be permitted to escape the pressure of opening options and choices for all of the people. The educational establishment has a major responsibility for creating and maintaining an open society.

American schools today are probably the chief contributors to institutional racism. Sexism and discrimination against the poor and against ethnic groups have most, if not all, of the same underlying characteristics as does racism. Schools which liberate their teachers and students from the constraints imposed by racism can also be liberating forces from all forms of domination which men and women unjustly impose on each other. The schools in an open society would be continually seeking to generate new alternatives for students. They would be self-renewing institutions which would not only be different from each other, but would foster differences within each school in the approaches used by staff and students for teaching and learning.

The operation of schools in such a society would be characterized by the principle that government and its institutions should seek to liberate men to live out their lives with maximum freedom of choice rather than to control, direct, or regulate people. The only limits to freedom for each individual would be the extent to which his actions interfere with freedom of choice by others.

Those who wrote chapters in Part Two focused on several areas of responsibility for the educational establishment. They describe the state of affairs in the areas of racism, the curriculum, instructional media, and teachers as professionals. There are also several exciting and innovative procedures suggested that will assist the educational establishment in moving toward an open society. According to our writers, there is still much work to be done within the educational establishment in order for the desired goals to be attained.

CHAPTER 3: OVERCOMING RACISM: THE ALTERNATIVES BEFORE US

CLARE A. BROADHEAD

THERE ARE TWO viable assumptions inherent in the title of this chapter. One is that racism prevails in our society, and therefore in our schools. The other is that something must be done about it and there are some choices to be made.

Our definition of *racism* is consistent with the concepts discussed in the previous and ensuing chapters: it refers to the institutional or societal practices which reflect the ability of the white power structure to discriminate systematically against blacks and other minorities. It is important to distinguish *racism* in this institutional or societal context from *prejudice* and *discrimination* as evidenced by an individual's attitudes and actions. A person can be racist, in the sense that he discriminates against a person or group of a different race. But *racism* is an institutionalized phenomenon which rests firmly on power to make and act upon decisions which are discriminatory.

We choose to dismiss the white-racism/black-racism question as irrelevant to the concerns of this discussion. Since all of the major social institutions of this nation are controlled by white people and reflect white values, "white racism" and "racism" are synonymous. If certain people and institutions of other races behave in ways which are discriminatory, this behavior has been well learned from white people. But discrimination in any form is destructive. The compelling need is for the white-controlled institutions to deal with the racism which inheres in their operations. It is to this task, and specifically this task in the schools, that we address ourselves.

For over 300 years we have perpetuated a system of education organized by and for the white middle class. The "melting pot myth" is now being exposed as just that when blacks and poor people are concerned. The large percentage of high-income whites who control most of the nation's goods and services have historically sent their children to private schools and colleges where the white superiority myth has been unchallenged and perpetuated. The white people who constitute approximately 85 percent of the population and who control the production of 95-98 percent of all goods and services have controlled the public schools, where the same white superiority myth has been perpetuated. This has been an economic necessity—a way of guaranteeing a cheap labor supply in both urban and rural areas. But two major developments of recent years have generated the beginning of change in this social and economic status quo: the technocratic revolution and the black revolution.

Mechanized production in factories and fields has left millions of our second-class poor and black citizens destitute. Most of them have sought economic opportunities in cities. The ensuing white flight to the suburbs has resulted in increased polarization—greater economic and social distance between whites and nonwhites, between middle class and poor. The increase in segregation of the schools since the 1954 Supreme Court decision, which is documented in the Kerner Report, inevitably followed this white flight. Thus, schools organized by and for the white middle class, while professing to be the great democratizing force of our society—"free public education"—are no longer viable social institutions in our multiethnic society.

The black revolution is also a social reality which is having impact on the schools. As is true of most revolutionary movements, the black movement began with a reform stage or struggle for integration in 1954. Blacks, seeking the satisfaction of needs denied them by our white-dominated institutions, have discovered that the reforms they sought were not granted and that the answers lie in taking power, power to control their own destiny. In the struggle for power, blacks are discovering the necessity to redefine the goals and methods of the schools and other institutions which have failed them. "Thus, even if black parents join the struggle for community control of schools with the aim of raising the reading achievement level of their children to that of white children, they are being led in the course of their struggle to challenge the fundamental philosophy and methods of contemporary education." [1]

What are these fundamental philosophies and methods of contemporary education which blacks are challenging? What are the manifestations of racism in our schools?

[1] Grace Lee Boggs. *The Black Revolution in America.* Number 6 in the Series: *A Black Look at White America.* Detroit, Michigan: University Center for Adult Education, 1968. p. 8.

The first and most obvious manifestation of institutional racism is found in the fact of segregated schools. Despite the Coleman Report and the Kerner Report—despite the knowledge that white America possesses about the nature and extent of the problem of race and schools—there are more black children attending segregated black schools today than was true in 1954. There are all kinds of explanations for this phenomenon—mainly the white exodus to the suburbs and the resulting concentration of blacks in urban centers, the "black separatist movement," etc. The fact remains, however, that white America does not come to grips with its problem.

Those of us who have clung to the notion that integrated education can and must be a national goal for the realization of equal educational opportunity are disturbed when the concept of integrated education is challenged. Preston Wilcox, a leading black scholar, wrote in 1970:

Education for humanism is far more relevant than integrated education —or even separatist education. Integrated education has largely been a subterfuge for white supremacy; little systematic effort has been undertaken to help black and white students relate as equals. Little has been done to help black and white students obtain the skills and desire to help solve the nation's problems without becoming a part of the problem themselves. Little has been done to aid black and white students to liberate themselves from a need to line up for the draft, on Wall Street, in racist churches, or in racist unions.[2]

Our answer is that no school *is* integrated unless black and white children and adults relate as equals. These components of "education for humanism" are essential goals for integrated schools.

But we recognize that the school as a social institution still, by and large, reflects the notions of the dominant power group—white middle and upper class Americans who keep the controls and dictate the policies and practices. Some of these prevailing notions are:

• If teachers will tell, explain, and clarify, children will learn. (The learner is a passive absorber of data.)

• Acquisition of facts and information must precede analysis. (You can't think critically until you have "mastered the subject.")

• The function of the school is to instill in youth certain values and attitudes. ("Democracy," "citizenship," "patriotism," "Judeo-Christian ethic," etc.)

[2] Preston Wilcox. "Integration or Separatism in Education: K-12." *Integrated Education: A Report on Race and Schools* 8 (1): 29-30; January-February 1970. Reprinted with permission from Volume 8, February 1970.

 • The role of the teacher is essentially authoritarian. (Successful students do what the teacher says.)

Black and poor people have been the most disadvantaged by such beliefs and practices. They have found very little in what teachers "tell" and in the values and attitudes "instilled" which legitimizes or relates to their real lives in their segregated communities; thus, their realities, their real selves, have been denied by schools.

Black House was established as an alternative school for high school youth in Berkeley, California, in 1970. Students there had found that because Berkeley High School did not allow black students to become whole persons, integration in the context of that school was impossible. And they rejected desegregation without integration. They had experienced embarrassment about their deficiencies in communications skills. They had not developed the ability to think for themselves, not because they did not have the capability but because the public schools had for so long ignored the importance of teaching responsibility and self-discipline. Black House students would not allow the perpetuation of "programmed irresponsibility." They were surprised to find themselves being held to their commitments as if they were adults. "Jiving" was out. They found the changes in their ability to think for themselves amazing and rewarding.[3]

This experience validates James Baldwin's challenge to teachers when he said that if America does not find the way to use the tremendous potential and energy which the black child represents, the nation will be destroyed by that energy. The Black House students who have discovered their energies and talents will find either useful or destructive channels for their lives, depending in large measure upon how open the society becomes.

We do not advocate segregated education. Rather, we advocate doing in *all* schools what the staff and students of Black House say they are doing: making teaching and learning relevant to the lives and the concerns of youth, and especially our most disadvantaged. If and when this occurs in response to the black challenge to our fundamental philosophy and methods, all children will benefit.

High school students of all racial and ethnic origins are becoming increasingly insightful about the nature and consequences of racism in schools and society. They speak from experience about the stereotyped concepts they hear from teachers and fellow students: "Blacks are

---

[3] Buddy Jackson and the Black Staff. "The Black House—An All Black Alternative School in Berkeley." *New School of Education Journal* 2 (3): 25-27; Summer 1971.

inherently lazy and less intelligent than whites," "Indians are content and well-off on their reservations except for a few militants." There is increasing conviction among concerned youth that most high school students, by the time they graduate, are so uninformed and brainwashed that they seldom think of questioning anything they are told. These thoughtful spokesmen for youth are convinced that schools have an obligation to furnish opportunities for students to learn the truth and stop the flow of propaganda and hypocrisy with which students are now being indoctrinated.[4]

We have some further concerns about racism in schools.

What is happening vis-à-vis curriculum reform? The proliferation of ethnic studies cannot be viewed, ipso facto, as a positive and constructive response to demands for change. As is true in all curriculum change, it is the uses of new content which make the difference, and not the facts by themselves. Larry Cuban sounds the alarm when he warns that "white instruction" will devitalize ethnic content. He characterizes "white instruction" as traditional and authoritarian, the kind that "locks students into the passive role of soaking up information." Where teachers of black students do in fact recognize this approach to ethnic studies as evidence of lack of respect for the ability of students to deal with emotion-laden, meaningful content, institutional racism is diminished. The alternative, continuing "teach and tell" methods, will, as Cuban states, "kill off one of the few reform efforts mounted to change instruction, especially in the social sciences."[5]

What is happening vis-à-vis school organization? The battle to eliminate the tracking system is still being fought. This system is one of the most blatant and destructive forms of institutional racism. Administrators, counselors, and teachers give voice to their low expectations of black and other minority students by their actions when they program large numbers of those students into the "non–college-bound" classes in schools—starting with ability grouping in elementary classrooms. In fact, historically the pecking order in school organization which awards higher status, smaller class size, and higher learning expectations to "traditional" or "academic" subjects and students enrolled in them is a neat way of perpetuating the cheap labor market and telling the "disadvantaged" youth that they can't make it into the mainstream.

[4] John Birmingham, editor. "A Case of the Student as Nigger and Racist." *Our Time Is Now.* New York: Praeger Publishers, 1970. p. 166.

[5] Larry Cuban. "Ethnic Content and 'White' Instruction." *Phi Delta Kappan* 53 (5): 273; January 1972.

Another message this conveys is that "academic" courses have far more value than any others and that the education of the privileged is the primary responsibility of the schools.

What about school staffing? The alternative school movement in both the public and private sectors is challenging traditional patterns of school staffing, organization, and curriculum. Students, staff members, and administrators of alternative schools are, in most instances, persons who are disenchanted with traditional, bureaucratic forms and content, and who are engaging in participatory processes they have not experienced before. They are attempting to take their own destinies into their own hands and find new bases for legitimacy. The influence of this movement on public education has not been studied systematically enough to draw firm conclusions, but the fact of proliferation should be saying something to public educators and education power groups about the urgency of bringing public education in line with the changing society.

Public pronouncements seem to indicate that more previously all-white school systems employ black teachers and that qualified minority applicants are employed in preference to Caucasians in some urban school districts. But after 300 years of miseducation and non-education of blacks in this country it will be a long time before there is true equality of employment opportunity for them in schools. The racism which permeates most suburban and rural areas of the country precludes most blacks from wanting to seek employment outside of urban schools. So the "short-changed children of suburbia" will continue to be shortchanged—deprived of the humanizing experiences to be gained from firsthand learning about and from human differences—until housing patterns created by our profit motive and our prejudices are eliminated. There is no "theoretical" way for children to learn about human worth. It only comes with day-to-day encounters with *all* kinds of humans, both peers and adults. In schools, this requires continuing commitment and struggle within the power structure and pressures from outside to change staffing patterns in ways which guarantee diversity; and, in the community, to change housing patterns for true open occupancy.

What about student grouping for instruction? How are classes put together in racially mixed schools? This is related to the earlier questions about tracking and ability grouping, but there is the broader question of resegregation and desegregated schools. Racism often dictates a kind of hypocrisy which says "Ours is a racially mixed school, so we are integrated," when in fact there is racial segregation within or among classrooms. When the adults in a school or community abide by the letter of the law but tolerate the perpetuation of segregated classes, this kind of decision-making behavior speaks loudly to young people involved—and their parents. No question about whose values are determining how, and with whom, they spend their school days. Dan Dodson has often said that who goes to school with whom is perhaps the most basic decision a board of education ever makes, for what children live, rather than what they study, teaches them lessons in ways which count. And Murray Wax speaks to this point when he says, ". . . it is the climate established by that peer society which determines the kind of intellectual and emotional growth of the youngsters in school."[6]

Up to this point we have discussed the first assumption that we made: that racism prevails in our society and in our schools. We made a second assumption: that something must be done about it and there are some choices to be made. The specific things to be done are dealt with extensively and in depth in the chapter which follows. There are some broad alternatives before us, however, which are urgent and require understanding, commitment, and action on the part of adults and youth in schools and society. Three alternatives confront us: continuing racism and repression in schools and society, radical reform in education, or revolution.

If the "fundamental philosophy and methods of contemporary education" which Grace Lee Boggs mentioned are not challenged and changed by whites as well as blacks, racism and repression will continue. The status quo prevails unless or until events cause it to change. The "professionals" in schools, as well as in most social institutions, have historically been slow to read the social landscape and respond positively rather than defensively to demands for change. Ours has been an ivory tower mentality; we are the product of the educational process which has prevailed in our lifetime. And we in schools, like all middle class professionals, have been decisively influenced by the economic base upon which racism rests. Robert Coles speaks to this:

A while back Julian Bond refused to be satisfied with a label like "white racist" even when applied to an obvious one, Lester Maddox. Mr. Bond took pains to emphasize that Maddox's struggles as a youth with bitter poverty require us to look at the Georgia Power Company, at the owners of textile mills, at the way the city of Atlanta and the state of Georgia are run—by

[6] Murray L. Wax. "How Should Schools Be Held Accountable?" *The Urban Review* 513: 15; January 1972.

whom, for whom, at whose overall expense. . . . perhaps we can, many of us, black, white, intellectuals, and workers, fight hard and politically so that children are well fed, so that their parents can find work and get good pay for that work—and most important, in the words a young welder once directed at me, so that "the working people of this country have more and more say about what goes on in this country." [7]

How we as educators and citizens feel when we read words like those, and what we do about what we feel, determine in some measure what happens in the schools where we work. Do we really believe that *our* schools (not somebody else's) should help youth learn to "have more and more say about what goes on in this country"? Do we believe that *all* youth should be helped to have more say? That is very different from just helping them know what goes on. Knowing is safe. Acting is risk taking. In elementary schools, children can learn who makes decisions about life in school, they can critique both the process and the results of decision making in the classroom and in the total school.

In secondary schools, youth can extend their learning about these matters to the school district, the community, the nation, and the world. They *can*—they have the interest and the ability—but whether they *do* usually depends on how much importance the adults-in-charge attach to this kind of learning for youth. And in racially mixed settings there is high risk for white educators who encourage *all* students to learn about and participate in decision making, because we have to be prepared then for shared power or changes in the power order. Racism and repression will continue until these changes occur. Which leads us to the second alternative.

Radical school reform means shared power. There is much movement in this direction abroad in the land at the local school level. In differentiated staffing the teachers share decision-making powers and administrative responsibilities which are traditionally those of the principal: how the money for instructional materials will be spent, how the school will be organized, which children will be assigned to which teachers, etc. This process often bogs down or stops at the point of decision about how much will be paid to whom for added responsibilities.

In individualized instruction, students share the teacher's power to decide who will learn what, how much, and when. The authority

---

[7] Robert Coles. "Understanding White Racists." *The New York Review of Books*, December 30, 1971. p. 12. Reprinted with permission from *The New York Review of Books.* Copyright © 1971 Nyrev, Inc.

role of the teacher *may* be modified in the direction of guiding and facilitating learning; but the structure does not guarantee the process. In these two instances, differentiated staffing and individualized instruction, the change process is often difficult at best, and it is compounded by racism in a racially mixed staff and student group where the white people in power customarily assume that blacks are not capable of sharing power, of making intelligent decisions.

At the school district level, change typically comes more slowly and reluctantly. The higher the echelons of power, the tighter the grasp becomes. The stakes are higher, in the view of the school officials and the community. The bureaucratic structure perpetuates itself. Final authority and responsibility, by law, rests with the board of education and its surrogate, the superintendent. Advisory committees proliferate in the name of democracy and "community involvement," but they are seldom composed of high stakeholders who have political clout. Thus power is "shared" in matters which do not rock the boat, or in matters which those in power already want changed.

The white power structure, in racially mixed school districts, will be highly sensitive to the "kind" of blacks appointed or elected to influential positions related to school management and operation or policy making. Certain racist assumptions are made about whom "he" represents, what "they" want, etc. Our history of repression burdens us with assumptions which get in the way of our seeing "them" as persons like ourselves. Thus, limitations inherent in radical school reform are determined in *all* districts by the degree of threat to power which is perceived by those about to share it and in racially mixed districts by the "Black Power" threat, real or imagined. *The black parent or community leader, whether he accepts the Black Power idea or not, has to be accepted and negotiated with as a peer, with just as much right to feel the way he does as the ruling whites have to feel as they do. This is an essential condition for radical school reform in racially mixed schools and in all schools.*

Radical school reform has succeeded in many districts in cooling the militants. Where revolutionary change is in the wind, it is incorporated into the system, as a "pilot program" or "experimental program," and the power to change then becomes shared with the officials in charge. This is not necessarily evil! Whether it is "good" or "bad" depends in the final analysis on what happens to the education of boys and girls. What is important is *not* how high they score on the standardized tests, though there *are* essential basic skills to be learned, but how fundamentally they become involved in the responsibility for and the consequences of their own learning or lack of learning. This can happen only in the context of shared decision making, shared assessment of learning, and social interaction.

Learning is a social process and it can take place only negatively under conditions of distrust, disrespect, exploitation, authoritarianism— the list could go on. These are some of the components of institutional racism. They are not unique to racism, but they are conditions which prevail overtly or "under the rug" in any institution which is character- ized by the preservation of discriminatory myths and values.

Radical school reform is under way in varying degrees in many schools. An important question for educators now is whether this is happening far and wide and fast enough in this multiracial, multiethnic society to provide equality of educational opportunity to all children and youth and, ultimately, to transform American society so that it becomes the good community where the good life can be lived. A big order!

We are talking about altering a culture. Educators have to raise their sights and find answers to questions such as: How can we educate children so the culture can and will be altered? How can teacher and administrator groups use the leverage of their organizations to these ends? How can they perform an advocacy role? *How can students be trained to be activists—to discover the ways to change things?*

We all need to listen to what black people are saying and feeling. Banks, Billings, and Ethridge speak to these questions and many more in their chapters in this volume. Some of their rather startling statements are: (a) that more important than the opportunity for an education is the opportunity to be a person, (b) that if we do not succeed in taking decisive steps to create an open society we face racial wars and chaos and the complete dehumanization of American Man, and (c) that the most valued persons in America are white Anglo-Saxon males with money.

Grace Lee Boggs says that the black city youth on the streets, many of whom are school dropouts, have recognized that they are expendable and will have to destroy this society or be destroyed by it.[8]

Robert Allen speaks to the necessity for white allies in the transi- tional stage between now and a state of full liberation through social revolution. Until white America becomes a humanistic society free of exploitation and class division, black America cannot be liberated.[9]

A Wisconsin black legislator, Lloyd A. Barbee, introduced a bill in the state legislature in 1971 which would repeal the compulsory school

[8] Grace Lee Boggs, *op. cit.*, pp. 3-4.

[9] Robert T. Allen. *Black Awakening in Capitalist America.* New York: Doubleday & Company, Inc., 1970. p. 281.

attendance laws.[10] He argued that schools do nothing more than repli-
cate and perpetuate racist middle class values and that parents who
are concerned with the development of human values in their children
would do better to keep them at home. What is our answer to this
proposal?

The alternatives posed earlier here—racism and repression, radical
reform in education, or revolution—intentionally imply that racism
and repression will continue to prevail in America unless radical reform
takes place in education. And if radical reform does *not* take place,
revolution is inevitable. The sequence of this "either-or" position is
not really quite that neatly identifiable or chronologically accurate. All
three of these conditions exist in American society today. Proponents
of each are contending for the power to prevail over the others. Racists
predominate, but their power bases in all our social institutions are
being exposed and challenged increasingly.

Radical reformers in education are effecting changes in schools
where they have the wisdom to win and maintain community support
for their efforts. Revolutionaries, both black and white, are gaining
support from many oppressed segments of the population—especially
youth, women, and homosexuals—who find no promise of change in
the existing economic and political structures which dominate their
lives. These are not the classic Marxist working class groups upon
whom the hope for revolutionary change has rested historically.

Whether school people find themselves in agreement or in disagreement with such serious challengers as these, we have decisions to make
about who we are in the context of the current social scene, and
especially what our commitments are and what we are doing about
institutional racism. Are schools a major or a minor force for change?
Should we confront the issues in schools or wait for solutions to problems of housing and unemployment? Do we believe the oft-repeated
maxim that if we are not part of the solution we are part of the problem? Will improvements in curriculum and methodology solve the
problem of racism in the schools? That is, can we help children become
thoughtful, knowledgeable, human people by prescribing the "right"
learning and using the "right" methods? John Holt would probably
call this creating "little worlds fit for children in a world not fit for
anyone else."

The broader perspective might be to conceive of the school as a
reality-oriented segment of society where children are free and encouraged *by the adult models with whom they live there* to think and

---

[10] Lloyd A. Barbee. "End Compulsory Attendance for Racism." *Integrated
Education: A Report on Race and Schools* 10 (1): 20; January-February 1972.

act on whatever exists in and out of school closest to their lives. This would put the reality of racism in the context of the other social institutions and problems and needs which impinge on the lives of children and youth—families, neighborhoods, churches, health and welfare agencies, the world of work, the law and the courts, to name a few. Where are the "basic skills" in all this? They are the vehicles for communication and understanding and problem solving, and they *are* basic, but not intrinsically valuable ends in themselves.

Clues to action for overcoming racism are found in subsequent chapters in this volume and in the people and organizations in the communities served by schools. When we know what our own commitments are, strategies for action can be devised confidently in concert with colleagues and parents. It is never easy, but the process is one of taking hold of life—the *real* life of the nation, not the mythical life.

CHAPTER 4: CURRICULAR MODELS FOR AN OPEN SOCIETY*

JAMES A. BANKS

It is .necessary to define an *open society* before we can design a curriculum that will enable students to develop a commitment to that kind of social system, and the strategies and skills needed to create and maintain it. This is essential, because each curriculum is normative since it is designed to create and sustain a specific set of beliefs, attitudes, and institutions. In this chapter, an *open society* is defined as one in which individuals from diverse ethnic, cultural, and social class groups have equal opportunities to participate. Each individual can take full advantage of the opportunities and rewards within all social, economic, and political institutions without regard to his ancestry or ethnic identity. He can also participate fully in the society while preserving his distinct ethnic and cultural traits,[1] and is able to "make the maximum number of voluntary contacts with others without regard to qualifications of ancestry, sex, or class."[2]

In an open society, rewards and opportunities are not necessarily evenly distributed, but they are distributed on the basis of the knowledge and skills which each person can contribute to the fulfillment of the

* I wish to express my gratitude for the perceptive reactions to the first draft of this chapter that were prepared by Professors Bernice Goldmark, Anna Ochoa, Jack Simpson, and Mrs. Barbara A. Sizemore. However, I assume total responsibility for the content of this chapter. I would also like to thank Mrs. Diane Collum, secretary in the Department of Curriculum and Instruction at the University of Washington, for her expert technical assistance in the preparation of this chapter.

[1] Talcott Parsons. "Full Citizenship Rights for the Negro American." In: Talcott Parsons and Kenneth B. Clark, editors. *The Negro American.* Boston: Houghton Mifflin Company, 1965. pp. 721-22.

[2] Barbara A. Sizemore. "Is There a Case for Separate Schools?" *Phi Delta Kappan* 53: 281; January 1972.

needs of his society. The societal needs referred to here consist of those systems and institutions which every society must have to function, such as a system of education, government, and the production and distribution of goods and services. The kind of society that we are proposing has never existed in the human experience. History and contemporary social science teach us that in every past and present culture individuals have had and still have widely unequal opportunities to share fully in the reward systems and benefits of their society. The basis for the unequal distribution of rewards is determined by elitist groups in which *power* is centered.

Ruling and powerful groups decide which traits and characteristics are necessary for full societal participation. *They determine necessary traits on the basis of the similarity of such traits to their own values, physical characteristics, life-styles, and behavior.* At various points in history, celibacy, sex, ethnicity, race, religion, as well as many other variables have been used by ruling groups to determine which individuals and groups would be given or denied opportunities for social mobility and full societal participation. In Colonial America, white Anglo-Saxon male Protestants with property controlled most social, political, economic, and military institutions. These were the men who wrote the Declaration of Independence and the United States Constitution. They excluded from full participation in decision making people, such as Blacks and Native Americans (Indians), who were different from themselves. Our "founding fathers" had a deep suspicion and contempt for individuals who were culturally and racially different. They invented and perpetuated stereotypes and myths about excluded groups to justify their oppression.

The United States, like all other nations, is still controlled by a few powerful groups who admit or deny individuals opportunities to participate in society on the basis of how similar such individuals are to themselves. White Anglo-Saxon male Protestants with money are the most valued persons in modern America; an individual who may be so classified has maximum opportunities to participate in America's social, economic, and political institutions. He is the "ideal" person in the United States, and all other individuals and groups are judged on the basis of their similarity to him. Black females without money are probably the least valued individuals in America.[3]

To create the kind of open society which we have defined here,

[3] Barbara A. Sizemore. "Social Science and Education for a Black Identity." In: James A. Banks and Jean D. Grambs, editors. *Black Self-Concept: Implications for Education and Social Science.* New York: McGraw-Hill Book Company, 1972.

we will either have to redistribute power so that groups with different ethnic and cultural characteristics will control entry to various social, economic, and political institutions; or we will have to modify the attitudes and actions of individuals who will control future institutions, so that they will become less ethnocentric and will permit people who differ from themselves culturally and physically to share equally in society's reward system on the basis of the *real* contributions which they can make to the functioning of society. We can conceptualize these two means to an open society as models.

Model I may be called a SHARED POWER MODEL. The goal of this model would be to create a society in which currently excluded groups would share power with dominant groups. They would control a number of social, economic, and political institutions, and would determine the criteria for admission to these institutions. The methods used to attain the major ends of this model would be an attempt to build group pride, cohesion, and identity among excluded groups, and help them to develop the ability to make effective political decisions, to gain and exercise political power effectively, and to develop a belief in the humanness of their own groups.

The alternative means to an open society may be called Model II, ENLIGHTENING POWERFUL GROUPS MODEL. The major goal of this model would be to modify the attitudes and perceptions of dominant groups so that they would be willing, as adults, to share power with oppressed and excluded groups. They would also be willing to regard excluded members of groups as human, unwilling to participate in efforts to continue their oppression, willing to accept and understand the actions by oppressed groups to liberate themselves, and willing to take *action* to change the social system so that it would treat powerless peoples more justly. The major goals within this model focus on helping dominant groups to expand their conception of who is human, to develop more positive attitudes toward exploited peoples, and to foster a willingness to share power with excluded groups. (See Figures 1 and 2 for a summary of these two models.)

Model I—Shared Power

Most oppressed individuals who are acutely aware of the extent to which excluded groups are powerless in America will perceive the SHARED POWER MODEL as more realistic than Model II. This model, if successfully implemented, would result in the redistribution of *power* so that groups which have been and still are systematically excluded from full participation in America would control such institutions as schools, courts, industries, health facilities, and the mass media. They would not necessarily control all institutions within America, but would control those in which they participate and which are needed to fulfill their individual and group needs. These groups would be able to distribute jobs and other rewards to persons who, like themselves, are denied such opportunities by present powerful groups. In recent years, the Nation of Islam has used this model to create employment and educational opportunities for poor and excluded Blacks. The community control movement was an unsuccessful attempt to implement this model, and elements within this model have been used by such

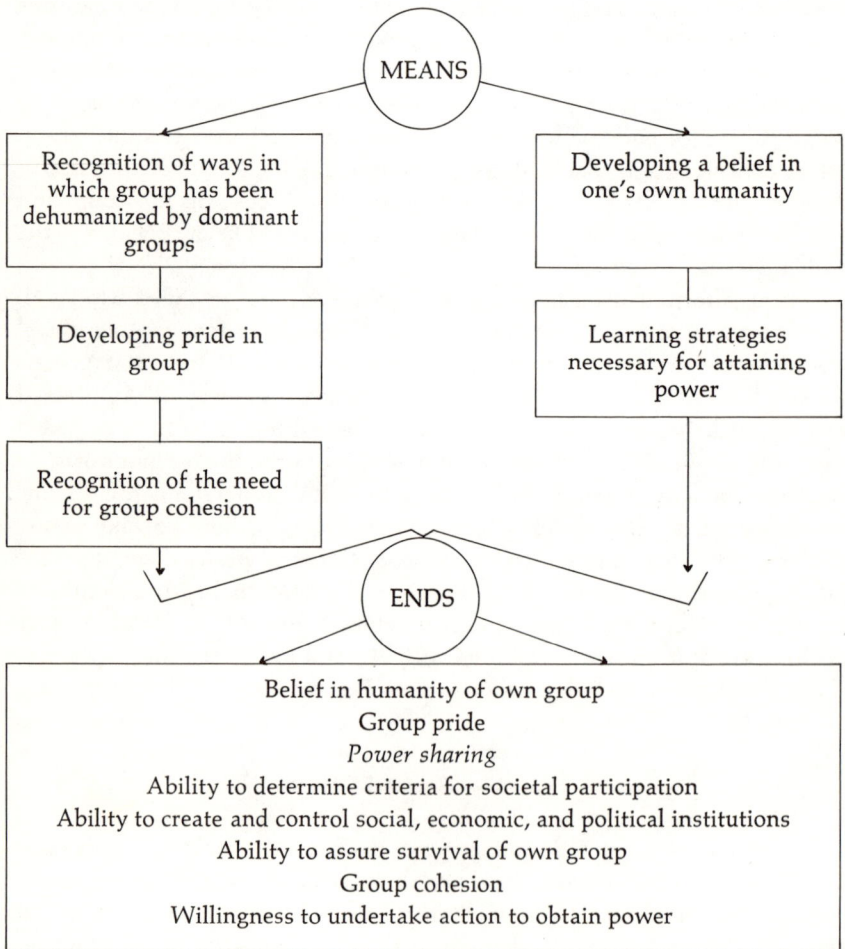

MEANS

Recognition of ways in which group has been dehumanized by dominant groups

Developing a belief in one's own humanity

Developing pride in group

Learning strategies necessary for attaining power

Recognition of the need for group cohesion

ENDS

Belief in humanity of own group
Group pride
Power sharing
Ability to determine criteria for societal participation
Ability to create and control social, economic, and political institutions
Ability to assure survival of own group
Group cohesion
Willingness to undertake action to obtain power

Figure 1. Model I—Shared Power Model

groups as Jews and Catholics to enable them to participate more fully in shaping public policy.

In a society in which power is shared by different groups, Blacks, Chicanos, women, Native Americans, Asian-Americans, Puerto Rican Americans, and other oppressed and colonized groups would control and determine the traits and characteristics necessary for sharing societal rewards and opportunities. IQ test scores may cease to be an important criterion, but the ability to relate to Third World peoples may become an essential criterion. A major assumption of this model is that present excluded groups, if they attained power, would, like present ruling groups, provide opportunities for those persons who are most like themselves physically and culturally. This assumption may or may not be valid, since some evidence suggests that oppressed groups have, at least in the past, idealized Anglo-Saxons with power and money, and held negative feelings toward their own cultures and groups.[4] This has been true even when previously oppressed individuals assumed power positions.

However, recent evidence reported by Arnez and Baughman indicates that this situation is changing and that exploited peoples are developing more group pride and cohesion.[5]

If the SHARED POWER MODEL is used to achieve an open society, we would have to think of ways in which such a model may be implemented without the genocide of powerless groups. We would also have to determine how essential societal cohesion may be maintained without conflict between competing and antagonistic powerful groups. There are valid reasons to believe that both of these concerns should be taken seriously by educators and policy makers if we intend to create a society in which a number of competing and alienated groups will share power.

History teaches us that people with power usually do not relinquish it without violence and bloodshed. The Black Revolt of the 1960's, which was a movement among Blacks designed primarily to attain power and influence over their lives, resulted in the murder of many Blacks who participated in protest movements and ghetto rebellions. Many of the victims were innocent bystanders. When the Black Panthers tried to

[4] See: James A. Banks. "Racial Prejudice and the Black Self-Concept." In: James A. Banks and Jean D. Grambs, editors. *Black Self-Concept: Implications for Education and Social Science.* New York: McGraw-Hill Book Company, 1972.

[5] See: Nancy L. Arnez. "Enhancing the Black Self-Concept Through Literature." In: James A. Banks and Jean D. Grambs, editors. *Black Self-Concept: Implications for Education and Social Science.* New York: McGraw-Hill Book Company, 1972.

gain control over their communities, they were hunted down and killed by police in a number of large cities.

The Fred Hampton murder which occurred in Chicago in 1970 is perhaps the most well known and notorious of such attacks by police on the Black Panther Party. Respected white-controlled newspapers such as the *Chicago Sun Times* and the *New York Times* concluded that the Hampton murder resulted from an unwarranted police attack on the Party. Between February 1968 and December 1969, it was alleged that more than 50 incidents involving the Panther Party and policemen took place in cities throughout the nation. Twenty-eight Panthers were killed by policemen in 1969 alone.[6] Many Blacks regarded the attacks on the Panther Party as a national conspiracy. The violent assassinations of Malcolm X, Medgar Evers, and Martin Luther King also suggest that excluded groups run the risk of genocide when they try to take power from ruling groups. Thus, recent history makes it clear that powerless groups, when making a bid for power, run the risk of extermination.

When excluded groups lead movements to free their people from oppression and colonialization, they also run the risk of imprisonment or, to use the phrase of some who are imprisoned, of becoming "political prisoners." In an anguished and touching book, *If They Come in the Morning*, Angela Y. Davis tells why she feels that she is a political prisoner: "The offense of the political prisoner is his political boldness, his persistent challenging—legally and extra-legally—of fundamental social wrongs fostered and reinforced by the state."[7] James Baldwin viewed Miss Davis as a political prisoner when he wrote, ". . . we must fight for your life as though it were our own—which it is—and render impassable with our bodies the corridor to the gas chamber. *For, if they take you in the morning, they will be coming for us that night.*"[8] (Emphasis added.)

Excluded groups clearly risk genocide and imprisonment (Martin Luther King was jailed many times) when they try to take power from ruling groups. However, a dilemma is created by the fact that throughout history, power has rarely been given to oppressed peoples by ruling groups; rather it is usually taken, and power struggles often result in

[6] James A. Banks. *March Toward Freedom: A History of Black Americans.* Belmont, California: Fearon Publishers, 1970. p. 107.

[7] Angela Y. Davis (and other political prisoners). *If They Come in the Morning.* New York: Signet Books, 1971. p. 31.

[8] James Baldwin. "An Open Letter to My Sister, Angela Y. Davis." In: Angela Y. Davis. *If They Come in the Morning.* New York: Signet Books, 1971. p. 23.

violence and deaths. Notes Clark, "No human being can easily and graciously give up power and privilege. Such change can come only with conflict and anguish and the ever present threat of retrogression." [9]

However, since violent strategies by America's powerless groups will most likely result in genocide, imprisonment, and further repression, the school must help them to develop other tactics to attain power and influence. Clark insightfully points out why violent revolution is an unrealistic way for excluded groups in America to get power: "The strategy of nonviolence reflects most obviously the fact that Negroes, in the minority, could not afford to be violent—except for the unplanned Watts type of violence, itself suicidal or a reflection of racial desperation. The historical and contemporary predicament of the Negro in America provides no basis for systematic military revolution." [10]

In translating the SHARED POWER MODEL into curriculum goals and strategies, our attention would focus primarily on the victims of oppression, such as Blacks, Native Americans, Chicanos, Asian-Americans, and Puerto Rican Americans. We would try to equip exploited peoples with the strategies which will enable them to attain power, while preventing their extermination and maintaining an essential degree of societal cohesion. We would help them see, through valid content samples, how previous oppressed groups in history have attained power, and how certain nonreflective and irrational *actions* and *inactions* can result in further repression or genocide. Case studies of groups such as unionized auto workers and teachers can serve as examples of groups which have successfully attained significant amounts of power in America with little bloodshed and violence. The cases of the German Jews and Native Americans could serve to illustrate the latter point.

Model II—Enlightening Powerful Groups

Model II, whose primary goal is to *help whites develop more positive attitudes toward oppressed peoples and a willingness to share power,* rests on a number of assumptions, the validity of which we have little evidence to support. If anything, current data give us little hope in this model as an effective way to achieve an open society. It assumes that people with power feel guilty about the ways in which exploited groups

---

[9] Kenneth B. Clark. "Introduction: The Dilemma of Power." In: Talcott Parsons and Kenneth B. Clark, editors. *The Negro American.* Boston: Houghton Mifflin Company, 1965. p. xv.

[10] *Ibid.,* p. xvi.

are treated, or can be made to feel guilty. For example, Myrdal, in his classic study of racism in America, *The American Dilemma*, suggests that American democratic ideals vis-à-vis the treatment of Blacks in

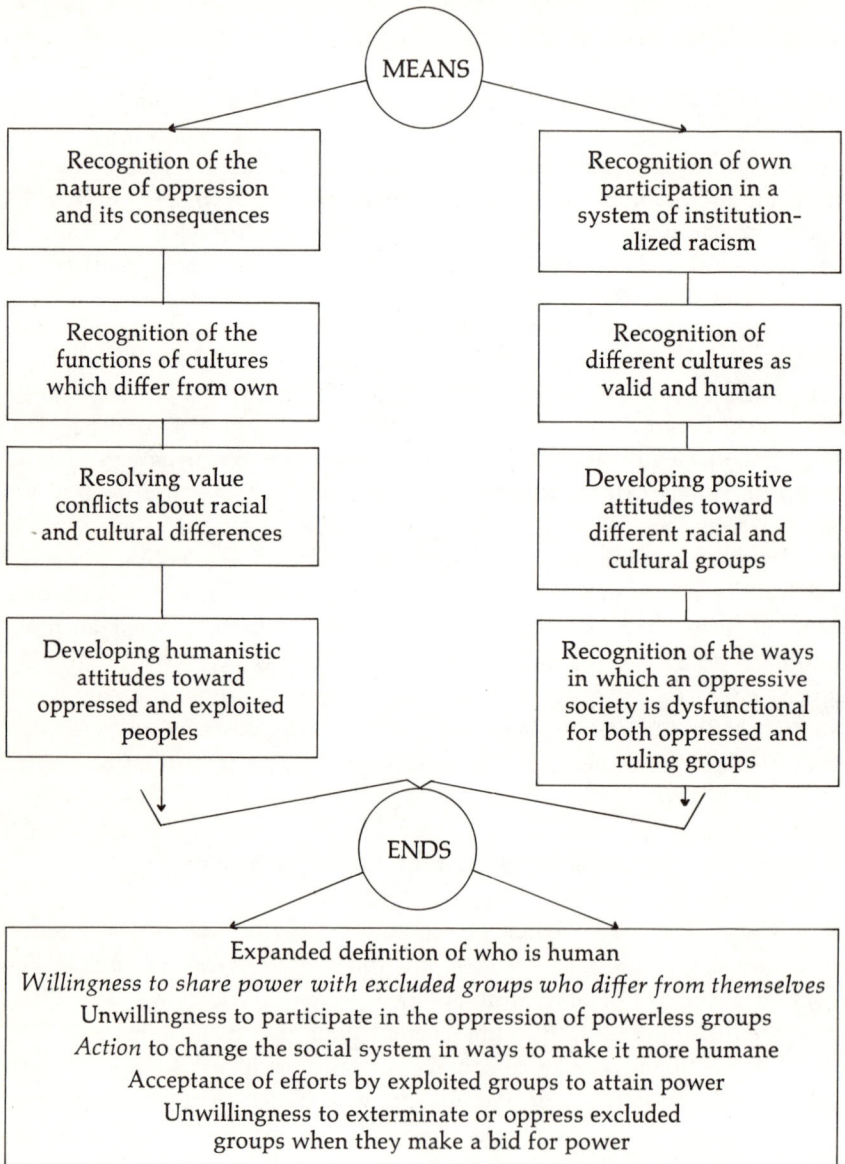

MEANS

| Recognition of the nature of oppression and its consequences | Recognition of own participation in a system of institution- alized racism |

| Recognition of the functions of cultures which differ from own | Recognition of different cultures as valid and human |

| Resolving value conflicts about racial and cultural differences | Developing positive attitudes toward different racial and cultural groups |

| Developing humanistic attitudes toward oppressed and exploited peoples | Recognition of the ways in which an oppressive society is dysfunctional for both oppressed and ruling groups |

ENDS

Expanded definition of who is human
Willingness to share power with excluded groups who differ from themselves
Unwillingness to participate in the oppression of powerless groups
Action to change the social system in ways to make it more humane
Acceptance of efforts by exploited groups to attain power
Unwillingness to exterminate or oppress excluded
groups when they make a bid for power

Figure 2. Model II—Enlightening Powerful Groups Model

America create a dilemma for most white Americans.[11] It may be that such a dilemma never has existed because whites have never perceived Blacks as *humans*. Writes Strom,

> . . . a new image of the Negro was created; he was for the first time endowed, by fiction rather than by God, as being somewhat less than human, a subhuman, a "nigger" whose natural inferiority to man justified his servant stature and allowed whites to see themselves as benevolent caretakers. . . . a group of enslaved people could be looked upon as subject to different rules and separate standards of conduct than real people, than human persons; these were "niggers." [12]

The differential reactions by the majority of whites to the killings of Blacks and whites in recent years suggest that many whites still do not consider Blacks and other Third World people as "human." [13] The majority of whites remained conspicuously silent when two Black students were shot by police on the campus of a Black college in South Carolina in 1969. The killing of four white students by National Guardsmen a year later at Kent State evoked strong reactions and protest by most white Americans. No similar strong reactions followed the Jackson State Massacre.

Thus, it may be unrealistic to assume that, by learning about the atrocities which have been committed against Blacks, whites will become more willing to share power with them, and to regard them as fellow human beings because of feelings of guilt. Some writers contend that the policies in our society which influence the ways in which excluded groups are treated are *deliberate* policies.[14] If this assumption is valid, then teaching whites about the brutalities of slavery, or the inhumanity of "Indian" reservations, cannot be expected to affect significantly the ways in which dominant groups treat Blacks, Native Americans, and other colonized groups in America.

This model also assumes that dominant groups may develop a commitment to change if they are helped to see the ways in which an oppressive and exploitative system is detrimental to the oppressor as

[11] Gunnar Myrdal. *An American Dilemma*. New York: Harper & Row, Publishers, 1962.

[12] Robert D. Strom. "The Mythology of Racism." Lecture delivered at Oxford University, England, Spring 1972. p. 1.

[13] James A. Banks. "The Imperatives of Ethnic Minority Education." *Phi Delta Kappan* 53: 268; January 1972.

[14] James Baldwin. "A Talk to Teachers." In: Everett T. Keach, Jr., Robert Fulton, and William E. Gardner, editors. *Education and Social Crisis: Perspectives on Teaching Disadvantaged Youth*. New York: John Wiley & Sons, 1967. pp. 263-68.

well as the oppressed. This assumption puts a lot of faith in the power of knowledge; yet evidence is quite clear that man often rejects knowledge which is antithetical to his *perceived* self-interests, and that the knowledge which becomes institutionalized within a society—and thus that knowledge which is taught in school—is designed to perpetuate the status quo, and to keep excluded groups from participating in shaping public policy.

Purposes of Models

While these two models represent what we feel are the basic ways by which we can create an open society, they are ideal-type constructs. And like any ideal-type constructs or models, they are best used for conceptualization purposes. The laws of the land, the current organization of schools, and the types of student populations in many American schools make it difficult, in many cases, to implement either Model I or Model II in *pure* form. However, these models can help the curriculum specialist to determine the kinds of *emphases* which are necessary for the curriculum for different student populations. While the curriculums for exploited and dominant groups should have some elements in common, we believe that the central messages which these groups receive in the curriculum should in many cases differ. In the following paragraphs, we will discuss, using the two models as departure points, the kinds of *emphases* which we feel should constitute the curriculums for *oppressed* and *dominant* groups in order to create and sustain an open society. We intend to take into account the limitations of each of the models in our recommendations, and to suggest ways in which they may be reduced. In those situations in which a teacher has students from both dominant and excluded groups, it will be necessary for him to combine elements from both models in order to structure an effective curriculum.

The Curriculum for Oppressed Groups: Curricular Implications of Model I

The curriculum which we recommend for oppressed groups will include most of the elements of Model I. However, it will also include elements from Model II because a "pure" SHARED POWER MODEL curriculum may result in a totally fragmented and dehumanized society.

Throughout history, oppressed ethnic minority groups have been taught by the larger society that they were less than human, and that they deserve the low status in society in which they most often find themselves. Notes Baldwin, "The American triumph—in which the American tragedy has always been implicit—was to make Black people despise themselves. When I was little I despised myself; I did not know any better." [15] A large body of evidence collected by the Clarks in the 1940's, and by Morland in recent years, indicates that minority groups often accept the definitions of themselves which are perpetuated by dominant groups. [16] Recent studies reviewed by Arnez and conducted by Baughman and his students suggest that the self-perceptions of minority groups may be changing, largely because of the positive results of the Black Revolt of the 1960's. [17] However, Goldschmid's intensive review of the literature indicates that ethnic minority groups often hold negative attitudes toward themselves and their race. [18] The curriculum for Blacks and other oppressed groups must recognize their feelings toward self, help them to clarify their racial attitudes, liberate them from psychological captivity, and convince them of their humanness, since the dominant society has made them believe that they are less than human. Writes Johnson:

The African descendants in America, having passed through three phases of education in America—de-Africanization, dehumanization, and, finally, an inferior caste status—through application of self-determination and the establishment of a voluntary self-separated school system, can educate themselves. [19]

Blacks and other ethnic minorities will be able to liberate themselves from psychological and physical oppression only when they know *how* and *why* the myths about them emerged and were institutionalized and validated by white "scholarly" social scientists and historians. A curriculum which has as one of its major goals the liberation of oppressed peoples must teach them the ways in which all social institutions within this society, including the schools and the academic community, have participated in a conspiracy to make them believe that they are less than human. [20]

[15] James Baldwin, "An Open Letter . . .," *op. cit.*, p. 20.

[16] James A. Banks, "Racial Prejudice and the Black Self-Concept," *op. cit.*

[17] Nancy L. Arnez, *op. cit.*

[18] Marcel L. Goldschmid, editor. *Black Americans and White Racism: Theory and Research.* New York: Holt, Rinehart and Winston, Inc., 1970.

[19] Edwina C. Johnson. "An Alternative to Miseducation for the Afro-American People." In: Nathan Wright, Jr., editor. *What Black Educators Are Saying.* New York: Hawthorn Books, Inc., 1970. p. 198. Reprinted by permission of Hawthorn Books, Inc.

[20] James Baldwin, "A Talk to Teachers," *op. cit.*, p. 268.

They must be taught how social science knowledge reflects the norms, values, and goals of the ruling and powerful groups in society, and how it validates those belief systems which are functional for groups in power and dysfunctional for oppressed and powerless groups. When teaching Black students about ways in which social knowledge has served to validate the stereotypes and myths about them, the teacher can use as examples Ulrich B. Phillips' racist descriptions of the nature of slavery, Moynihan's disastrous study of the Black family, Jensen's and Schockley's denigrating work on Black-white intelligence, and Banfield's distorted and myopic interpretations of the Black ghetto rebellions. Textbook descriptions of Asian-Americans, Native Americans, Puerto Rican Americans, and Chicanos can also be used to teach oppressed peoples about ways in which social knowledge has been used to keep them at the lower rungs of the social ladder.[21]

While studying about the ways in which they have been psychologically and physically exploited and dehumanized is necessary to help exploited groups to liberate themselves, it is not sufficient. They must be helped to develop the ability to make *reflective* public decisions so that they can gain *power* and shape public policy that affects their lives. They must also develop a sense of *political efficacy,* and be given practice in *social action* strategies which teach them how to get power without being exterminated and becoming further oppressed. *In other words, excluded groups must be taught the most effective ways to gain power.* The school must help them become effective and reflective *political activists.* We are defining *reflective* decision making and social action as those kinds of decisions and social action which will enable oppressed groups to attain power, but will at the same time ensure their existence as a group and essential societal cohesion. Opportunities for social action, in which students have experience in obtaining and exercising power, must be emphasized within a curriculum which is designed to help liberate excluded groups. Since oppression and racism exist within the school as well as within all other American institutions, students can be provided practice in shaping public policy and in gaining power within their classroom, school, or school system.

The social studies curriculum for oppressed groups must not only help release them from psychological captivity, and focus on social action, it must also help them to develop *humanistic* attitudes toward members of their own group, as well as toward other excluded groups, since

---

[21] See: James A. Banks. *Teaching the Black Experience: Methods and Materials.* Belmont, California: Fearon Publishers, 1970. See also: James A. Banks, editor. *Teaching Ethnic Studies: Concepts and Strategies.* 43rd Yearbook. Washington, D.C.: National Council for the Social Studies, 1973.

coalitions among Third World peoples are necessary for them to gain and exercise political power. The fact that individuals are more likely to attain power when working in groups than when working alone is a highly important generalization which must be incorporated into a curriculum which has *liberation* as its goal. Write Bailey and Saxe:

> Individualism, a Euro-American value imposed upon Blacks, is dysfunctional for us when internalized, because of our precarious position in this society. Cooperation is far more valuable and necessary. Achievement-motivation directed toward the goal of liberation, coupled with a desire to work with others in an organized fashion to end oppression, and training to do so effectively—this is what a twentieth century education for black children demands.[22]

The school must also make an effort, when teaching oppressed groups how to attain power and to develop an appreciation of their cultural identity, to prevent them from becoming chauvinistic and ethnocentric, and from developing the kinds of attitudes and perceptions about different cultural groups which present ruling groups have toward people who are different from themselves. While presently excluded groups must learn to value their own cultures, try to attain power, and develop group solidarity and identity in order to participate fully in this society, they must also learn that there are other ways of living and being, and that even though dominant groups treat them in dehumanizing ways, it would not be to their advantage to treat other groups similarly if they attained power positions. To imitate the behavior of the oppressor would be the highest compliment which powerless peoples could pay to him. The humanism which exists among oppressed groups would be killed if they, once having attained power, were to act like current ruling groups; and the opportunity to humanize this society would be lost.

We stated that a curriculum for oppressed groups should help them to develop group pride, ways in which to attain power, and humanistic attitudes toward all cultural, ethnic, and social class groups. Most of these elements are Model I components, but we feel that the *humanistic* emphasis, which is a Model II component, must be incorporated into a curriculum for oppressed groups to prevent them from developing ethnocentric attitudes that are similar to the detrimental attitudes which dominant and powerful groups have today.

[22] Ronald W. Bailey and Janet C. Saxe. *Teaching Black: An Evaluation of Methods and Resources.* Stanford, California: Multi-Ethnic Education Resources Center of Stanford University, 1971. p. 31.

Curriculum for Dominant Groups:
Curricular Implications of Model II

Since we have no reliable ways of knowing that a Model I type curriculum *would* lead to an open society as we have defined it in this chapter, the curriculum builder should also implement elements of Model II in appropriate settings; that is, in settings which contain dominant groups. What we are suggesting is that since both of these models have severe limitations, and since we know little about ways to create an open society because we have never made a serious effort to create one, we should take a *multiple* approach to the problem. Also, the two models are complementary and not contradictory. If we succeed in enlightening or changing the attitudes of dominant groups so that they become more willing to share power with excluded groups, then the struggle for power among oppressed peoples will consequently be less intense, and thus less likely to lead to violence and societal chaos.

The elements which constitute Model II have been among the most widespread methods used by educators and policy makers to create a more humane society and better opportunities for Blacks, Native Americans, Chicanos, Asian-Americans, and other powerless groups in America. This approach is suggested by such terms as *intergroup education, intercultural education, human relations,* and *race relations.* Massive efforts were undertaken by such organizations as the American Council on Education and the Anti-Defamation League of B'nai B'rith in the forties and fifties to implement workshops to change the attitudes of teachers and children toward ethnic minority groups.

Hilda Taba and her colleagues developed a theoretical rationale for intergroup education, conducted numerous workshops, and published a number of books for the American Council on Education. Taba identified four major goals of intergroup education: (a) to provide pupils with facts, ideas, and concepts basic to intelligent understanding of group relations; (b) to develop the ability to think objectively and rationally about people, their problems, relationships, and cultures; (c) to develop those feelings, values, attitudes, and sensitivities necessary for living in a pluralistic society; and (d) to develop skills necessary for getting along with individuals and for working successfully in groups.[23]

[23] Hilda Taba, Elizabeth H. Brady, and John T. Robinson. *Intergroup Education in Public Schools.* Washington, D.C.: American Council on Education, 1952. p. 36. This summary of Taba's theory is taken from: June V. Gilliard. "Intergroup Education: How, For What, and For Whom?" Unpublished paper, University of Washington, Seattle, 1971. p. 2.

Jean Dresden Grambs, another leader in intergroup education, states the assumption of the approach:

> If a person can learn to hate and distrust others, he can learn to like and trust others. . . . This is the basic assumption of intergroup education. . . . Intergroup education similarly assumes that, as a result of selected materials and methods, individuals will be changed, that their attitudes and behaviors toward persons of other groups, and toward members of whatever group they themselves belong to, will be changed. The change will result in *more* acceptance of persons who differ and *more* acceptance of one's own difference from others.[24]

Other leaders in the field also assume that we can teach people new attitudes toward excluded groups. Trager and Yarrow write,

> Children learn what they live; in a culture which practices and condones prejudice, one behaves and thinks with prejudice. If children are to learn new ways of behaving, more democratic ways, they must be *taught* new behaviors and new values.[25]

The seminal study by Trager and Yarrow supports the assumption that democratic attitudes can be taught to children if a *deliberate* program of instruction is designed for that purpose.[26]

The primary goal of intergroup education (Model II elements) is to "enlighten" dominant groups by changing their attitudes toward excluded groups. Attempts are made to enlighten whites by conducting workshops and courses, often called *"Human Relations,"* in which whites are told about the sins of institutionalized racism, and are exposed to readings and materials which illustrate the ways in which racism has adversely affected excluded groups. Often, in these courses and workshops, ethnic minority speakers who are perceived as "militant" by whites serve as consultants and speakers, and they "tell it like it is." Frequently in these sessions anger and hostility reign. However, there is little evidence that these kinds of sessions achieve much, except to serve as a catharsis forum for both whites and ethnic speakers.

It would be premature to say that Model II approaches have *no* value. *They have never been tried on a mass level.* Whites are not usually exposed to a Model II type experience until they are adults.

[24] Jean Dresden Grambs. *Intergroup Education: Methods and Materials.* Englewood Cliffs, New Jersey: Prentice-Hall, Inc., 1968. p. 1. © 1968. Reprinted by permission of Prentice-Hall, Inc., Englewood Cliffs, New Jersey.

[25] Helen G. Trager and Marian Radke Yarrow. *They Learn What They Live: Prejudice in Young Children.* New York: Harper and Brothers, 1952. p. 362.

[26] *Ibid.*

Such adults usually attend a workshop two or three weeks or a course in race relations for a quarter or a semester. Evidence suggests that these experiences usually have little *permanent* impact on adults' racial attitudes, although other kinds of experiences (used in conjunction with lectures and readings) seem to have *some* lasting influence on the racial attitudes of adults.[27] It is predictable that a short workshop would have limited effect on adults' racial attitudes, since an experience of 20 hours or less cannot be expected to change attitudes and perceptions which an individual has internalized over a 20-year period, especially when the basic institutions in which he lives reinforce his pre-experimental attitudes.

Because of the meager results which have been obtained from Model II approaches, many ethnic minority spokesmen feel that this model should be abandoned, and that a shared power model is the only realistic way in which to achieve an open society. As a Black person who has conducted many *race relations* workshops, I greatly respect individuals who endorse this point of view. However, I feel that Model II approaches should be continued, *but the ways in which they are implemented should be greatly modified.* They should be continued and expanded because: (a) We have no assurance that a shared power model will succeed in this period of our history (however, we also have no assurance that it will not); (b) Model II strategies have never been implemented on a mass level, rather they are usually used in experiments with children or with teachers when a racial crisis hits a school district; (c) research suggests that the racial attitudes of children can be modified by curriculum intervention, especially in the earliest years—the younger children are, the greater the impact that curriculum intervention is likely to have on their racial feelings;[28] and (d) racism is a serious, dehumanizing pathology in this society which the school has a moral and professional responsibility to help eradicate, and most schools are controlled by whites. If we recommend the elimination of Model II approaches to an open society, we will in essence be telling people in power (dominant white groups) that they should play no role in humanizing this society, and should fiddle while our ghettos are burning. This kind of advice to dominant groups would be myopic, since the widespread repression within America is a powder keg that can explode and result in bloodshed and the destruction of this nation.

Earlier we discussed the severe limitations of Model II, and the

---

[27] For a summary of the research on which this discussion is based, see: James A. Banks, "Racial Prejudice and the Black Self-Concept," *op. cit.*
[28] *Ibid.*

questionable assumptions on which it is based. Later we argued that elements of this model should be implemented in appropriate settings. We do not see these two positions as contradictory; rather, we feel that when the curriculum builder is aware of the limitations of his strategies, he can better use, evaluate, and modify them. A knowledge of the limitations of a curriculum strategy will also prevent the curriculum builder from expecting unrealistic outcomes. For example, a knowledge of the limitations of Model II will help a teacher to realize that a unit on race relations during Black Heritage Week will have little impact on the racial attitudes of his pupils. Rather, he will know that *only* a complete modification of his total program is likely to have any significant impact on his students' racial attitudes and beliefs, and that even with this kind of substantial curriculum modification, the chances for alteration of racial attitudes will not be extremely high, especially if he is working with older students or adults.

Despite the severe limitations of Model II as it is currently used in the schools and in teacher education, I believe that substantial modifications in the *implementation* of Model II components can significantly increase this model's impact on the racial attitudes and perceptions of dominant groups. The ultimate result of an effective implementation of a model *may be* that children of dominant groups, as adults, will be more likely to perceive oppressed groups as *humans*, and thus more likely to share power with them, and allow them to participate more fully in America's social, economic, and political institutions. All of these statements are, at best, promising hypotheses, but I base them on experience, gleanings from research, and *faith*. In the next few paragraphs, I would like to suggest ways in which the implementation of a Model II type curriculum can have maximum opportunity to "enlighten" or modify the racial attitudes, beliefs, and perceptions of dominant and ruling groups.

By the time that the child enters school, he has generally already been inculcated with the negative attitudes toward ethnic minorities which are pervasive within the larger society. Although this fact has been documented since Lasker's pioneering research in 1929,[29] teachers are often surprised to learn in workshops that even kindergarten pupils are aware of racial differences and assign different values to Blacks and whites. This fact alone gives us little hope for effective intervention. However, a related one does. The racial attitudes of kindergartners are not as negative or as crystallized as those of fifth graders. As children grow older, and no systematic efforts are made to modify their racial

[29] Bruno Lasker. *Race Attitudes in Children*. New York: Henry Holt & Company, 1929.

feelings, they become more bigoted. The curricular implications of this research are clear. To modify children's racial attitudes, a *deliberate* program of instruction must be structured for that purpose in the earliest grades. The longer we wait, the less our chances are for success. By the time the individual reaches adulthood, the chances for successful intervention become almost—but not quite—nil.

Effective intervention programs must not only begin in the earliest grades, the efforts must be *sustained* over a long period of time, and material related to cultural differences must permeate the *entire* curriculum. Also, a variety of media and materials improves chances for successful intervention. A unit on Native Americans in the second grade, and a book on Chicanos in the third grade, will do little to help majority group youngsters to understand or accept cultures which are different from their own. A "hit and miss" approach to the study of cultural differences may do more harm than good. While there may be times when an in-depth study of an American ethnic minority culture is educationally justified in order to teach a concept such as *acculturation* or *enculturation,* most often when ethnic groups are studied in this way the students are likely to get the impression that ethnic minorities have not played an integral and significant role in the shaping of this society and its institutions, and that they are not "real" Americans. Most often Blacks, Native Americans, Chicanos, Puerto Rican Americans, and Asian-Americans are studied only when they are presented as "problems" by the textbook writer or curriculum builder. Thus most information about Blacks in textbooks focuses on the topic of slavery. Substantial information about Blacks does not appear again in most textbooks until the Black Revolt of the sixties. Native Americans are discussed when Columbus "discovered" them, and when they later become a "problem" when Anglo-Saxons expand westward.

If white students are to be helped to perceive other cultures as valid and legitimate, *a totally new conceptual framework must be used to view and teach about the American experience.* Most textbooks and curriculum materials are written from a white Anglo-Saxon point of view. Books on the "American Experience" usually begin with a discussion of the Crusades, the Vikings, and other Western European institutions and movements. Native American cultures are considered only as Columbus "discovers" them and they become an obstacle to the expansion of the colonies. Not only is this approach to American studies blatantly ethnocentric, it interprets the American experience strictly as a political entity which was an extension of Western European institutions and culture into the Americas. This totally Anglo-Saxon way of viewing the American experience cannot be tolerated in a curriculum which is designed to achieve an open society. America must be viewed as a land which was made up of a rich variety of cultures centuries before Europeans arrived. The introduction to American studies should deal with the nature of these complex and diverse cultures, and the ways in which they structured institutions to meet their needs for survival.[30]

After students have studied early America as a *culture area,* made up of a wide diversity of peoples and cultures, they can then learn about the foreigners who came to America from Europe. They can study about the ways in which the Europeans renamed Native Americans *Indians* (even though whites knew that America was not India), eradicated their cultures, committed genocide against the Natives, took their land, and created the most technologically advanced nation in the world. In any serious and honest study of American culture, the tragic experience of its Native peoples must be seen from new and humanistic perspectives. The point which I am trying to emphasize is that the study of America must be seen through the eyes of the vanquished, since students now study it primarily from the viewpoint of the victors. While both views can add to our understanding of the American experience, we must stress other viewpoints since the Anglo-Saxon view of American history is so distorted and widespread within our school and the larger society. Only by trying to see this nation from the viewpoints of oppressed peoples will we be able to fully understand the complexity of the American drama.

White students must also be helped to expand their conceptions of what it means to be human, since many whites assume that people who possess physical and cultural traits which differ markedly from their own are less than human. One promising way to help dominant group children to understand that there are many ways to be human is to expose them to a wide variety of cultures both within and outside the United States, and point out the similar needs which all groups have, and illustrate how they have used a wide variety of ways to satisfy them. Cross-cultural studies will help students understand that all cultures find ways to satisfy the needs of their members, and that a culture can be evaluated only within a particular social context. Thus, a cultural trait that is *different* does not mean that it is nonhuman or inferior, but rather it is different because it is functional for a different group of *human* beings.

Majority group students must also be helped to come to grips with the value dilemmas which are pervasive within our society and with

[30] See: Alvin M. Josephy, Jr. *The Indian Heritage of America.* New York: Bantam Books, Inc., 1968.

their own interpersonal value conflicts. Many students verbally claim that they value freedom for oppressed groups, but harshly condemn efforts by these groups to liberate themselves from oppression. Teachers must help students to see why these two feelings are contradictory and inconsistent. They have a professional responsibility to help students to see the contradictions and conflicts in their beliefs, to analyze reflectively their values, and to express a willingness to accept their implications. Some beliefs are inherently contradictory, and education should create men who have clarified, consistent beliefs which can guide meaningful and purposeful action of which the individual will be proud. A number of valuing inquiry models and strategies are available for use by teachers to help students to confront and analyze value problems and conflicts.[31]

The contradictions between the values expressed in our national documents and the ways in which minority groups are treated in our society should constitute an important part of a curriculum which purports to enlighten dominant groups. By reading case studies and documents on the experiences of ethnic minority groups, students will be able to conclude that only the wealthy persons within our society enjoy the "best" of America. The schools, the courts, and medical institutions respond best to the needs of the powerful groups in society. Poor people get an inferior education, little justice in the courts, and minimal medical care.

These facts about American life may or may not cause future powerful individuals to share power with the poor. However, many people in powerful positions today have never had to confront these issues in the school or elsewhere. *If for no other reasons, these facts need to be taught to students in order for them to obtain a sound education and liberated minds.* The school must help to liberate the minds of both dominant and exploited groups; both have been victimized by the myths and illusions which are rampant within America. Writes Paynter,

It should be obvious today that few American youth, black or white, will settle for illusions over reality where the past is concerned. By continuing to put forth a mythology in our history books which has little basis in fact, we shall be teaching contempt for history and for the white world which is its purveyor, as well as contributing to the already considerable degree of cynicism among many American young people today. . . . in studying various atrocities, some students would have trouble avoiding the conclusion that inhumanness

---

[31] A number of such strategies are presented in: James A. Banks (with contributions by Ambrose A. Clegg, Jr.). *Teaching Strategies for the Social Studies.* Reading, Massachusetts: Addison-Wesley Publishing Company, 1973. pp. 445-75.

was a necessary consequence of whiteness. . . . these students should be helped to see that simply to condemn the past has no more merit than mindless celebration of it.[32]

In summary, we have argued that in order to create an *open society* it is necessary to define clearly such a social system, and to design a curriculum specifically to achieve and perpetuate it. We have defined an open society as a social system in which individuals from diverse ethnic, cultural, and social class groups can freely participate, and have equal opportunities to gain the skills and knowledge which the society needs in order to function. Rewards within an open society are based upon the contributions which each person, regardless of his ancestry or social class, can make to the fulfillment of the society's functional requirements.

We conceptualized two models by which we may achieve and maintain an open society. Model I, or the SHARED POWER MODEL, focuses on helping oppressed groups to attain power so that they can control a number of social, economic, and political institutions, and determine who may participate in these institutions. These groups would also determine how rewards would be distributed. A second model, the ENLIGHTENING POWERFUL GROUPS MODEL, focuses on changing the attitudes of dominant and ruling groups so that they will share power with excluded groups, regard them as *human,* and take action to eliminate institutionalized racism within America.

The complexity of our society makes it impossible for either of these models to be implemented in *pure* form. Also, both models are ideal-type constructs which are based on a number of unverified assumptions. However, these models can help the curriculum builder to determine the kinds of focuses which should constitute an open society-curriculum for excluded, dominant, and mixed groups, for planning programs, and for ascertaining the effectiveness of various curriculum strategies. The urgency of our current racial crisis demands that we take decisive steps to create a more open society if we are to prevent racial wars and chaos and the complete dehumanization of the American Man.[33]

[32] Julie Paynter. "An End to Innocence." In: James A. Banks and William W. Joyce, editors. *Teaching Social Studies to Culturally Different Children.* Reading, Massachusetts: Addison-Wesley Publishing Company, 1971. pp. 333, 336. Reprinted by permission. *Journal of Current Social Issues* 7 (4); January 1969. Published by the United Church Board for Homeland Ministries.

[33] James A. Banks, "The Imperatives of Ethnic Minority Education," *op. cit.,* p. 269.

CHAPTER 5: INSTRUCTIONAL MEDIA FOR AN OPEN SOCIETY

LaMAR P. MILLER

THE HISTORY OF American education reveals that our schools have perpetuated the myth of a monistic America, which in effect has denied the pluralistic nature of our society with its multiracial and multiethnic culture. According to Hogg and McComb, "cultural pluralism has been a dominant feature in man's recent history, and yet there has been a general failure to consider its meaning and to examine its implication for American culture in general, and the field of education in particular."[1] We have also had a tradition of believing that education is a means of achieving equality, yet we find ourselves in the midst of an era in which social scientists have brought that assumption into question. The issues raised by the 1954 Supreme Court decision, *Brown* v. *Topeka*, have been contaminated by political questions related to public policy as well as emotional, often racist attitudes which color such considerations. Thus progress toward desegregation has been haltingly slow.

One has only to look at the segregated situation in Northern schools to know that insofar as education is concerned many doors are far from open. Historically, the situation with respect to the school program is similar. In general, instructional programs, methods of teaching, and our use of instructional materials are geared to a traditional and outmoded philosophy of education which is based solely on the transmission of knowledge model of learning. At the very least there are serious doubts that an open society, let alone an open-ended educational system, is possible in this country. It would be a serious omission if the skepticism that lies just beneath the surface of our hopes

[1] Thomas C. Hogg and Marlin R. McComb. "Cultural Pluralism: Its Implications for Education." *Educational Leadership* 27 (3): 235-36; December 1969.

for the future were not pointed out with respect to the use of instructional media in an open society.

In the 1960's and 1970's we witnessed a sustained assault on accepted traditional notions of education, and even on the hope that we could overcome those aspects of life that keep our society closed, particularly to Blacks and other minority groups. Clearly some of the results of the war on poverty, the impact of compensatory education, and the persistence of racism in the United States have dented the optimism of a variety of educators, social scientists, and policy makers. However, it is precisely these apparent failures which have given rise to new questions and encouraged scholars to seek new ways of looking at old problems.

Out of this continued inquiry and optimism, and to no one's surprise, we discovered that one of the most formidable agents for keeping our society closed has been our instructional materials, especially the textbook. The widespread reliance upon textbooks and other media which falsely depict our educational system as a model that is free and open to children from all religious and cultural backgrounds and the influence of these materials on learners during their early years are important contributing factors in maintaining the status quo of a closed and separate system. More important, we tend to take the contents of books and other materials and the way they are used for granted and, therefore, whatever debate we have had has been curiously superficial. "The most important thing that we can know about a man," says Lewis Wirth, "is what he takes for granted, and the most elemental and important facts about a society are those that are seldom debated and generally regarded as settled." [2] We can ill afford that luxury with regard to instructional media, if we are to achieve the elusive goal of a free and open society.

Open Education and Cultural Pluralism

It should be stated at the outset that this author's hopes for education represent a bias toward an open educational system based on cultural pluralism and acculturation without assimilation. There is a great need to assist learners, particularly Black and other minority youngsters, in attaining the skills necessary for competition in American life without pressuring them to reject totally their own individual

[2] Lewis Wirth. Preface in: Carl Mannheim. *Ideology and Utopia: An Introduction to the Sociology of Knowledge.* New York: Harcourt, Brace and World, 1936. pp. 10-30.

cultural style. A basic element of an open society is valid intercultural dialog based on cultural distinctiveness and not on assimilation. Only upon acceptance of cultural differences can we grow toward a mature acceptance of others and an awareness of the value of cultural diversity.

In a similar vein it makes sense that an open society requires an open system of education. This means a system based on the belief that knowledge is unique to each individual and that a child learns from the direct personal exploration of his environment. An open educational system would require that, if we accept the notion that learning and knowledge result from the learner's primary experience with the real world, our emphasis must shift from secondhand recorded knowledge to the problem of selecting and providing the materials which will extend each child's knowledge. We can believe, as Rousseau did, that skills can develop from firsthand exploration as well as from those educational experiences that are often abstract and irrelevant. It is important to note these differences with regard to the development of instructional media since others may have surveyed the same territory and mapped it very differently.

Rethinking Educational Needs

In considering instructional media in an open society, it is extremely important that we rethink educational needs for our children. Perhaps it is time we acknowledge that we have done considerable damage to children who must grow up in what is basically a consumer society. That youngsters need to be needed is accepted by most of us, but vital experiences in this area are almost impossible. In a system where there is little opportunity for young people to participate in such things as simple manual work, where parents do all the caring for their children that they conceive is necessary, and where we are united as consumers rather than producers, it is possible for children to grow up without having any experience of being needed or of being anything more than one more consumer.

Another important notion is that children learn by *needing*. One of the most disastrous results of the emphasis on so-called skill learning, out of any context of a need to learn, is that learning becomes enforced drudgery or a way of pleasing adults or deferred gratification. To put it another way, we place more emphasis on teaching the child to live in the future than in the present. In developing materials today there is also the tendency to rely on those instructional devices which foster the whole dogma of teaching to concepts. This can be very damaging in the development of instructional materials for an open society. The problem here is that these materials often seek to supplant individually arrived-at perceived meaning with publicly shared belief, which often goes unexamined. If our youngsters are to grow up to be autonomous, to have competence in decision making based on alternatives that they can live with, they must have an opportunity to develop those virtues which we claim mature members of our society ought to have.

Finally, we must also consider the shortcomings of American textbooks. During the past 10 years the publishers of textbooks have been subjected to serious criticism. This criticism has not been confined to one particular subject nor to one particular grade level. It covers the entire range of textbooks from the kindergartner's reading readiness workbook to the high school senior's American history text. As Drachler pointed out, "In 1970, nearly 200 years after Pike's publication of his arithmetic book, textbooks and instructional materials are still a subject for disagreement and debate."[3] Drachler's remarks are not aimed solely at publishers for he suggests that we, as educators, are equally responsible if teaching materials do not fully meet sound educational objectives. Richard Margolis agrees when he states that,

> In the final analysis the responsibility for improving our textbooks rests with the public and with the schools (which are presumably an instrument of public will). Since publishers are first and foremost businessmen, they must act out the myth that the customer is always right, even when the customer is obviously dead wrong.[4]

Suffice it to say here that textbook criticism is certainly not new. During the past century, there have been as many demands for studies and recommendations for improving texts as there have been for improving schools. And it is because the textbook is such an important educational tool that it ought to be evaluated critically for its strengths and weaknesses. As for the use of textbooks in an open society, Drachler is correct in his assertion that we should reexamine our texts and our history, not to distort the truth or to conceal shortcomings, but to reevaluate the questions, "What is an American?" and "What is a worthy American deed?"

[3] Norman Drachler. "Shortcomings of American Textbooks." *Bulletin of the National Association of Secondary School Principals* 54 (345): 15-25; April 1970. "In 1788 Nicholas Pike published a textbook called, 'A New and Complete System of Arithmetic Composed for the Use of Citizens in the United States.'"

[4] Richard J. Margolis. "The Trouble with Textbooks." *Redbook Magazine* 124: 64-65, 123-29; March 1965. Reprinted from *Redbook Magazine*, March 1965. Copyright © 1965 by The McCall Publishing Company.

Teachers have complained for a long time now about the great need for proper materials and guidance in introducing, into their classes in elementary and secondary schools, information on the role of minorities. There is, in fact, a vast literature which is critical of the interpretation of American history in our texts. Yet it ought to be clear that the blatant mistreatment of minorities is by no means confined to history or literature books. While instructional media dealing with science, mathematics, grooming, and even driver education have improved as far as updating information is concerned, the fact is that with respect to minority groups, most materials fall far short of what is relevant in an open system. And to be perfectly frank, media that are insensitive to one group, Blacks for example, are likely to be insensitive to other groups and, in all probability, to mankind. The following example of insensitivity taken from an arithmetic book published by a large national publisher and printed in 1961 is illustrative.

Once upon a time a ship was caught in a severe storm. It looked as if the ship, its crew, and 30 passengers would be lost. In order to save the ship and its crew, the captain decided that one-half of the passengers would have to be thrown overboard. There were 15 Christians and 15 Turks aboard the ship. . . . Now the captain was a Christian. So he arranged the 30 passengers in a big circle . . . and announced that he would count the passengers and that every ninth one would be thrown overboard.

The question was: how could the 15 Christians and 15 Turks be placed in the circle so that all the Turks would be thrown overboard and then all of the Christians would be saved? [5]

In the past five years a rush has been under way from coast to coast to make up for past inadequacies. Minority groups have been exerting pressure to bring about quick changes in the curriculum, such as the inclusion of Black and Native American Studies. These pressures and the development of a rash of new programs in urban, suburban, and rural school districts provided an opportunity for the publishing industry to produce new integrated textbooks and supplementary materials by and about ethnic groups. Indeed, the publishers have rushed in, but for the most part materials have been produced in haste with little thought given to their appropriateness. While it is not the purpose here to specify the inadequacies, let it suffice to say that there has not been a combination of providing appropriate and adequate content based on sound principles of learning and realistic appraisals of the wide range of learning situations.

[5] Norman Drachler, *op. cit.*, pp. 21-22.

Developing Instructional Media in an Open System

A number of school districts, state departments of education, and other agencies have established policies for evaluating instructional media, and some publishers have developed guides for selecting materials. For the most part the primary emphasis of these criteria is improving the treatment of minority and ethnic groups. More recently some school districts have focused on the treatment of women in their material. It is doubtful, however, whether any of these groups have approached the development of instructional media from the broad perspective of an open society.

In setting forth what needs to be accomplished it must be recognized that we face a complicated, long-range undertaking. Nevertheless some suggestions are offered, based on what a variety of other groups have said. The guide which follows is certainly not exhaustive and is only meant to be broad and general. Hopefully it is consistent with our view that the representation of diverse groups in an open setting is an asset and not a liability in instructional media. Instructional media for an open society should:

1. Advance the learning and personal development of young people from very diverse regional and ethnic groups.

2. Emphasize an open-ended inquiry approach to learning and represent a balance between the immediate social environment and the larger social world.

3. Focus on an interdisciplinary approach which reflects experiences that relate to the individual's real world and not divide knowledge into neatly separated categories or disciplines.

4. Assure an accurate and balanced inclusion in presenting historical contributions as well as present status of ethnic groups and women.

5. Avoid stereotyping. Present a range of roles and human characteristics for any group. Include portrayals of ethnic groups that include the accurate presentation of the group culture from the point of view of that group.

6. Be functional. Stress skills necessary for one to cope with life, particularly for those who come from minority backgrounds.

7. Take into account new instructional strategies that include a balanced combination of written, visual, and new technological developments.

8. Stress the dignity and worth of the individual.

9. Assist students in identifying with the educational process.

10. Seek to motivate students to examine their own attitudes and behaviors, and to comprehend their own duties and responsibilities as citizens in a pluralistic open society.

New Concepts and New Information

In considering the foregoing suggestions there are some specific areas that should be discussed in more detail. The first is the need for development of new concepts and new information for American history. Inclusion of the participation of minorities in our history has really required a new look at our past. For example, the prevalence of Poles, Blacks, and Indians in Jamestown provides a very different picture of this first colony than that offered by traditional versions of Captain John Smith, Pocahontas, and John Rolfe. In 1619 the House of Burgesses, America's first representative assembly, met in Jamestown. But Africans were then present and laboring in Jamestown's fields; and Poles, denied the right to vote because they were not Anglo-Saxons, marched on the House of Burgesses and staged the nation's first civil rights demonstration until they did win the right to vote for Burgesses. The story of Jamestown must be told with this new information about its multiracial and ethnic nature and conflicts.

Another example typical of the kind of information needed can be found in a book called *The Black West*,[6] a documentary of the Afro-American in the American frontier. For example, the history of Jim Beckwourth, a Black hero in 1860, who was as famous as Kit Carson, has been left out of most Western histories. Few of us had the opportunity to learn of the U.S. Army's Black fighters known as the "Buffalo Scouts," nor do we know anything about Bill Pickett, a fabulous rodeo performer and master practitioner of bulldogging, who at various times was assisted by two unknown cowpunchers—Tom Mix and Will Rogers.

New figures need to be introduced into the U.S. history curriculum. Their patriotism was manifested in their fearless championship of reform against great odds: Dr. W. E. B. DuBois; Indian chieftains; Jacob Riis, the Danish immigrant whose camera and writing exposed ghetto conditions; and Lillian Wald, the Jewish immigrant whose settlement house in New York sought to correct social inequities.

The story of Orientals as a minority group cannot be overlooked either and, more important, it cannot be told in isolation from any other

[6] William L. Katz. *The Black West*. New York: Doubleday & Company, Inc., 1971.

group of people. As Shibutani and Kwan put it, "there are often more than two ethnic groups on a given frontier of contact and all of them interlock in a common system; they must be studied together."[7] The study of Orientals in China, Japan, and Southeast Asia must be seen in the context of the place they occupy and within the world they knew and touched, rather than to describe them as isolated human beings and, therefore, to perpetuate an unjustified stereotyping.

Similar comments can be made with regard to Hispanic peoples in the United States. The primary fact is that the first White settlers in the Southwest were Spanish. As Valdes reports,

For centuries Spain was England's superior, most powerful, and hated enemy. Both the English and Dutch founding colonists of eastern United States were envious of Spanish wealth and influence, and afraid of the Spanish and the Spanish church. It was natural, then, that English historians and their allies should feed the propaganda mills that poured out such a collection of myths, exaggerations, and lies about the Spanish that the phenomenon became known as the "Black Legend." Anglo-Americans took up the legend and even embellished it. The legend is still very much alive today, although some American historians of today, with admirable honesty, have done much to discredit and destroy it.

Valdes goes on to note another important fact:

The most important cultural and racial antecedents of the Hispano of the U.S. Southwest are Spanish, but the Indian racial and cultural admixtures in most Mexican Americans, and the Negroid and Indian elements in the makeup of many Cubans and Puerto Ricans, should not be ignored.[8]

Recent surveys have pointed to the general lack of knowledge about the importance of ethnic groups in American society. Many Americans, themselves members of one or another ethnic group, are unaware of the diversity of American culture, of the heritage, struggles, and achievements of other ethnic groups. They continue to think of such groups in terms of stereotypes and to use clichés to describe them. And the average American history textbook provides little or no information that could counter their clichés. In fact, the members of any one ethnic group are almost as deprived of valid information about their own past as they are about the past of another ethnic group. Black Americans are especially interested in studying their roots; and other groups, sensing

[7] Tamotsu Shibutani and Kian M. Kwan. *Ethnic Stratification: A Comparative Approach.* New York: The Macmillan Company, 1965.

[8] Daniel R. Valdes. "The U.S. Hispano." *Social Education* 33 (4): 440-42; April 1969.

the similarities in their own situations, have also begun to show an interest in acquiring more accurate information about their heritage.

Insofar as the nation's schools are concerned, they are beginning to discover that they have been perpetuating a great injustice to ethnic minority groups. A major part of the problem, pinpointed by the groups themselves and by concerned educators, is now clearly in focus: The role of the Black, Mexican American, Indian, and Oriental in American life has often been ignored or inaccurately portrayed in curriculum materials.

Open-Ended Inquiry

A second important consideration in developing instructional media is the assumption that knowledge is a *means* of education and not its *end*. It is questionable, if not impossible, that there is a minimum body of knowledge that is essential for everyone to know. This is a premise upon which advocates of open education, open schools, or open-spaced schools claim to base their programs. While it is not the purpose of this chapter to determine a precise definition of open-ended education, most educators will agree that knowledge is unique to each individual. In any event, if we were to search for a term it would more likely be called *open-ended inquiry*. One of the features of materials based on this notion would be the provision for opportunities for students to study in areas that they recognize as significant to themselves. Open-ended inquiry is somewhat different than discovery, because it does not require that teachers guide students toward a foreknown end. This is not to suggest that materials based on the discovery method are not important, since they may play a part in some aspects of the curriculum in motivating students and challenging them to new understandings.

Materials based on this notion would allow for wide-ranging conceptualizing. They should be written engagingly and slanted emphatically toward open inquiry with the aim of provoking deeper involvement of the learner with topics that are important to him. It is true, however, that in developing materials about ethnic minority groups, writers and publishers need to be concerned with validity and how various aspects of an ethnic group culture are conceptualized. This is a problem regardless of the approach one uses, but one can choose to focus on any significant aspect of a group and, by careful use of open-ended inquiry, maintain validity. The fact is that any particular focus can create distortions. Unless instructional media are totally representative of each aspect of a culture, they are bound to create grounds for wrong assumptions. This is particularly true with groups such as the Native American, with a vast array of tribal customs, but it is equally as much a risk with other ethnic groups in developing appropriate instructional media.

While it is difficult to proceed from the specific to the general without some degree of stereotyping, it might be possible if the creators of instructional media moved in random ways into an examination of a people's art, for instance, and if supportive illustrations of life styles were offered. In fact, we need new approaches to replace the often dull materials used by students in the past. These should be a combination of exciting reading and visual materials that capture the history of ethnic minority groups. Eyewitness accounts of slaves, indentured servants, sweatshop operators, tenement dwellers, civil rights crusaders, and people imbued with a sense of their own racial or ethnic importance should enrich learning in the classrooms of the nation. At the same time, based on the process of open-ended inquiry, we need to develop some conceptions that are not usually made. For example, if some Mexican Americans (but by no means all) do menial farm labor in Southern California, it means some are employed only seasonally. If this is so, it would be safe to hypothesize that some Mexican Americans are probably poor.

On the other hand, if we depict an artistic medium in a form of illustrations that are distinctly Indian, Oriental, or Mexican, could it not follow that these practitioners will maintain their cultural lineage, and that this example of cultural lineage may prevail in other aspects of their lives? An illustration of Puerto Ricans filling eight hardball diamonds in Central Park may be a valid clue to acculturation—at least in New York City—where 90 percent of the Puerto Ricans in the United States dwell. The point is that by using open-ended inquiry one illustration may be vastly more useful and interesting than a flat-out statement regarding how many Puerto Ricans play baseball in the major leagues. While an emphasis on history and literature is important, there is a strong possibility that conveying cultural lineage by emphasizing an artistic medium would be not only fruitful, but exciting.

Revising Our Philosophy of Education

Although the thrust of this chapter has been to cite the necessity for developing instructional media that are appropriate for an open society, it is the need for a revision of our philosophy of education that is the essence of this report. The instructional materials of our schools must reflect the total dynamics of our society past and present. The concept of the "melting pot" is not an appropriate guide for new educational directions. It suggests that differences which exist among Americans of varying backgrounds can be ignored. It implies a cultural monolog rather than a cultural dialog. Instructional media based on this concept reflect neither a pluralistic society nor its common aspirations, but instead tend to reinforce a pattern of racism or separate attitudes in our society.

In the final analysis, the blends and patterns of education which should overcome former educational deficiencies in favor of a system that respects the life styles of Blacks and other ethnic minority groups clearly necessitate creative leadership. It is the commitment to such patterns rather than the polemics which should be the greatest concern for those who make crucial decisions in the purchasing and use of instructional media. The pressures that have led to the development of instructional media and ethnic studies programs can only mean a healthy development for education. The goal of education must be to preserve the ethnic identity of Black, Indian, Chinese, Puerto Rican, Mexican, and all other American children through a system of education that emphasizes the value of cultural diversity in an open society.

References

James A. Banks. "A Content Analysis of the Black American in Textbooks." *Social Education* 33 (8): 954-57; December 1969.

James A. Banks. "Teaching Ethnic Minority Studies with a Focus on Culture." *Educational Leadership* 29 (2): 113-17; November 1971.

Gloria T. Blatt. "The Mexican American in Children's Literature." *Elementary English* 45 (4): 446-51; April 1968.

Frank M. Cordasco and Leonard Covello. "Studies of Puerto Rican Children in American Schools: A Preliminary Bibliography." *Journal of Human Relations* 16: 264-85; Second Quarter 1968.

Joanne Dale. "Literature By and About Minorities." *Educational Leadership* 28 (3): 289-91; December 1970.

Norman Drachler. "Shortcomings of American Textbooks." *Bulletin of the National Association of Secondary School Principals* 54 (345): 15-25; April 1970.

"Education for Self-Identity." *Educational Leadership* 27 (3): 213-324; December 1969. An issue containing articles relevant to problems of bias and pluralism.

Sol M. Elkin. "Minorities in Textbooks: The Latest Chapter." *Teachers College Record* 66 (6): 502-508; March 1965.

Geneva Gay. "Ethnic Minority Studies: How Widespread? How Successful?" *Educational Leadership* 29 (2): 108-12; November 1971.

Geneva Gay. "Needed: Ethnic Studies in Schools." *Educational Leadership* 28 (3): 292-95; December 1970.

Warren J. Halliburton and William Loren Katz. *American Majorities and*

Minorities: A Syllabus of United States History for Secondary Schools. New York: National Association for the Advancement of Colored People, 1970.

Nelson H. Harris. "The Treatment of Negroes in Books and Media Designed for the Elementary School." *Social Education* 33 (4): 434-37; April 1969.

Thomas C. Hogg and Marlin R. McComb. "Cultural Pluralism: Its Implications for Education." *Educational Leadership* 27 (3): 235-38; December 1969.

An Index to Multi-Ethnic Teaching and Teacher Resources. Washington, D.C.: Professional Rights and Responsibilities Commission, Committee on Civil and Human Rights of Educators, National Education Association, 1967.

Agnes M. S. Inn. "The Orientals." *Social Education* 33 (4): 443-46; April 1969.

Harry Alleyn Johnson, editor. *Multimedia Materials for Afro-American Studies.* New York: R. R. Bowker Co., 1971.

William Loren Katz. "The Past and Its Presence." *Southern Education Report* 4: 20-22; July/August 1968. (Reprint available from NAACP Special Contribution Fund, New York.)

Milton Kleg. "Ethnic Relations Media: Exercise Care When Selecting!" *Social Education* 36 (2): 192-98; February 1972.

Lloyd A. Marcus. *The Treatment of Minorities in Secondary School Textbooks.* New York: Anti-Defamation League of B'nai B'rith, 1961.

Charles F. Marder and Gladys Meyer. *Minorities in American Society.* New York: American Book Company, 1962.

Richard J. Margolis. "The Trouble with Textbooks." *Redbook Magazine* 124: 64-65, 123-29; March 1965.

LaMar P. Miller. "Black Studies: A Pedagogical Device for a Pluralistic Society." *New York University Education Quarterly* 11: 17-26; Winter 1971.

LaMar P. Miller. "Materials for Multi-Ethnic Learners." *Educational Leadership* 28 (2): 129-32; November 1970.

National Education Association, Commission on Professional Rights and Responsibilities. "The Treatment of Minorities in Textbooks." *School & Society* 95 (2293): 323-24; Summer 1967.

Red, White, and Black: Minorities in America. The Combined Paperback Exhibit. Briarcliff Manor, New York: The Combined Book Exhibit, Inc., 1969.

Armando Rodriguez. "Education for the Spanish-Speaking: Mañana in Motion." *National Elementary Principal* 49 (4): 52-56; February 1970.

Textbook Report. Detroit, Michigan: Intergroup Relations Department, School-Community Relations Division, Detroit Public Schools, 1968.

Daniel T. Valdes. "The U.S. Hispano." *Social Education* 33 (4): 440-42; April 1969.

CHAPTER 6: TEACHERS FOR AN OPEN SOCIETY

R. BRUCE IRONS*

It is amusing to hear people suggesting education as a solution to the race problem. *Education in America cannot solve the race problem because education in America is part of the race problem.* The education process perpetuates the control and subordination of black people, and it is vitiated from top to bottom by a class bias which mystifies the poor and the black.— *Lerone Bennett, Jr.*†

TODAY THE STRUGGLE to create an open society in the United States is, most fundamentally, the struggle to stop the genocide of people of color. This genocide is partly physical (three black babies die in this country for every white baby who dies) and partly psychological (black and brown children are forced to internalize teachers' beliefs in their innate inferiority). A dense web of myth and illusion systematically obscures the origins and maintenance of genocide. Movement toward an open society requires the identification of those myths and illusions, and subsequent changes in consciousness—values, assumptions, feelings, perceptions, and even cognitive styles. Because teachers of European descent (Euro-Americans) constitute the vast majority of the teaching force, it is they who can and must change, if education is ever to stop being part of the problem of genocide, and become part of the solution.

This chapter argues that to promote an open society, teachers must uncover these myths, change our cultural consciousness, and act on our new vision to remake schools and communities. This action is the responsibility of Euro-Americans, while Third World people continually monitor and assess the appropriateness of such actions and their effects.

* *Author's Note:* I am grateful to Alfred Alschuler, Pat Bidol, Edith Sparago, and Rhody McCoy for commenting on earlier drafts of this chapter.

† Lerone Bennett, Jr. "Student Power, Black Power, and the American Dream." Speech at the Association for Supervision and Curriculum Development Annual Conference, Philadelphia, Pennsylvania, March 5, 1972.

What are the steps leading to the acquisition of these new patterns? First, the *processes* of Euro-American innocence and illusion need to be identified. Second, the *content* of these illusions needs to be outlined to suggest goals for "new white consciousness." Finally, strategies must be designed to accomplish these goals in pre- and in-service teachers' personal/cultural consciousness. One of these strategies involves defining the crucial characteristics of teachers who foster a more open society. These characteristics become the criteria for selection, certification, or hiring staff for educational enterprises. A second strategy is relatively novel. Newly clarified principles of psychological education can be used to facilitate individuals' efforts to transform their world and consciousness simultaneously.[1]

"The Perfection of Innocence Is Madness"—Arthur Miller

Euro-American culture shapes institutions that socialize Americans to be innocent about manifest inhumanities exemplified by the genocide of people of color. Yette,[2] Citron,[3] and Knowles and Prewitt,[4] among others, lucidly document the reality of cultural and institutional racism in the United States. Intellectual understanding has not derailed the cultural, psychological, historical, and social processes which apparently allow teachers to remain innocent of this reality. The search for freedom from racism has not yet touched the illusion-based innocence that is a knot of madness ". . . tied very, very tight around the throat of the whole human species."[5] Teachers participating in this illusory innocence reinforce the environment for racism in the United States and act as instruments of it, not only destroying children of people of color, but also diminishing the potential humanity of Euro-American children and their own humanity.

The dominant ethical pattern of the United States only tightens this knot. Based on the emphasis on Reason and Individualism in the Renaissance, we learn to stand up for what we believe in, even if we must go against the crowd. Euro-Americans deny or remain *pseudo-*

---

[1] A. S. Alschuler. *Developing Achievement Motivation in Adolescents.* Englewood Cliffs, New Jersey: Education Technology, Inc., 1973.

[2] Samuel F. Yette. *The Choice: The Issue of Black Survival in America.* New York: G. P. Putnam's Sons, 1971.

[3] Abraham F. Citron. "The 'Rightness of Whiteness.'" Detroit, Michigan: Michigan-Ohio Regional Educational Laboratory, 1969.

[4] L. L. Knowles and Kenneth Prewitt. *Institutional Racism in America.* Englewood Cliffs, New Jersey: Prentice-Hall, Inc., 1969.

[5] R. D. Laing. *The Politics of the Family.* New York: Vintage Books, 1972. p. 124.

innocent, in Rollo May's words, of the consequences of their actions on others. There is a lack of identification with the powerless and the unwillingness to assume responsibility for ensuring equity for the powerless. The mechanisms of this denial are varied. All point to the need for a new ethical framework that does not forfeit our valuing of *all* individuals and their integrity. We need to balance values of individualism with values of collective responsibility for guaranteeing equity. As teachers, we must be held and we must hold ourselves accountable for our actions *and* for becoming as aware as we can of the effects of our actions.

To accomplish such an expanded ethical framework requires a change in conceptual patterns basic to Western thought. From Aristotle to Nixon, the "either/or" conceptual approach characterizing most Euro-American thinking *necessarily* leads to racial conflict rather than to racial harmony. *Union* of opposites characterizes typical African conceptual patterns, while Euro-American thinking typically denies one polarity to affirm the other. If white is human, black is not human. If I am good, I cannot acknowledge even my potential for evil. If I do not admit having power, I do not hold myself accountable for the effects of failing to exercise it. When one makes sense of the world in this conceptual style, it guarantees "innocence" of the effects of one's action or inaction, as well as the maintenance of the illusions that justify those actions.

Thus, many teachers have told Third World children to have reasonable (low) career aspirations, as Malcolm X's teacher did, *believing* they are doing the children a favor. Some teachers fail to teach children to read, but remain in the classroom *believing* the children have failed. Other teachers organize successfully to double their wages in 10 years, while *believing* in their impotence to confront "the system" that does not provide adequate food, shelter, and health care for children. The fabric of assumptions which supports this belief system is relatively inaccessible. There is an unspoken rule against exploring that fabric. R. D. Laing found this unspoken rule operating in the families of so-called schizophrenics. As in all families, there were rules and assumptions that governed interaction among the members. However, in these families there were "rules against seeing the rules, and hence against [seeing] all the issues that arise from complying with or breaking them." [6] Paradoxically, the one who sees or names such assumptions or rules in the family is often the one labeled insane. The teacher who sees and names the assumptions and implicit rules supporting racism in

[6] *Ibid.*, p. 106.

schools is often labeled radical, idealist, naïve, or a troublemaker instead of a problem solver.

Many teachers, along with the larger population, consciously or unconsciously assume that people of color, women, or the poor are innately inferior to white males, that these oppressed people *deserve* their subordination, and that "these problems" (racism, sexism, etc.) would go away if everyone just accepted Jesus as their savior, or experienced Gestalt therapy, or did whatever they "could" in their own way. However, these apparent solutions avoid the crucial power issues and ignore the limitations of the teachers' own cultural perspective.

Given such teachers, what is a plausible intervention strategy to break the cycle of the perpetuation of racism? The cyclical process is one in which culture is shaped by institutions which, in turn, socialize people into cultural patterns. The patterns, in turn, actively reinforce the existing social, economic, and cultural institutions. Defining the cycle this way implies that racism is learned and might be eliminated by some "unlearning" process. This broadly held hypothesis, at least, acknowledges Euro-American racism as "the problem." The belief that racism is learned, instead of being an inherent aspect of human nature, is an example of the either/or pattern in Western thought. This either/or conceptual pattern, in itself, partially causes our racism. Thus, we must train ourselves simultaneously to affirm that (a) people are by nature racist and demand action policies designed to control their racism, *and* that (b) people learn racism and demand action policies designed to eliminate it. For example, portions of teachers' salaries can be made contingent on equal ultimate educational attainment of Euro-American and Third World children from those teachers' schools, while simultaneous attempts are made educationally to promote more humane awareness, attitudes, and actions by the same teachers. The often debated choice between trying to change people or institutions is simply a symptom of our illusory either/or way of thinking. In such a double solution process, the pseudo-innocence and illusions providing the environment and justification for oppression can begin to be burned away. Especially among those who teach young people, such a process cannot be left to chance.

New White Consciousness for Teachers

We must begin to understand that *all* whites are racist, because they benefit from inequitable, illegitimate privileges coming to them by virtue of their whiteness. A white arrested for the same crime as a Third World person typically receives lower bail, better legal representation, a shorter sentence, and is paroled sooner, everything else being equal. Similar negatively different results for Third World people occur in our schools in spite of educators' good intentions. The essence of teachers' movement toward "new white consciousness" involves their internalizing a new realization of the inequity and illegitimacy of existent white privilege. Once aware of this, teachers may mobilize their resources to promote decision-making and standard-setting processes that support equitable outcomes for all students.

The paradoxical nature of the suggested "new white consciousness" and its expression in action are described by Robert Terry.

New white consciousness is a way for us to understand ourselves simultaneously as white racists and as creators of justice.

As new conscious whites we have at least six urgent tasks:

1. Become conscious agents of change—recognize new directions are possible.

2. Seek ethical clarity—know what we ought to stand for and why.

3. Identify the multiple forms and expressions of white racism—know who we have been, and why.

4. Develop social strategies for change to eliminate and move beyond racism—experience what our society might be.

5. Discern the appropriate tactics—assess our power for change.

6. Experiment, test, and refine personal styles of life congruent with our newly affirmed values—experience who we might be.[7]

However, *whites cannot eliminate racism by themselves,* and to suggest they can perpetuates paternalism. Whites need continual Third World assessment and monitoring when struggling against racial oppression. Thus, the seventh task of "new white consciousness" is to find ways to implement accountability to the oppressed without creating new oppression.

Conceptual and cultural patterns, thus, combine with psychological defensiveness to prevent white engagement with the tasks of new white consciousness. Part of the fundamental white fears of confronting racism issues spring directly from cultural myths of "rugged individualism" and the "success fantasy." Rugged individualism implies that individual, courageous action solves problems, for example, David and Goliath. The "success fantasy" implies one should choose action based on the likelihood of accomplishing goals rather than the con-

[7] Robert Terry. *For Whites Only.* Grand Rapids, Michigan: Wm. B. Eerdmans Publishing Co., 1970. pp. 20-21.

sistency of chosen actions with one's values regardless of probable outcome. These cultural patterns imprison whites, because effective anti-racist action can rarely be individual or unambiguously successful *by definition*. For instance, the following catalog of statements of conventional wisdom in relation to each task illustrates the interdependence of either/or conceptual patterns, cultural patterns of individualism, and psychological patterns of defensiveness in typical white resistance to self-knowledge concerning racism.

1. *Become a conscious agent of change.* "You can't beat city hall. I'm a follower not a leader. I'm afraid to stick my neck out. I don't know *how* to start."

2. *Seek ethical clarity.* "I believe in freedom, whatever the cost. I'm not a racist, but I can't be held accountable for my colleagues' behavior. People aren't responsible for evil they don't know about. Everyone has an equal chance to succeed or fail in my classroom."

3. *Identify the multiple forms and expressions of white racism.* "Blacks held each other as slaves. They have no history or civilization. The problem is motivation. The problem is their language differences. I expect everyone to work up to their potential, but it's no good to push youngsters beyond themselves. Families can help by encouraging excellence in school work. Things *are* getting better."

4. *Social change strategies.* "You don't understand the political realities. Conflict just hurts everyone, nobody wins. I'm just one person. I don't know *how* things happen around here. We tried once, and it didn't work. I don't dare speak up."

5. *Tactics.* "Look out for number one. It's not what you know; it's who you know. Violence is always wrong. I don't like to make people uncomfortable. They must know what they're doing. We *tried* a petition. Majority rules. I don't dare."

6. *Experience new values, life styles.* "I'm old-fashioned, I guess. Things are changing so fast, I get confused. I got some mod clothes and my friends laughed. If I do what I should, I'll lose my job and friends— I guess I can't do anything."

7. *Third World accountability.* "What do they want from us? It's just reverse racism to do everything Blacks say."

A similar catalog could be compiled of resistance to seeing and acting against the oppression of other people: women, youth, the old, the ethnically and religiously identifiable. The creating of conditions for allowing teachers to overcome such deep, complex resistance and to engage the tasks of new white consciousness comprises an agenda for teacher reeducation, as well as suggests criteria for teacher selection.

This agenda is fundamentally different from those underlying most existing efforts to select and train teachers to combat racism. Up to now most attempts to confront this problem have focused on training teachers to change negative attitudes toward Third World people. Such programs may increase or reduce racial tension. However, by definition the training cannot change the dominant cultural framework or the institutions from which racial oppression springs. Nor can we move toward a more open society using the same assumptions on which the present one was created.

Attitude change efforts are futile as more than a partial strategy in the needed individual and collective cultural revolution. A typical program of human relations training conducted for a school's administrators, teachers, and custodians illustrates this futility. Participants' attitudes toward minority people "improved" on a racial attitudes inventory. These changes were confirmed by increased measured acceptance of oneself and others, as well as a self-report of reduced "prejudiced" behavior. However, no *observable* behavior change, or change in institutional policy, occurred.

One can assume that the teacher who never touches black students, or compulsively wipes her hands after touching a black child, who never calls on a black youngster except to berate or scold, or calls blacks by their last names and whites by their first, is not consciously aware of these behaviors. Indeed, these *same* teachers were the most enthusiastic about the effects of the workshop in changing their behavior. Yet children, black, white, brown, red, or yellow, observe these behaviors, and racial prejudice is taught in the most effective way possible, through the subtle modeling of the approved social behavior of the adults they seek to emulate.[8]

Teachers' racist behaviors are stable, reflect the cultural context, and are *not* controlled through attitude change programs. We desperately need to find ways to control the expression of subtle or overt racist teacher behaviors. Such control must be a primary objective of anti-racist educators. "New white" educators must simultaneously go to the roots of the disease by fostering cultural revolution *and* preventing the *expression* of Euro-American teachers' racism in the present moment. Teacher selection and reeducation programs should reflect both these goals.

[8] G. C. Fauth. "Attitude and Behavior Change in Teachers During a Human Relations Laboratory Training Experience." Unpublished doctoral dissertation, University of Michigan, Ann Arbor, 1972. p. 165.

The cultural revolution alluded to is *not* the current "counter-culture" movement of the white middle class, which is steeped in the American norm of individuality without social responsibility. Rather it is a revolution that involves the confrontation of culture itself: the values, myths, norms, and structures that formed and preserve it. Wide-spread adoption of superordinate goals based on the value of the sacredness of human life, and the interdependence of humans among themselves, as well as with the natural earth shared by all living beings, will signal progress in that revolution. The United States is in a survival crisis that is total. The solution involves total reconstruction of the values and assumptions of all U.S. institutions. Nowhere is this more true than in the educational system. Persons of power who make decisions in that system, even provided they can *see* alternatives, have rarely decided to pay the price required to begin such reconstruction.

Some teachers can and have decided to "pay the price," to fight the debilitating web of assumptions and illusions into which they have been socialized, and to pursue the tasks of "new whiteness" in the context of their role as teachers. Those who educate, license, and hire teachers can make such a decision the core objective and criterion for success of their work.

Goals for Reeducation and Criteria for Teacher Selection and Retention

To promote the cultural revolution *and* block continuing racism, school and program goals must reflect (a) the need to control *and* eliminate personal, cultural, and institutional racism, and (b) the need to revolutionize the consciousness that makes change possible. Under-standing the power structures, the influence practices, and the control of physical resources of educational institutions means little without new values and consciousness. New consciousness, on the other hand, is impotent without understanding the underlying causes of racism in relation to the distribution of power and wealth and an understanding of the ways present racist policies and practices support that distribution.

Successfully putting in place basic realignment of power and norms in support of anti-racist teacher behavior *both* depends on and should result in progress in the cultural revolution. The control of overt, covert, conscious, or unconscious behavior that either damages children of color or teaches the appropriateness of such behavior to white children *can* be accomplished. Along with institutionally racist prac-tices like much tracking, standardized testing, and "guidance" that channels Third World children to educational programs with little promise of future success, the individual teacher's racist behavior can be controlled by educators with power and the will to use it.

In Flint, Michigan, the union negotiated dismissal as the penalty for overtly racist behaviors. In Dayton, Ohio, parents are suing for damages those administrators and teachers who fail to successfully teach black children to read. Criminal fraud and psychological tort (injury) charges against teachers and school districts are also being experimentally pursued there with the help of the Center for the Study of Student Citizenship, Rights, and Responsibilities. The examples illustrate the rule.

No white person has ever been executed in the United States for murdering a black person. Few white teachers have been disciplined or fired for overt racism, let alone for failing to teach successfully. No teacher training institutions or state departments of education refuse to grant white teachers credentials for their demonstrated inability to understand and confront institutional and cultural racism. In many states, teachers must understand and affirm the written provisions of the U.S. Constitution in order to be licensed to teach, but no state requires them to demonstrate their understanding of how that Constitution is being subverted and ignored to support Euro-American privilege and the genocide of Third World people.

Teacher education institutions are a *potentially* effective agency for controlling the entry of the destructive, pseudo-innocent teachers into schools. No such institution presently accomplishes such control. The following suggestions are visions of what might be, should be. If teacher education institutions begin serious attempts to accomplish such control, the frequent expressions of concern about racism by teacher educators might develop a more authentic ring.

Teacher Accountability and "New Whiteness"

Specifying the characteristics of "new white consciousness" as long-term goals determines some crucial objectives for teacher education. The ability to "see" through the myths and illusions supporting white supremacy, increased psychological strength, and demonstrated commitment to the tasks of new whiteness can be made objectives of teacher education programs and requirements for graduation, certification, or recertification. We cannot continue to ignore the illusions and fears that block educators' effectiveness in teaching, as well as political affairs. The following suggestions are intended to invite exploration of the outcomes of a program requiring beginning teachers to demonstrate an understanding of and an ability to operate on a culturally, ethically, and psychologically expanded frame of reference.

Such a program would require a demonstration of *understandings* in the form of responses to tests and interview; a documentation of *participation* in experiential learning opportunities designed to provoke increased ethnic sensitivity, value clarity, etc.; and *appropriate behavioral responses* to planned, structured stimuli. The compulsory nature of these requirements may seem problematic to those of us committed to open education and self-directed learning. There is widespread commitment to the notion that, in order to prepare teachers to operate in open classrooms and facilitate self-directed learning, teacher education programs must themselves be open-ended and self-directed. However, teacher trainees are not presently discovering, on their own, the values, courage, and competence to effectively combat racism in their schools and communities. Consequently, the norm against coercion in teacher preparation operates to perpetuate policies and practices that ensure, rather than combat, racism.

"Seeing Through" the Myths and Illusions of White Supremacy

Requirements to promote such "seeing" may include the demonstrated ability to take alternative perspectives on a variety of issues. For example, consider presenting teacher trainees the following problems:

1. You believe that a charge of genocide of people of color by Euro-American controlled institutions is warranted in the United States. Provide as convincing a case as you can for this allegation. (See: *The Choice: The Issue of Black Survival in America*, by Samuel Yette.) [9]

2. You believe that "blaming the victim" [10] occurs regularly in most schools. Make the best case you can to support your belief. Pay special attention to tracking and channeling practices, and to the often heard: "I taught it, they just didn't learn it."

Take the opposite point of view, and make a case indicting the "victims." Make the best argument you can that the people of color, the old, the young, the poor, and the sick *are* to blame for their condition.

[9] Samuel Yette, *op. cit.*

[10] William Ryan in *Blaming the Victim* (New York: Pantheon Books, 1971. p. 10.) describes present U.S. ideology as (a) identifying a social problem, (b) seeing how those affected are different from the rest of us as a consequence of deprivation and injustice, (c) defining these differences as the cause of the problem, and (d) developing a program to *correct* the differences.

3. You believe, as Barbara Sizemore [11] says, that, "One function of social science has been to legitimize the values of the white European culture by producing for distribution and dissemination a body of knowledge supportive of a model which guarantees success to white male Europeans."

a. Outline your strategy for holding Euro-American "social scientists" accountable for destructive beliefs and public policy outcomes of their work. Pay particular attention to the following: Moynihan's [12] assertion that the Negro family is disintegrating, Jensen's [13] assertion that average black IQ is genetically lower than average white IQ, and Myrdal's [14] assertion that the solution to the U.S. "race problem" only awaits Euro-Americans' deciding to live up to their explicit ideals.

b. Visit several public schools and, adopting an anthropologist's attitude, "discover" all the evidence you can that the schools are guaranteeing the success of white males of European ancestry.

4. Brag about aspects of the history and culture of Chicanos, Africans, Orientals, and Native Americans that you would be particularly proud of, *as if you were a member of each of these victimized groups*. Also, summarize the history of your group before and after contact with Europeans.

5. Brag about superiorities in the values, cultural patterns, and humanness of these Third World peoples compared to the dominant U.S. culture.

6. You believe that Euro-Americans hold myths about the cultures and histories of Third World peoples in order to justify their oppression. Debunk these myths by providing evidence contrary to *false* commonplaces, such as, "blacks never rebelled," "blacks retained no culture when they came to this country," "*Columbus* discovered America," or "the government *bought* Chicano landholdings after the treaty of Guadalupe-Hidalgo."

White supremacist illusions result only partially from cognitive ignorance that can be diminished by understanding alternative perspectives. There are motivations, feelings, values, and habits of mind not accessible to rational analysis. There is a range of potentially effective strategies for attacking these as well. For instance, human relations laboratory approaches can reduce defensiveness through the promotion

[11] B. A. Sizemore. "Social Science and Education for Black Identity." In: James A. Banks and Jean D. Grambs, editors. *Black Self-Concept: Implications for Education and Social Sciences.* New York: McGraw-Hill Book Company, 1972.

[12] D. P. Moynihan. *The Negro Family: A Case for National Action.* Washington, D.C.: Department of Labor, 1965.

[13] A. R. Jensen. "How Much Can We Boost IQ and Scholastic Achievement?" *Harvard Educational Review* 39 (1): 1-123; Winter 1969.

[14] G. Myrdal. *An American Dilemma.* New York: Harper & Row, Publishers, 1962.

of new norms in unique, often isolated, settings. Third World/Euro-American confrontations often lead to increased awareness and readiness to act. Internships and involvement in a variety of community settings often generate greater acceptance and valuing of cultural differences. Most meaningful, however, are experientially-based, anti-racism training sequences that (a) explore historical, cultural roots of racism reflected in existing institutional practices and power inequities; (b) analyze, prepare, and execute change strategies that reflect the foregoing; as well as (c) resolve conflicts of feeling or attitudes that interfere with effective anti-racist action.

All these strategies belong in comprehensive teacher education. Evaluation of these widely-used experiences is difficult, partially because their goals involve changes in attitudes, internal states, and consciousness. Only crude beginnings have been made in measuring the actual behaviors that new, more humane, attitudes should imply. While avoiding the either/or trap of "success or inaction," teacher educators and administrators can push for demonstration of training program effectiveness through the documentation of actual changes in teacher behavior. At the same time, sanctions to support the desired new behavior must be developed in the school and community.

Psychological Strength and Ethical Clarity

Efforts to increase teachers' psychological strength and ethical clarity also require action practice. Teacher education programs make increasingly wide use of experiential learning opportunities designed to increase participants' psychological strength, sensitivity, and value clarity.

Intense, provocative laboratory situations also generate the data for a widely used value-clarifying strategy, developed by Sidney Simon and others,[15] which provokes teachers to confront their relative ability to choose, affirm, and act on their increasingly explicit values. These strategies have been successfully modified for developing values and training in behaviors needed to productively confront racism and youth oppression in the school and community. Trainee self-reports and anecdotal evidence need to be supplemented with controlled research, because the obvious changes in a laboratory situation do not necessarily predict the maintenance of such changes in classroom practice.

Educators should understand that to focus on psychological

[15] S. B. Simon, L. Howe, and H. Kirschenbaum. *Values Clarification*. New York: Hart Publishing Co., Inc., 1972.

strength, sensitivity, and value clarity without making explicit the connections to racism-related issues will not necessarily lead to anti-racist behavior in classrooms, or to reductions in institutionally racist policy and practice in schools. However, when combined with the efforts heretofore suggested to provide teachers opportunities for new cultural, conceptual, and ethical frames of reference, such action training is more likely to lead to action in the world.

Change Strategies

Efforts to eliminate naïveté concerning institutional and social change strategies and tactics strike directly at Euro-American fear, ironic in the extreme, about power and the potential for its abuse. Educating, or reeducating, teachers requires that they understand, experience, and act on the full range of strategies and tactics that may be used in their schools and communities. Teachers need experience with strategies that, even if not consistent with their values, teachers are likely to encounter in the communities they serve. Specifically, teachers meeting these objectives would (a) display diminished pseudo-innocence about power and its exercise; (b) have increased their understanding of change strategies and tactics, whether these are consistent with their values and cultural biases or not; (c) have clarified and acknowledged their relative personal power and powerlessness; and (d) have moved toward overcoming the alienation which divides so-called public and private lives by clarifying the inextricable interdependence of school and community.

Accomplishing these objectives requires alternative perceptions and assumptions about (a) schools as organizations, (b) appropriate strategies and tactics for change, and (c) desegregation, integration, and community control. The ability to take such alternative perspectives could be demonstrated in response to problems such as the following:

1. Describe evidence that supports the assumptions about schools as organizations reflected in this statement: "There are real differences in values and beliefs among the students, teachers, and parents of this school. Those who have similar beliefs should organize together to argue and negotiate for what they want. We'll never all agree on the same thing, and we need to face and work through the conflict."

Describe similar evidence for this statement: "If people will just communicate with one another, respond to each others' needs, we'll be able to come to a trusting consensus."

(The second perspective fits with previously indicated aspects of Euro-

American illusion by encouraging individual vs. group action, denying cultural and value differences, and reinforcing innocence of power realities. Nevertheless, both perspectives give guidance to change efforts. Understanding the assumptions on which individuals and groups are operating is important diagnostic information.)

2. You believe that the mythology in the United States about how social justice is promoted (or denied) has the effect of preventing justice. You believe (with Robert Terry) it is *not* true that

"Justice can be brought about legally through the courts, politically by voting, and economically by selective buying. In other words, the basic mechanisms of the American system—the courts, the political process, and the market system—are equitable systems that only demand use to be effective." [16]

Provide evidence that supports your belief, especially concerning the *exclusion of youth* from these mechanisms of justice. Describe the due process children can expect from schools.

3. What perceptions of the United States and learning lead many Third World educators to struggle for racially separate schools (politically, psychologically, academically)?

What perceptions lead overtly racist Euro-Americans to struggle for racially separate schools?

4. You believe that liberal teachers (among others) destructively promote the ridiculous falsehood that Third World children need white classmates in order to learn and that interracial "contact" in childhood will eliminate racism. Provide as much evidence as you can that this proposition is *unsupportable*. Describe what anyone can presently see in most multiracial public schools that exposes this falsehood.

Required Experiences for reducing naïveté about change include structured simulations like Star Power,[17] Serfdom, and Seven Minute Day.[18] These often intense experiences encourage integrating thoughts, feelings, and actions around issues of structural and personal power. In addition to such simulations, schools of education themselves provide very challenging *real* laboratories for diagnosis of racist practices in admissions, hiring, decision making, and exploration of the relative effectiveness of various change strategies and tactics. Such change efforts require choosing at least a temporary situational emphasis on

[16] Robert Terry, *op. cit.*, p. 81.

[17] G. Shirts. "Star Power: A Simulation." La Jolla, California: Western Behavioral Institute, n.d.

[18] P. A. Bidol. *Developing New Perspectives on Race*. Revised edition. Detroit, Michigan: New Perspectives on Race, 1972.

(a) the "trust-truth" [19] assumption that more trust and better communication lead to consensus and universal satisfaction, or (b) the "power conflict" assumption that real, important irreconcilable differences are best negotiated and resolved by well-organized groups with clearly common values advocating their position.

A variety of teacher education and reeducation programs share some of these objectives and learning activities. However, if we are to specify, as one of the major objectives of teacher education, that we are preparing teachers to be active anti-racists, then our teacher education programs must begin careful implementation and evaluation of a variety of comprehensive, committed efforts to do *exactly* that. Assuming scarce resources, *critical* antecedents in the development of "new white consciousness" require continuing definition and analysis. We cannot permit the lack of such a conceptual framework to paralyze us into inaction on the obvious.

Whether or not systematic training programs exist, educators can begin to utilize the powers they already have to create educational environments which are not racist. Educators can use their powers of selection and employment to demand teachers who have the understandings, experiences, and behaviors necessary to combat racism. The more difficult task may be the development of strategies and tactics to accomplish meaningful reeducation of *experienced* teachers. The success possible in this task may depend on the movement of power and culture toward or away from totalitarianism and racism. Successful collaborative efforts among many government and community agencies in structuring long-range, in-service, anti-racism interventions necessary to reeducate experienced teachers do exist, although they are understandably rare.

Reeducating Experienced Teachers for Conscientization

The reeducation of experienced teachers must involve changes in consciousness and promotion of internal controls of the destructive expression of their racism. The technology available for accomplishing this task is profoundly inadequate. Understandably, the power to control expressions of teachers' racism has not been effectively mobilized. Effective reeducation should result in spontaneously occurring behaviors by teachers that humanize their own and others' consciousness

[19] M. A. Chesler and J. E. Lohman. "Changing Schools Through Student Advocacy." In: R. A. Schmuck and M. A. Miles. *Organization Development in Schools.* Palo Alto, California: National Press Books, 1971. pp. 185-212.

and action, in addition to changing destructive institutional practices and structures.

Thus, the familiar educational problem arises of trying to determine whether an intervention results in long-term desired changes in behavior across diverse situations. Evidence for long-term changes resulting from psychological reeducation programs can come from coding spontaneously occurring thought samples (from dreams, fantasies, TAT responses, etc.), but is not typically found in respondent measures, such as questionnaires or structured interviews. We presently lack a systematically, experimentally developed coding system to screen spontaneous thoughts of Euro-Americans for images signaling change toward "new white consciousness," which are subsequently reflected in action. An effort to develop such a coding system is under way at the Center for Humanistic Education, University of Massachusetts.

Progress toward "new white consciousness" should be evident in the spontaneously occurring thought samples of people being successfully reeducated. Such progress, "conscientization" as Freire calls it, is characterized by "a deepening awareness of experience that people experience as they critically reflect on their experience and act to transform it." [20] Although useful with Brazilian campesinos, such a process may not be directly transferable to the United States. Nevertheless, Freire's basic assumption,

... that man's ontological vocation . . . is to be a subject who acts upon and transforms his world, and in so doing moves towards ever new possibilities of fuller and richer life, individually and collectively,[21]

does characterize the task of Euro-American liberation and provides a liberating definition of humanness.

The pedagogical process leading to the conscientization described by Freire involves collaborative development of goals, processes, needs, and evaluation. It explores generative themes in dialog, the content of which is determined by the focus of participants' energy (usually related to some form of domination). The process results in new cultural synthesis and action on the world, as persons' awareness, reflection, and action all expand. The conceptualization of a similar process for Euro-American liberation remains to be created and documented. However, a process resulting in successful psychological reeducation of other stable

---

[20] Paulo Freire. *The Pedagogy of the Oppressed.* New York: The Seabury Press, 1970. © 1970 by Paulo Freire. Used by permission of the publisher, The Seabury Press, New York.

[21] R. Scaull. Foreword in: *Ibid.*, pp. 12-13.

human characteristics in our culture is documented by McClelland,[22] Alschuler,[23] and others.

A variety of programs at the frontiers of psychology and education have successfully increased achievement motivation or personal efficacy, as reflected both in spontaneous thought-samples *and* related long-term behavior changes. The principles developed in these programs, synthesized with Freire's insights, may give direction to a process of liberating teacher reeducation. Such a process could only begin in a special reeducation "program," and would by definition be a lifelong struggle with the contradictions in U.S. education and culture.

Experience with psychological education to promote achievement motivation resulted in development of strategies (how and with whom) and tactics (what and in what order) for formal training ranging in length from a day to a year. Empirically supported *strategizing principles* for structuring psychological reeducation involve systematically focusing many experiential methods (fantasy, role-play, nonverbal communication, simulation, etc.) on a single characteristic of consciousness, seeking internalization rather than just arousal of the characteristic, intervening during critical periods of development (for example, the development of role-taking ability in 9- to 12-year-olds), and changing a sufficient number of environmental pressures to promote opportunities to act on the desired characteristic.

Well-documented optimal training sequences derived from these strategies are also available. Optimal training outcomes typically require getting attention through moderate novelty; having an intense, integrated experience of the thoughts, feelings, and actions associated with the characteristic; and clearly conceptualizing the experience. Additionally, participants must relate the experience to their real life situation; practice the characteristic actions associated with the change, both in simulations and reality; and, finally, internalize the characteristic and progressively withdraw from external supports.[24] These principles were used in educating teachers toward goals resembling conscientization. Strong evidence for at least short-term positive change in consciousness and commitment among many students was noted, but highlighted the need for evaluation techniques that are less equivocal.

Teachers and teacher educators find these principles from psychological education helpful in avoiding ineffectiveness in anti-racism

---

[22] D. McClelland and D. G. Winter. *Motivating Economic Achievement.* New York: The Free Press, 1969.

[23] A. S. Alschuler, *op. cit.*

[24] *Ibid.*, Chapter 11.

education. A partial list of commonly used but, by the criteria of these principles, *ineffective* practices includes:

1. Black/white confrontation with no systematic conceptualization of the experience or opportunity to practice the alternative behaviors suggested by increased awareness

2. Exposure to "negative" aspects of urban life (in terms of middle class, white norms and values) without processing and conceptualizing the aroused thoughts and feelings—not "practicing" the new *internal* responses allowed by new data or organizers

3. Lecture presentations, readings, and intellectual discussions which do not involve participants' feelings and actions in an integrated experience

4. "Prescribing" *correct* responses to situational injustice, thus short-circuiting the necessary sequence of connection to one's real life, practice, and internalization

5. Focusing on changing attitudes or people without changing or addressing the power and structural elements of the trainee's real environment, resulting in punishment of expressions of tentative "new white consciousness"

6. Trainers acting as "leaders," "parents," "gurus," or "judges" rather than catalysts in the model of the client-centered therapies. This often results in a lack of openness and trust required during training to allow practice and internalization of fundamental conceptual and affective changes. This does not rule out confrontation as an "integrated experience," but *does* rule it out as an assumed complete, powerful strategy for changing consciousness.

The effort to develop a technology of reeducation that can actually make a difference is important, but should not be even fantasized as *the* answer. The myth of "the one right answer" blinds Euro-Americans to obviously necessary partial actions to control racism and genocide. The emphasis on consciousness and understanding is a "half-vision," if it results in Euro-Americans waiting around as powerless individuals for their leaders magically to "see the light." Some can change through the processes described here, while others will be "reeducated" by the changes in the power realities which they confront.

In summary, this chapter has explored the content and processes of Euro-American self-delusion and innocence which support the racism and genocide of people of color. This web of illusion prevents their clear understanding of effective action. Seeing the control of racism as the central priority accentuates the parallel need to humanize schooling by ensuring that *all* children have access to environments in which they acquire the competence to maximize their potential social contribution. Also, children must experience schooling as a collaborative, participative venture in which the needs, concerns, and growth of all people are equally attended to.

The task of teachers who want to promote an open society is to act now, whatever their psychological or power resources, and to participate in the necessary cultural revolution. By focusing on the difficult tasks facing Euro-American teachers, it was not the intention to downplay the overwhelming need for Third World teachers in all education settings. The role of Third World teachers, and the necessary education of those teachers, is being defined by Third World people in the process of their own liberation. Euro-American solidarity with that struggle may be best expressed by teachers actively confronting their own racist institutions and promoting their own cultural revolution. Only if Euro-American teachers learn to *see* and act can their instruction be less destructive.

PART 3

THE USE OF POWER IN AN OPEN SOCIETY

THE USE AND MISUSE of power is probably the single most effective block to an emerging open society. A large segment of the violence and disruption during the past decade, in schools and society, has been caused by those who wanted a piece of the action—a larger share of the power and decision-making activity. In recent years, we have heard from groups who heretofore have been silent—Blacks, women, students, and teachers. The cry for Black Power left many Americans angry and afraid. Student violence and disruptions, because of a desire of students for more involvement in their own education, caused many to say that the schools had lost control. Teachers walking on the picket line suggested a loss of professionalism. At issue, in each instance, was a desire to see a more equitable redistribution of power.

One thing was discovered from these confrontations: those who have power are not going to share it without a struggle. The writers of the chapters in Part Three look historically at those who seek additional power and suggest the degree of achievement. The lead chapter reviews power and authority as they are exercised in our public schools. The real challenge to us is to find a way of realistically involving those who should legitimately be involved in the power process. An open society is one model for bringing all segments of our population into the decision-making process. Such a model would involve using power not only for the needs of individuals and groups, but also for the mutual benefit of all groups and individuals in creating and maintaining an open society.

CHAPTER 7: AUTHORITY, POWER, AND EDUCATION

DAN W. DODSON

THE BASIC ISSUE confronting American education is that, today, it serves a society characterized by dissension and conflict, and its organization is still for a society in which there was a high degree of consensus. Hence, the old rituals and practices are no longer relevant.

Admittedly, this is a simplistic analysis of a complicated problem. Let us examine the case for it.

The Consensus Model

Historically, education evolved from a society which fitted the consensus model.[1] The power arrangement of the society was monolithic. It was scarcely challenged. Its myths and values were accepted as being "The American Way." The myth of the American Dream was widely communicated through all channels of indoctrination. Minorities who sought to rise in status disciplined themselves to the ethos of this power group, and strove to make themselves worthy of being accepted. They had faith in the system. They believed that if they did their part to become worthy they would be recognized.

These minorities of the past may have complained of discrimination at times, but fundamentally they subscribed to the basic tenets of the society and accommodated themselves to it. Those who had power were able to hold the society to a more-or-less steady course, for they embodied the ideals for which the people strove.

In this historical period the schools embodied the consensual nature of the society. Education was a privilege which was not available to all. Hence, children and their parents cooperated to make the school the

[1] Robert A. Dahl. *Pluralist Democracy in the United States: Conflict and Consent.* Chicago: Rand McNally & Company, 1967.

99

place of optimum learning. Rituals, such as rising to recite in class, the deference to the teacher, the respect for his authority, all attest the support education had among the people. Both parents and children consented for the school to exercise whatever authority was needed to make education good.

In this situation, the teacher's authority arose from two basic sources. He was, in many respects, an extension of the family, that is, he was *in loco parentis*—in place of parents. Also he was an authority in his field, that is, his authority stemmed from his expertise. This latter was recognized by licensure or other means of credentialing. He was usually much better educated than either the children or their parents.

Organizations such as the Parent-Teacher Association evolved in response to the need for close cooperation between the school and the home, and allowed these two institutions to work more closely in the interest of development of the child. The emphasis, for the most part, was on the development of the individual child, not on such issues as socializing children from outside the power arrangement into the mainstream.

In all too many instances the children of the poor and powerless were discriminated against, or considered of worth only to the extent that they conformed to the demands of the power group in the society. The Catholic population withdrew into parochial education which they could control. The Jewish group mobilized parents and community resources to complement the services of the schools, but stayed engaged in the encounter with the WASP group. To shield their children from the shock of assimilationist efforts, they organized after-school programs to teach the religious and cultural heritage. All in all, then, there was little challenge to the goals, objectives, and methods of the schools.

A major ingredient of this consensual model which is difficult to describe, but nevertheless real, relates to this legitimation of authority. Authority is power legitimated. The Declaration of Independence stated that "just powers" are derived from the "consent of the governed." In political matters, men were elected from remote places who went to halls of decision making and enacted the laws which regulated conduct and provided public policy. Information dissemination, at that time, was not sufficient for the people to be completely informed about issues. Those who were elected were given "consent" to make the decisions, because they were where the information existed.

From this "consent of the governed" also came the trust in the expert. It was not presumed that people would be informed on technical matters. They tended to give the expert their consent, for he knew best. Thus medical doctors still decide our fate, for we have confidence that they know better what is good for us than we know ourselves. Educators were given considerable latitude in curriculum development, methods of instruction, and many other areas. Since the teacher was better educated than most parents, they gave him their "consent" to practice authority in the school.

Another aspect of the consensual model relates to social change. Many educators gave lip service to education as a change agent. George Counts[2] and many others suggested that schools should have a role in determining the direction of the society. However, change which would upset the equilibrium of the social order was shunned. Conflict was avoided at all costs—even at the cost of repression in many instances.

Most would contend that the role of the school in the consensual model should be that of developing a problem-solving approach to life, with examination of all sides of a question, open-mindedness, and suspended judgment. This would produce a "built-in" pressure to change which would be "evolutionary and not revolutionary."

Clark Wissler,[3] one of America's outstanding anthropologists, once said that education had taken the place of religion as the dynamic for social change. What we once prayed God to send us, we now expect education to provide. That faith was placed in education because the social order felt it was safe, and did not disturb the equilibrium of the societal arrangement.

The Conflict Model

Today, this consensus era is passing. We are now coping with a society which better fits the conflict model. Power has been fragmented and diffused. The society is held together more by force rather than consensus. The growing preoccupation with "law and order" is an indication of the lack of cohesiveness among the groups in the society. Crime is increasingly committed by alienated individuals and groups who are political and social deviants outside the system, rather than by sick persons within the system. Civil disobedience and insurgency tactics of disruption indicate the lack of consensus within the society. The alienation from the system, or "establishment" as it is sometimes called, is widespread and tremendously baffling.

We have moved away from the "consent of the governed" concept

[2] George Counts. *Dare the Schools Build a New Social Order?* New York: The John Day Company, 1932.

[3] Clark Wissler. *Man and Culture.* New York: Thomas Y. Crowell Co., 1923. p. 8.

of political process. For an era we operated on the precept that public opinion was the basis of authority in political process. The school administrators made lists of their publics and tried to figure how to win their support. Corporations employed "public relations" firms to help them with their varied publics. Old-line politicians could make up slates of candidates for office in smoke-filled rooms and balance the slates so as to appeal to the varied publics without having to involve them in political process.

We are now in an era of participatory democracy. People are no longer content just to give their "consent" for authority which is practiced upon them. They insist that they be included in the decision-making process. Not even the expert is trusted in this phase of participatory democracy. Professional people are being required increasingly to allow the consumers of their services to participate in determining the goals toward which "expertness" is directed. The populace wants "a piece of the action."

In this development we have seen the parents pull away from the traditional Parent-Teacher Association into organizations of their own, such as the United Parents Association in New York City. The transition has moved them away from the consensus model of participation, in which they worked hand in glove with the staff of the school, to a power group which will fight for the schools when they think it in the interest of their children but, equally important, will fight the schools when they deem it necessary. Ellen Lurie's manual on *How To Change the Schools*[4] is suggestive of the conflict model I have described.

By the same token, teachers have sought collective security in their organizations. As teachers fell from their place of high esteem they ceased identifying with the professional middle class type of white collar vocation in which it was deemed unethical to unionize—and beneath their dignity to strike—and adopted a blue collar type of collective bargaining pattern. Thus, they ceased depending upon their services to the community for their status, and in turn are expecting the community to reward them adequately for such effort. They became a power group which demands adequate wages and working conditions. Their security is in their union.

With the growing concentration of minorities in the inner cities, they, too, found it possible to create a power base from which they can operate, which had not been possible before to a comparable extent. The poor performance of the schools in educating their youths

---

[4] Ellen Lurie. *How To Change the Schools, A Parents' Handbook on How To Fight the School System.* New York: Random House, Inc., 1970.

has led minorities to mobilize as a power group to demand varied considerations, ranging from simply a higher quality of education to local control of the school.

One observer described the encounter this type of power group had with the teachers' power group in one ghetto school. This observer said that a meeting was arranged for a dialog between the teachers and the parents at the time of a strike. In the heat of the discussion the teachers got up and somewhat haughtily said, "We don't have to take this," and started walking out.

The parents responded, "You are fired."

The teachers replied, "That's what you think. We do not work for you."

Whereupon the parents said, "We will see."

When the strike was settled and school resumed, the parents pulled all but a dozen children out of this large elementary school until the board of education replaced the teachers involved in the incident.

This need for minorities to develop power blocs becomes more and more acute. As whites with children flee to the suburbs, the schools become disproportionately minority in makeup. In New Brunswick, New Jersey, for instance, blacks constitute only 15.5 percent of the total population of those 15 years and over. Yet 77 percent of all the children in the first grade are black. Politically, these blacks do not have enough leverage to demand anything. Inner city schools of this type become "charity schools for the poor."

In Dallas, Texas, the superintendent of schools reported recently that approximately 40 percent of the black youths drop out before they finish high school. Of the 1,400 who stayed to finish, only 84 scored high enough on tests to indicate that they could succeed in even the most marginal colleges. Eighty percent scored in the bottom 20 percent on national norms. The superintendent's panacea was massive "inequality of education" to compensate them for their deficits. The Dallas community has resisted desegregation. It seems patently clear that if the white segment of the community will not share community, and if the pressure for sharing through desegregation is removed, there will be no compensatory funds either. Compensatory education was unheard of until it was clear that some black children were going to go to school with some white ones. At that point at which the pressure is removed, such funds will dry up again almost inevitably. Under these conditions, without political leverage, the only alternative for the minorities is mobilization, disruption, and harassment until they can make their interests felt in communal decision making.

What of students? High school students are showing a restlessness previously unknown. Sometimes this is based on racial status, as minorities demand more attention to their needs and interests. Often, it does not involve racial matters at all, but stems from a growing feeling which was characterized by the title of the book, *The Student as Nigger*,[5] that is, that the student increasingly feels himself a second class citizen with few rights.

In many of these instances the students have become a power bloc. It is reported that in New York City between ¼ and ⅓ of the high school principals either retired or resigned between February and June of 1972. They were unable or unwilling to deal with the community and student power blocs.

Legitimacy

Added to this changing power arrangement which transforms schools from consensus models to conflict ones is the loss of legitimacy which the schools have suffered in the past two decades. In the consensus model of the society the teacher stood in relation to the children as a parent surrogate. As suggested earlier, he was *in loco parentis*. His authority was supreme. He could use corporal punishment. Students had few rights he was bound to respect. In LeRoi Jones' African Free School, one is impressed that all teachers are addressed as "Mamma" along with whatever their African names may be. It is an indication of the family relatedness of the teacher.

Today, few teachers are parent surrogates any more. They are not *in loco parentis* either in the minds of the children or their parents. Another aspect of the teacher's authority is also changing. This is his authority as it relates to subject matter. Often he is not the expert he once was. Many of his children have traveled more, seen more on television, and, through other channels of mass communication, become more experienced than their mentors. Hence, on both counts, the authority of the teacher has declined.

If the students and their parents do not give their consent to be under the authority of the teacher, and if they are not privy to the decision making which affects them, the teacher's authority is not legitimated in their lives. Anyone who practices authority on another without his consent, in an institution which requires attendance, is running a custodial operation. No such agency has ever gotten creativeness out of people. Children, under such circumstances, do what all people so

[5] Jerry Farber. *The Student as Nigger*. North Hollywood, California: A Contact Book, 1969.

compromised do: they harass hell out of whoever represents authority to them. Increasingly schools are referred to in this custodial role, rather than in their educational aspect. In other words the consensus model of society no longer exists in many, if not most, urban schools.

Children are kept in school by power—not by their consent. Teachers hold their jobs by power—not by consent of the governed. A major item included in negotiations of new contracts is the physical protection of teachers from both children and parents. Their jobs are secure largely because they have the power of collective bargaining behind them. Parents in many communities are challenging the right to place tenure above what they consider "accountability." The parents wield their influence through mass action—not PTA's.

Truly, the educational enterprise has moved from the consensus model to that of the conflict one. Groups meet each other in jousts over their differences in a school organization which was designed to serve the consensus era—an era that is largely no more.

What Are the New Designs?

What then is the new type of educational organization which would be more responsive to this conflict model? School administration specialists will have to perfect the designs. A social scientist can only sketch in the broad framework of it. Such a design has to make room for all the actors who have power to participate in the process of decision making. The skills of political process will have to be adapted to the operation. Opportunity will have to be provided periodically for these groups to come together, as peers, to deal with the issues which arise. Teachers as a power group will be one interest group to be involved. Parents will be another. In mixed neighborhoods there may be two or more parent interest groups. This may be true of the teachers as well.

Students will compose one or more interest groups. The business and professional groups of the community will no doubt want to be involved in the process. Religious groups may represent their interests by bloc pressures. Boards of education will probably be restricted in their authority. Legal authority which is not legitimated does not count for much. These officeholders represent only a segment of the community in most instances—regardless of whether they are elected or appointed.

In other words, all power groups of the community that have an interest in education will have to be involved in the decision-making process. They will be in on the action. They will not be just electing somebody to represent them.

The model for such a program would probably be on the order of the *Charrette* which has been experimented with by the U.S. Office of Education. In such a model, the actors who have an equity in schools come together in assembly. Groups caucus before they vote on an issue. They make coalitions with other groups to get their wishes translated into policy. They have to wrestle with problems through compromise, negotiation, arbitration, and all the other skills required in group decision making.

The important thing is that what used to be called "publics," which are now power groups, would all become involved in process in a political way. All would be in on the decision-making process. All would combine to polish the abrasive edges of the special demands of each group. Apathy would be sloughed off and a new basis of legitimacy acquired for the school. School leadership would no longer possess the capacity to manipulate the affairs of the community to an administration's special interest. The superintendent and his staff would be part of a power bloc, but they would also have the role of experts as they brought data, information, alternative plans, and programs for the assembled power groups to use in decision making.

An illustration which comes nearest to what is envisioned in this type of policy determination was the political convention of the Democratic Party in the summer of 1972. In Chicago at their convention four years earlier there was violence, bloodshed, and acrimony. Several hundred youths were arrested. The reorganization of the party toward the conflict model brought these youths into the decision-making processes. The 1972 convention came off without disruption, and only one youth was reported arrested.

If one fears that learning might suffer if a community launched such a program, he should observe the growth of sophistication among these political novices. Eighty percent of them had never attended a convention before. Yet they were disciplined. They ran circles around old-line politicians and labor leaders who were considered extremely specialized in political manipulation. It seems safe to say that there is a much higher degree of education than before among the rank and file of these youths because they had to address themselves to the issues before them. This is where real learning takes place. If one has power, he must learn to use it responsibly. If he does not have power he either resigns in apathy, or else disrupts the process.

Some feeble intimations of how this process would work show through in some of the current school controversies. When a student conference on unrest was being planned, one bright White Plains High School girl said, "If you want us to come to a conference so you can hear us rap, forget it. You have listened to your young folk for a long time, and nothing happened. If you want the students to participate, let us have our caucus in advance. You have yours. Let's define our positions, and then meet in power negotiations and open dialog."

In one high school when several teachers were dismissed because of budgetary difficulties, students became disruptive. An astute superintendent, however, was able to get them involved in examining the facts. The students appeared before the board of education and other public bodies. Whether they got the teachers back is not as important, perhaps, as what they learned about taxes, budgets, and government. They also learned how to require those who make decisions concerning the students' lives to become accountable to those they serve.

At George Washington High School in Manhattan, parents and some students proposed that a conference table be set up in the hallway so that issues could be negotiated there. The teachers union vetoed the agreement, and used its power to require removal of the table. The school's leadership was unable to involve all the power blocs in the decision making, hence the school was paralyzed for several days by the disruption.

Toward the Future

The conflict model of society implies shared power. It implies political process as a major vehicle through which power is redistributed. Instead of consensus in the traditional sense, it implies decisions collectively arrived at by a participatory set of actors who have an equity in the issues.

No longer can a board of education make policy decisions unilaterally—such as one did recently with regard to discipline. This statement presented the rules and regulations by which the board would act with regard to discipline matters. It was an excellent statement. In developing it, however, the board consulted no students and no parents. It was the board's "legal" prerogative to develop it and adopt it. The only limitation was that it had no legitimacy in a large portion of the community.

Teachers face comparable problems. They can walk out of an encounter with parents—as cited earlier; they can demand tenure and job security; they can even demand a policeman standing by the door to protect them; but they cannot perform educational tasks unless they have the support of the parents and the cooperation of the children.

Advantages of the conflict type of approach should be explored as they relate to the content of the curriculum. One of the thorny issues is that of what is taught to children concerning race. Some blacks contend that the present curriculum practices cultural genocide upon them. In a sense they are correct. An adequate curriculum cannot be developed by any one power unit of the community. America cannot escape an apartheid society unless we educate children into a common culture, and until the part with power relinquishes its demands that the other be educated as second class citizens. What is taught has little relevance unless its content provides a sense of comfort for all the community.

Today, we are in great need for some type of sex education. The reason we have so much trouble about it is that the community is divided about the issue. Unless the power blocs can come together and have dialog about their differences, little can be accomplished. There is no mechanism of consequence through which reconciliation can be accomplished if we are to move through consensus.

Public schools are at a watershed point at the present time. Costs of education have soared at a time when there is a growing realization that inputs of money, better training of teachers, better libraries, and other related items do not make much difference in children's learning.[6] The schools are without legitimacy in a growing segment of the American society. Teachers who formerly commanded the highest respect are now demanding protection from hostile children. Children who formerly accepted opportunities for schooling as a privilege now look upon the schools as custodial institutions. Alternatives to public education are popularly advocated—even at public expense.

If this malaise is to be overcome, the educational establishment must be brought in line with the changing nature of the society. The time may well come when we again achieve the consensus model of society. In the meantime it seems patently clear that educational rituals designed to serve a past era of consensus are not adequate today— at least in urban education. Perhaps the time has come for us to experiment with alternate models of organization. If this sketchy examination of the problem stimulates further examination of the matter, it will have served its purpose.

[6] James Coleman. *The Equality of Educational Opportunity.* Washington, D.C.: Office of Education, U.S. Department of Health, Education, and Welfare, 1966.

CHAPTER 8: COMMUNITY POWER AND EDUCATION

BARBARA A. SIZEMORE

On December 1, 1955, Rosa Parks, a black seamstress in the Montgomery Fair Department Store, refused to relinquish her seat to a white man in accordance with the statutes of Alabama and the mores of Montgomery. Mrs. Parks was promptly arrested. She made no disturbance. There was no disorder. This single, small incident exploded into a massive movement for freedom.

Mrs. Parks deserves more credit than she gets, for her courage forged unity where before there was little. Her determination released the first burst of Black Power. She had something more than sore corns and bunions or chronic fatigue. Mrs. Parks had power—the power to revolt.

Social scientists later commenting on the incident failed to understand the meaning of her act, and even Martin Luther King, Jr., did not see that it was black power that brought segregation to an end throughout the South. Certainly, litigation cleared the way, but at no time have laws alone assured rights to blacks in this country. Black power overcame the brutal racist police and their vicious dogs. Black power repelled the insults, brickbats, and hoses. Black power kept the Montgomery buses empty month after month after month. This glorious show of strength lured others to join in the war against injustice. King and many more missed the crucial lesson of Rosa Parks' act because they mistook black power for a movement instead of a resource.

A Healthy Black Community

But, indeed, the miracle of the Montgomery bus boycott was the application and the use of this resource. Rosa Parks sparked the spirit of the black masses, and perhaps her greatest gift to them on that day was a unified, healthy community where sociologists had said there was none. From that point on, the black community was in control of its transportation. Over time, the spirit of the masses diminished. That this spirit was not sustained is a problem of maintenance. Yet, for that time and event, under Martin Luther King's leadership, the black community responded.[1]

Although definitions of community are often imprecise and incomplete, community is generally described as a social system with a geographical base and economic interdependence.[2] To understand the concepts better, however, Parsons' definition may be useful:

Reduced to the simplest possible terms, then, a social system consists in a plurality of individual actors interacting with each other in a situation which has at least a physical or environmental aspect, actors who are motivated in terms of a tendency to the "optimization of gratification" and whose relation to their situations, including each other, is defined and mediated in terms of a system of culturally structured and shared symbols.[3]

Hawley and Zimmer add another important and useful dimension to the concept of community, and that is organization. They say:

Conceptually a social system is an organization adapted to the performance of a set of functions. Organization is the means of mobilizing and coordinating the power required to execute one or more functions.[4]

Haskins explains a black community as a continuum of black relationships starting with one black family and ending with the black people of the world.[5] The Montgomery victory renewed this sense of

---

[1] Donald H. Smith. "The Black Revolution and Education." In: Robert L. Green, editor. *Racial Crisis in American Education.* Chicago: Follett Educational Corporation, 1969. p. 56. For information about the Montgomery boycott, see: Louis E. Lomax. *The Negro Revolt.* New York: Signet Books, New American Library, Inc., 1962; Robert F. Williams. ". . . from Negroes with Guns." In: Floyd B. Barbour, editor. *Black Power Revolt.* Boston: Porter Sargent Publisher, 1968. p. 154; and Charles E. Silberman. *Crisis in Black and White.* New York: Vintage Books, Random House, Inc., 1964. pp. 141-42.

[2] Morris Janowitz. "Introduction: Converging Perspectives in Community Political Analysis." In: Morris Janowitz, editor. *Community Political Systems.* New York: The Free Press, Inc., 1961. p. 14.

[3] Talcott Parsons. *The Social System.* New York: The Free Press, Inc., 1951. pp. 5-6.

[4] Amos H. Hawley and Basil G. Zimmer. "Resistance to Unification in a Metropolitan Community." In: Morris Janowitz, editor. *Community Political Systems.* New York: The Free Press, Inc., 1961. p. 148.

[5] Kenneth W. Haskins. "Community Control of Schools." p. 5. Mimeographed.

community for blacks across the country and emphasized the need for organization to attain power. This was the period of nonviolence, civil disobedience, and integration.

Then came the period of Black Nationalism embodied in the philosophy of Malcolm X and providing the inspiration for a new black quest for self-determination.[6] The drive for Black Studies, Black Literature, and curricular change was strong [7]; and there were many advocates for cultural nationalism. This was the period of rioting, violence, and separation. During this time community meant a base of organization or "a frame of reference for an analysis of power relations" or "a primary power center." [8]

Out of this period of constant protest and confrontation, "Black Power" became an operational term. For Brazier, black power articulated three major feelings: (a) pride in color, (b) self-determination, and (c) the recognition of the necessity of some form of power organization.[9] His basic premise was that the black community should organize for self-determination. But the "Black Power Ideology" was best stated by Carmichael and Hamilton, who said:

> The concept of Black Power rests on a fundamental premise: Before a group can enter the open society, it must first close ranks. By this we mean that group solidarity is necessary before a group can operate effectively from a bargaining position of strength in a pluralistic society.[10]

This was the time of the tiki, the ghele, the dashiki, and the "Afro." Black pride was the theme and "Black Is Beautiful" the motto. "Sister" and "Brother" were descriptive membership labels and handshake rituals reinforced this belonging. A renaming occurred as Negro gave way to Black and African-American. Community control was born from this union of community and black power. Local control returned for a rerun, but this time in color and in Spanish.

[6] Donald H. Smith, op. cit., p. 61.

[7] See: James A. Banks. "Imperatives in Ethnic Minority Education." Phi Delta Kappan 53 (5): 266-69; January 1972; James A. Banks and William W. Joyce, editors. Teaching Social Studies to Culturally Different Children. Reading, Massachusetts: Addison-Wesley Publishing Company, 1971; James A. Banks. "Racial Prejudice and the Black Self-Concept." In: James A. Banks and Jean Dresden Grambs, editors. Black Self-Concept. New York: McGraw-Hill Book Company, 1972. pp. 5-35.

[8] Floyd A. Hunter. Community Power Structure. Garden City, New York: Anchor Books, 1963. p. 2.

[9] Arthur M. Brazier. Black Self-Determination. Grand Rapids, Michigan: William B. Eerdmans Publishing Co., 1969. p. 18.

[10] Stokely Carmichael and Charles V. Hamilton. Black Power. New York: Vintage Books, Random House, Inc., 1967. p. 44.

Community control is a power concept and, therefore, political.[11] Using Hunter's definition, "power involves relationships between individuals and groups, both controlled and controlling." [12] Power is a word he uses to describe "the acts of men going about the business of moving other men to act in relation to themselves or in relation to organic or inorganic things." [13] It involves decision making and the function of executing determined policies.[14] Words often used to mean power are: control, self-determination, authority, and influence. To understand the use of power more clearly, consider Sol Tax's formula "A/B" where "A" represents groups with power and "B" represents groups with no power.[15] In this situation, "A" moves "B" about to act in relation to "A" and what "A" wants.[16] Additionally, the American economy is based on a highly interdependent competitive paradigm which guarantees losers.[17] When "A" wins, "B" loses and vice versa. The relevant question is not whether there will be losers (unemployed), but who will it be? Gittell says that community control is an instrument for social change primarily concerned with the redistribution of this power.[18] Redistributing and mobilizing power are political acts.

[11] See: Charles E. Billings. "Community Control of the Schools and the Quest for Power." *Phi Delta Kappan* 53 (5): 277-78; January 1972; and Rodney J. Reed. "The Community School Board." *School Review* 81 (3): 357-63; May 1973. Also see: Marilyn Gittell. "Community Control of Education." In: Marilyn Gittell and Alan G. Hevesi, editors. *The Politics of Urban Education.* New York: Frederick A. Praeger, Publishers, 1969. pp. 363-75; Marilyn Gittell. *Participants and Participation.* New York: Frederick A. Praeger, Publishers, 1967; and Marilyn Gittell and T. Edward Hollander. *Six Urban School Districts.* New York: Frederick A. Praeger, Publishers, 1967.

[12] Floyd A. Hunter, *op. cit.,* p. 5.

[13] *Ibid.,* p. 2.

[14] *Ibid.*

[15] Sol Tax. "The Freedom To Make Mistakes." In: Fred Gearing, Robert McNetting, and Lisa R. Peattie, editors. *The Documentary History of the Fox Project.* Chicago: University of Chicago Press, 1960. pp. 245-50.

[16] Barbara A. Sizemore. "Making the Schools a Vehicle for Cultural Pluralism." In: Madelon D. Stent, William R. Hazard, and Harry N. Rivlin, editors. *Cultural Pluralism in Education.* New York: Appleton-Century-Crofts, 1973. p. 45.

[17] Morton Deutsch. "Cooperation and Trust: Some Theoretical Notes." In: Warren G. Bennis, Edgar H. Scheine, David E. Berlew, and Fred I. Steele, editors. *Interpersonal Dynamics.* Homewood, Illinois: The Dorsey Press, Inc., 1964. p. 566.

[18] Marilyn Gittell. "The Balance of Power and the Community School." In: Henry M. Levin, editor. *Community Control of Schools.* Washington, D.C.: The Brookings Institution, 1970. pp. 115-37. See also: Marilyn Gittell. "Supervisors and Coordinators: Power in the System." In: Vernon F. Haubrich, editor. *Freedom, Bureaucracy, & Schooling.* 1971 Yearbook. Washington, D.C.: Association for Supervision and Curriculum Development, 1971. pp. 161-73.

Politics, according to Banfield and Wilson, is conflict management or "the way by which politicians and others get the power they must have to govern."[19] The period of the seventies is one of black political organization for the mobilization of power. As Watson puts it:

> The question, when all is said and done, is not whether government can effectively intervene or whether schools make a difference. The evidence of history, unbiased observation, and common sense is very clear: it is all a matter of expectations—and the power to see that expectations are met.[20]

The black community has one important task: to mobilize and use the power dormant in the masses for the redistribution of resources belonging to all. Efforts are now underway to co-opt community control endeavors with decentralization which restructures the system so that "A" group power is brought closer to "B" group. Decentralization does not redistribute power. Power remains in the hands of group "A."

Excluded minority communities continue their attempts to mobilize power for full participation in this social order with preservation of ethnic differences. Yet, education is but one element of these trials. Other institutions subject to community control are: police, fire, and transportation departments, health facilities, housing, food delivery systems, and jobs (unions). This chapter attempts to: (a) explain community control within the context of the mobilization of people power; (b) describe examples of community control of education as exhibited by the majority community; and (c) present a more detailed description of one attempt at community control of education by a minority community. Although it will deal primarily with examples from the black community, comparable situations exist in all excluded minority communities.

The Rationale for Community Control

Many reasons have been cited for the reemergence of community control. Some have attributed its appearance to the failure of integration.[21] An oft-mentioned example is New York's I.S. 201 case.[22] Others

---

[19] Edward C. Banfield and James Q. Wilson. *City Politics*. New York: Vintage Books, Random House, Inc., 1963. p. 22.

[20] Bernard C. Watson. *Stupidity, Sloth, and Public Policy: Social Darwinism Rides Again*. Washington, D.C.: National Urban Coalition, 1973. p. 25.

[21] Robert L. Green. "Community Control and Desegregation." *School Review* 81 (3): 348; May 1973.

[22] David Rogers. *110 Livingston Street*. New York: Random House, Inc., 1968. pp. 29-30.

have blamed the political failure of schools and the inability of teachers to affect achievement scores in poor and minority communities.[23] A few have charged it to the appearance of black power arising from the failure of nonviolence and violence to attain inalienable rights.[24] This renewal of interest in community control may be viewed as a consequence of an increased political awareness created by all of these factors, the rigidity and unresponsiveness of overcentralized bureaucracies, the concentration of a black majority in the public school system of several major cities, and the increased feeling of community.

Iannaccone points out that any structure of policy making or system of governance involves the mobilization of bias. He says,

> Not all groups have equal access to policy making in any arena of governance. Characteristically, the politics of education has been a low visibility, insider, educational elite dominated game conducted in separate arenas of government.[25]

Furthermore, Iannaccone says that the autonomy of the large urban school districts, which have special legislation separating their powers from those of the state, and the political coalitions found in them have increased the power of urban education bureaucracies.[26] He comments that no government structure or political process is neutral, and that the political system is usually biased toward some actors or interests, giving them a major voice in the making of decisions.[27]

Iannaccone believes that "the governmental system of the typical school district is relatively closed to most district citizens" and the local board has few powers: (a) to hire and fire the superintendent and (b) to support or reject his recommendations.[28] The organized efforts of school employees, especially principals (particularly secondary school principals), have appeared in many studies to hold virtual veto power over the implementation of board policies. Koerner agrees with Iannaccone and says that the local board enjoys nowhere the degree of

[23] Preston Wilcox. "The Thrust Toward Community Control of the Schools in Black Communities." In: Robert L. Green, editor. *Racial Crisis in American Education.* Chicago: Follett Educational Corporation, 1969. pp. 300-17.

[24] Harold W. Pfautz. "The Black Community, the Community School, and the Socialization Process: Some Caveats." In: Henry M. Levin, editor. *Community Control of Schools.* Washington, D.C.: The Brookings Institution, 1970. pp. 26-30.

[25] Laurence Iannaccone. "Politics of Education." Paper prepared for The National Panel on High Schools and Adolescent Education, March 1973. p. 15.

[26] *Ibid.,* p. 31.

[27] *Ibid.,* p. 41.

[28] *Ibid.,* p. 37.

local control that most people think, being limited by its "preoccupation with housekeeping details, its own failure to assert its authority, and the external controls forced on it by other bodies." [29] Iannaccone warns further that "we can no longer assume that . . . board policies will be supported or implemented by teachers or principals at the building level." [30] The revolt of white taxpayers against financing education may be an indication of the validity of Iannaccone's and Koerner's points of view. Feeling the school board's powerlessness, that constituency took to the polls.

Many other outside forces affect education. Education is relegated to the state and is one of its constitutional responsibilities. The state delegates these powers to the local school district. The federal government sends money and constraints to the local district through the state. Additionally, education is influenced by teachers' organizations, national and regional organizations, and statewide groups and their lobbyists. Except when critical and crucial issues arise, however, local control is in the hands of the educational establishment.

The schools then become responsive to the needs and demands of these groups. Rogers explains this phenomenon in New York City where he says most municipal employees' unions and associations are well developed:

> The power of these groups is manifested in a variety of ways. Under the protective facade of "professionalism," they control entry into their agencies, and through civil service are able to limit the access of "outsiders." Particular agencies and civil service groups become the centers of ethnic power, despite the existence of a merit system. Thus, in New York City, the Irish dominate the police and fire departments, the Italians, the sanitation department, the Jews, the school system and welfare agencies.[31]

On May 1, 1973, local school board elections were held in New York City to determine who would occupy the 288 seats on the city's 32 community school boards. The turnout was 11 percent, less than the 15 percent which voted in the 1970 turnout. This has been regarded as an indicator of public disinterest. The United Federation of Teachers (UFT), politicians, antipoverty employees, and staff members ran one of the biggest political campaigns in history to advance their favored

[29] James D. Koerner. *Who Controls American Education?* Boston: Beacon Press, Inc., 1968. p. 124.

[30] Iannaccone, *op. cit.*

[31] David Rogers. *The Management of Big Cities.* Beverly Hills, California: Sage Publications, Inc., 1971. p. 37. Reprinted by permission of the publisher, Sage Publications, Inc., Beverly Hills, California.

candidates. The low voter turnout and poor representation of minorities among the winners clearly demonstrate the lack of mobilization of people power in those communities.

Kenneth B. Clark, a member of the Board of Regents of the State of New York and noted black social scientist (famous for the research leading to the 1954 *Brown* decision), has reportedly damned decentralization efforts because some local boards and groups, including the teachers union, have been more concerned with power and their special interests than with improving schools.[32] What Clark does not seem to consider is that power is needed to improve them. According to Haskins, the original purpose of the black community in seeking control was to try to stop the miseducation of the black children and to remove them from the influence of a system that was insensitive to their needs.[33] Minority communities have never mobilized enough cohesion around community goals; consequently, they have never reaped the fruits from their people power. Describing efforts in Cleveland, Rogers says:

The fragmented ecological and ethnic structure of the city, then, has determined its political superstructure. The careers of councilmen depend on appealing to separatist local interests, and these politicians reinforce the divisiveness that geographic and ethnic identity created. Black councilmen function much like their white colleagues. They even oppose many of Mayor Stokes' programs on the grounds that their neighborhood interests are not being adequately met.[34]

The mobilization of people power in minority communities is more important now than ever, because of the Nixon administration's determination to delegate more control and authority over social programs to the states. This move is particularly regressive because of the long history of failure on the part of state legislatures to deal effectively with urban problems. The State Senate of Illinois approved a bill requiring an elected and salaried Chicago School Board in April 1973, about three years after Chicago voters had overwhelmingly defeated such a proposal in a referendum. According to some senators, their action was justified because they felt that the referendum, in which only 9 percent of the registered voters participated, did not represent the views of the majority.[35]

[32] "Decentralization: Will It Pass the Big Test?" *New York Times*, April 29, 1973. p. 11.

[33] Haskins, *op. cit.*, p. 6.

[34] David Rogers, *The Management of Big Cities, op. cit.*, p. 114.

[35] David Gilbert. "State Senate OK's Elected School Board for Chicago." *Chicago Tribune*, April 26, 1973.

This new Federalism and the intent of the Nixon administration to solidify power in the hands of Small Town, America, will create agencies and programs even less responsive to the hard-core poor, local employers, and institutions.[36] Moreover, Rogers says, "It (Small Town, America) represents an insignificant and diminishing number of Americans (75 percent of the population live in metropolitan areas), and an even smaller proportion of the nation's problems." [37] Planning the future of America rests primarily with minorities, and this depends on their ability to mobilize power.

The Mobilization of People Power

There seem to be two approaches to the mobilization of people power: (a) the "issue" approach and (b) the "ideology" approach. Probably the best known example of the issue approach is The Woodlawn Organization (TWO) of Chicago, Illinois. Woodlawn is one of the ten poorest of the 75 community areas of Chicago, located on the central south side adjacent to the University of Chicago—less than two square miles, bounded by 60th Street on the north, Stony Island Avenue on the east, King Drive on the west, and 67th Street on the south.

According to Brazier, pastor of the Apostolic Church of God in Woodlawn and former president of The Woodlawn Organization, "People outside the Establishment must confront the Establishment with a crisis situation and seize upon it so that relevant change can be brought about. The only way for black people to bring this about and to get their fair share of the affluence of America is through a power organization." [38] He sees power as the means to goal achievement and community organization as the way to mobilize power. He explains his process in this way:

A power-based community organization must also bring about confrontation and conflict. Where there is no controversy, there is no issue. It is only when two groups or two people disagree that the issue is drawn. No vital community organization can exist without controversy. And this controversy must not be limited to one issue but must take up a multiplicity of issues.[39]

[36] David Rogers, *The Management of Big Cities, op. cit.*, p. 137.
[37] *Ibid.*, p. 139.
[38] Brazier, *op. cit.*, p. 19.
[39] *Ibid.*, p. 20.

For Brazier, there is a difference between an organization and a social movement, the former being goal oriented and the latter simply action oriented.

Brazier sees two sources of power: money and people.[40] His aim is to organize the latter. Founded in 1959 and led by ministers from the church, TWO was advised by the Industrial Areas Foundation to organize around issues. Some of the early issues were: the exploitation, lying, and cheating by businessmen in the area; unfair treatment by absentee landlords who hid behind land trusts; and the unequal and inadequate education provided by the public schools. Later issues were: housing, urban renewal, and the University of Chicago; the Blackstone Rangers and youth unemployment; and Model Cities and the political structure of education, health, and other services. TWO was an integrated organization, led by blacks, defined by blacks, but open to all who lived or led in Woodlawn.

Brazier feels it is significant that the religious leaders of Woodlawn and not the political or business leaders first saw the need for a strong organization in the community because he believes that the church has a responsibility for the elimination of injustice, poverty, oppression, and racism.[41] In spite of Brazier's strong leadership and moral courage, TWO was never able to deal effectively with the massive forces arrayed against it and eventually it was co-opted.

"Community organization falters," according to Marris and Rein, "because it cannot offer any future to the neighborhood leaders and because it provides no hierarchy of affiliation from local to national levels and thereby trivializes major interests by its parochial bias." [42] Brazier resigned in 1970, and there are allegations of corruption in the 1973 leadership. One resident, speaking of the present leadership, said, "They are in bed with the University of Chicago and the politicians for personal gain." Moore, Livermore, and Galland say that the devastation of Woodlawn began in 1960 at approximately the same time that TWO was founded. They comment as follows:

In 1960, at the beginning of Woodlawn's disastrous decade, the community was a crowded, largely rental-occupied black neighborhood, most of whose housing was at least 40 years old. An awesome collapse followed. During the 1960's Woodlawn's population declined from 81,000 to 52,000,

40 Ibid., p. 21.
41 Ibid., p. 30.
42 Peter Marris and Martin Rein. Dilemmas of Social Reform. New York: Atherton Press, 1967. p. 186.

a drop of 36 percent, and it is still dropping: the core of Woodlawn, between Cottage Grove Avenue and Jackson Park, lost 41 percent of its population. These losses exceeded those suffered by any other Chicago community. Between 1965 and 1971, the city demolished over 400 Woodlawn buildings. Lately the city has been demolishing at a rate of 500 dwelling units a year in Woodlawn, and currently has a demolition backlog there of over 1,500.[43]

TWO's strategy was based on winning. Brazier said that the selection of issues was of prime importance and the criterion of action was not necessarily the largest or most important issue, but the one the organization most likely could win.[44] As the forces against it mobilized effectively, TWO won fewer and fewer issues. Thus, its constituency became disillusioned, and the community collapsed.

The most celebrated example of the ideology approach in the black community is the Nation of Islam. It is based on the concepts of religious redefinition and nationalistic separation.[45] Ideology is used here as a particular definition of reality attached to a concrete power interest.[46] While both approaches, the issue and the ideology, proclaim the importance of self-determination and self-reliance, the former deals with action, the latter deals with power. While TWO is losing a community, the Nation of Islam is building one.

The ideology of most previously excluded groups is derived from religion and nationalism and has been described as a Power-Inclusion Model.[47] In this model, people power is mobilized from a separatist approach involving three steps: (a) the development of a pseudospecies declaration, (b) the acceptance of an identity specification, and (c) the creation of a territorial imperative. The first step is the religious process of believing in a God who has chosen the group as His Own (above all other groups). It says, "We are the chosen people made in the image of God." Erikson argues that man has survived as a species by being

[43] Winston Moore, Charles P. Livermore, and George F. Galland, Jr. "Wood-lawn: The Zone of Destruction." *The Public Interest* 30: 44-45; Winter 1973.

[44] Brazier, *op. cit.*, pp. 31-32.

[45] Elijah Muhammad. *Message to the Blackman in America.* Chicago: Muhammad Mosque of Islam No. 2, 1965. See also: E. U. Essien-Udom. *Black Nationalism.* New York: Dell Publishing Company, Inc., 1962.

[46] Peter L. Berger and Thomas Luckmann. *The Social Construction of Reality.* Garden City, New York: Doubleday & Company, Inc., 1966. p. 113.

[47] Barbara A. Sizemore. "Separatism: A Reality Approach to Inclusion?" In: Robert L. Green, editor. *Racial Crisis in American Education.* Chicago: Follett Educational Corporation, 1969. pp. 266-70. See also: Barbara A. Sizemore. "Is There a Case for Separate Schools?" *Phi Delta Kappan* 53 (5): 281-84; January 1972.

divided into pseudospecies, and this development becomes the program of group cohesion and group solidarity to protect the group from other pseudospecies.[48] Such cohesion causes the rejection of others, which Erikson explains as negative identity, "perversely based on all those identifications and roles which are most undesirable" and "dictated by the necessity of finding and defending a niche of one's own." [49]

The second step is that of self-definition and explanation: it must answer three questions. The first is: "Who Am I?" Erikson calls this the personal identity, the perception of the continuity of one's existence in time and space and the perception of the fact that others recognize one's sameness and continuity.[50] The second question is: "How good am I in relation to these others?" This is the ego identity, concerned with the quality of that existence or the awareness of the fact that there is a selfsameness and continuity to the ego. The last question is: "What is my group from which I come?" This is the group identity, representing that group's basic way of organizing experience, which is transmitted through child training to the foundation of the ego.[51]

The third step necessary for separatism is the creation of a territorial imperative. In man's effort to survive and reproduce he has come into conflict with land, nature, and other men. Sékou Touré defines culture within this context as an "expression in particular and specific forms of a general problem—that of the relationships linking man to his environment." [52] Every man must have a land base from which he springs and toward which he feels allegiance and love. Once the separatism process is completed, the power exists for the creation of myths, rites, and rituals to socialize the young and to build associations, institutions, and organizations for renaming and reclaiming this world.

Some critics of the Nation of Islam say that it is capitalistic, sexist, and elitist.[53] They also feel that the Nation will collapse when the present leader dies. Whether or not this prediction is valid remains to be proved. One thing is certain: the Nation has met the needs of many of the black poor. It has purchased land and houses, built bakeries and

---

[48] Erik H. Erikson. *Identity, Youth, and Crisis.* New York: W. W. Norton & Company, Inc., 1968. p. 41.

[49] *Ibid.,* p. 175.

[50] *Ibid.,* p. 67.

[51] *Ibid.*

[52] Sékou Touré. "A Dialectical Approach to Culture." *The Black Scholar* 1 (1): 13; November 1969.

[53] Barbara A. Sizemore. "Sexism and the Black Male." *The Black Scholar* 4 (4-5): 2-10; March-April 1973.

markets, established temples and farms, solved juvenile delinquency and drug addiction. This makes it a landmark for study in the mobilization and use of power.

Presently, some sources say that the Nation of Islam does not participate in politics. If it should do so at any time in order to protect its interests, it may have the power necessary to project these interests into the political arena with reasonable parity, providing it can recruit larger numbers of blacks to make a significant force. Its present anti-female, anti-Christian method of proselytization impedes this recruitment.

Community Control in Education: The Majority Community

One justification for the mobilization of community control often heard in the minority community is that minorities only want what the majority already enjoys. There is much disagreement among the experts about that statement. Mayer says that this minority view is entirely erroneous because lay boards have no power. He supports the finding expressed by Iannaccone that the professional staffs run the schools everywhere because nobody else can. Mayer argues that the function of a lay board of education is to improve the performance of these professionals by feeding into the system information about what the community thinks is wrong and by asking the questions which force the professionals to look for intelligent answers.[54]

Iannaccone discusses his findings in terms of routine and non-routine decisions; moreover, he reveals differences between small towns and large urban areas. He says that most of the issues in the politics of education are mundane and routine and the more routinized the policy making proves, the more the managers of the organization influence it. But,

. . . when factors such as population changes within governmental units, general credibility of government, and periodic national or international waves of concern about education elevate that routine politics into an episodic issue involving more political actors, the traditional managers of school systems lose a degree of control over that policy.[55]

Iannaccone shows that although larger cities display a mix and coalition of heterogeneous political subcultures in which persistent

[54] Martin Mayer. "The Local Board in New York City: A Personal Document." In: David Street, editor. *Innovation in Mass Education.* New York: John Wiley & Sons, Inc., 1969. p. 230.

[55] Iannaccone, *op. cit.*, p. 9.

political cleavages of municipal reform and city machine elements appear, the studies of urban school politics concerned with a range of social issues have found that the city school bureaus are central to the politics of urban education.[56] These findings show that the professional bureaucracy influences decision making over routine matters which prove to be the vast bulk of the issues in the politics of education. But, when abnormal issues arise, other constituencies become important to the policy making. Studies of desegregation, decentralization, and community control confirm this finding.

In the case of desegregation in the North, Crain found that there were six stages in the decision process and three groups of prime actors.[57] The issue usually appeared as a result of the activity of civil rights groups that generally were residents of integrated neighborhoods or members of civil rights organizations such as the NAACP. Demands for integration generally did not come from all black neighborhood groups or from the black political or civic elites. Residents of integrated neighborhoods were concerned about preventing a white flight from their communities and maintaining integrated schools. The struggle for desegregation in the North might be viewed as a struggle to stop the white flight. In none of the eight school systems studied by Crain did the civil rights movement succeed in integrating a particularly large number of black students. In fact, he found no relationship between the number of blacks in integrated schools and the extent to which the movement was satisfied. These data suggest that integration was not the real issue.[58]

Handlin gives two definitions of integration.[59] One refers to an open society, to a condition in which every individual can make the maximum number of voluntary contacts with others without regard to qualifications of ancestry. This definition requires solutions which eradicate segregated housing, deny unequal job opportunities, eliminate inadequate medical and educational services, and remove unequal taxation regulations. If this definition had been chosen, all barriers to association would have been leveled except those based on ability, taste, and personal preferences.[60]

[56] *Ibid.*, p. 32.

[57] Robert L. Crain, Morton Inger, Gerald A. McWorter, and James J. Vanecko. *The Politics of School Desegregation.* New York: Anchor Books, 1969. pp. 10-176.

[58] *Ibid.*, p. 12.

[59] Oscar Handlin. "The Goals of Integration." In: Talcott Parsons and Kenneth B. Clark, editors. *The Negro American.* Boston: Houghton Mifflin Company, 1965. pp. 659-77.

[60] See also: Barbara A. Sizemore. "Is There a Case for Separate Schools?" *Phi Delta Kappan* 53 (5): 281; January 1972.

The other definition refers to integration as racial balance. This means that individuals of each racial or ethnic group are randomly distributed throughout the society so that every realm of activity contains a representative cross section of the population. This definition is desegregation. Integration affords free choice to equals with the same limitations; desegregation assures free choice to the superordinate. Handlin says that the civil rights movement has never made a clear choice between these two definitions. As a result the groups with power, the "A" groups, rejected the open society definition, and models of desegregation which accommodated racist goals were implemented.

In an "A/B" situation, "A" group has the power to distribute and disseminate knowledge, information, and skills as well as to make decisions. Other powers exist too, such as:

. . . power is also exercised when A devotes his energies to creating or reinforcing social and political values and institutional practices that limit the scope of the political process to public consideration of only those issues which are comparatively innocuous to A. To the extent that A succeeds in doing this, B is prevented, for all practical purposes, from bringing to the fore any issues that might in their resolution be seriously detrimental to A's set of preferences.[61]

The hidden issue is that of open housing, since one of the major forces operating to integrate schools is the need to maintain racially stable neighborhoods or white majorities in the major cities.

In fact, in four cases studied by Crain, interracial neighborhood groups and white liberals were in the forefront of the protest. These pro-integration community groups wanted to maintain a sufficiently high percentage of whites, or a sufficiently low percentage of blacks, to prevent whites from moving out. Stated in this way, their position sounds like it might be closer to the "Keep the Blacks Out" demands of segregationist white communities than those of the black community.[62] A symbolic goal, integration, was substituted by "A" group for a welfare goal, housing, which was submitted by "B" group.

The hidden truth is that the U.S.A. had been faced with the "progressive ghettoization of whole series of great urban conglomerations."[63] The whites had been fleeing to suburbia and the blacks had

[61] Peter Bachrach and Morton S. Baratz. "Two Faces of Power." *American Political Science Review*, December 1962. pp. 948-49.

[62] Robert L. Crain *et al., op. cit.*, pp. 112-22. See also: Barbara A. Sizemore and Anderson Thompson. "Separatism, Segregation, and Integration." *Educational Leadership* 27 (3): 239-42; December 1969.

[63] Joseph Alsop. "No More Nonsense About Ghetto Education!" *The New Republic* 157: 18-23; July 22, 1967.

been concentrating in the central cities. In 1951-52, for the first time in the urban centers, the schools of Washington, D.C., had a black majority (53 percent). The predictions that this would occur in city after city threatened white political control of the "Free North." Commerce, banking, and industry took up the pattern of flight to the safe suburbs, leaving the central city open to black power, black self-determination, and black control. Realizing their plight, white leaders found it necessary to select some alternative to keep black people out of control. These were the conditions which influenced the thinking of the Justices of the Supreme Court in 1954. The 1954 decision reflects this thinking. It says:

> Segregation of white and colored children in public schools has a detrimental effect upon the colored children. The impact is greater when it has the sanction of the law, for the policy of separating the races is usually interpreted as denoting the inferiority of the Negro group. A sense of inferiority affects the motivation of a child to learn.[64]

This language implies that segregation does little or no harm to white children; therefore, segregated schools must support whites. If an institution reinforces the superiority of one group, how can that institution reinforce another group? What the decision really upheld was the contention that black schools are bad; and, even when they are not bad, they are bad if white people think so. Consequently, no schools should be all black.

Crain found that traditional civil rights groups tend to have symbolic goals, while the black community as a whole held both symbolic and welfare-oriented goals. He suggests that the civil rights movement can best be understood, not as the representative of the black community, but as a special interest group which is concerned with a limited range of social problems.[65] The civil rights movement, although generally supported by the black community, has begun to lose its credibility as welfare programs have been caught under the hammer of hard-hat hard-headedness. The recent controversy between the local NAACP director and the national director in Atlanta, Georgia, over desegregation, is an example of this conflict. The local chapter in Atlanta is supporting the welfare goals of the black community and the national office advocates the symbolic interests of the power groups.

The hard-hat revolt resulted from the pursuit of welfare goals. The black community interests were not being met by the civil rights movement programs. Welfare-oriented community leaders separated

[64] 347 US 843 (1954).
[65] Robert L. Crain et al., op. cit., pp. 143-44.

from the movement and began pushing for jobs. This demand hit the union organization with a lightning bolt which it hurled back in the form of political protest. School bond issues were defeated. School board members were recalled. School superintendents who supported integration were fired. Additionally, these "unmeltable" ethnics made their feelings about busing known to their elected representatives to affect the national elections of 1970, thereby determining the posture of the Congress, the President, and the Supreme Court and limiting goal achievement by the black community for years to come.

The most celebrated case of union-community conflict in education is the Ocean Hill-Brownsville experiment in decentralization. People in Ocean Hill and the upper end of Brownsville in the old District 17 in Brooklyn wanted to stimulate an inactive parents' association in the area; to seek out interested teachers who wanted to work together with the community for the improvement of education; and to form, at each of the schools, school-community advisory boards consisting of parents, teachers, and community persons to participate in the running of the public schools.[66] Their proposal was submitted to the New York City Board of Education and was later funded by the Ford Foundation. This was an attempt on the part of "B" group to make "A" group institutions accountable to "B" group.

The United Federation of Teachers (UFT) had a long history of opposition to decentralization and community control. The teacher strikes of September 1967, held to attain higher salaries, smaller classes, and the right to expel disruptive students, occurred at the time the Ocean Hill-Brownsville governing board had appointed replacement principals of its own choice. Those chosen had certified qualifications but had not come from the approved waiting list through which the teachers union and principals association exercised influence over appointments. The local board refused to support the strike and the teacher representatives resigned from the board, never to resume their membership. As a result, many union teachers withdrew their support of the experiment, requested transfers, and left. The governing board repeatedly asked for aid in this situation from the central board of education but received no action.[67]

The big conflict occurred in May 1968, when the local governing board "fired" 19 teachers. Ward reports that the fact is that the governing board requested the city's superintendent of schools to trans-

---

[66] Rhody McCoy. "The Formation of a Community-Controlled School District." In: Henry M. Levin, op. cit., p. 172.

[67] Agee Ward. "Ocean Hill." The Center Forum 3 (3): 3; November 13, 1968.

fer out of Ocean Hill-Brownsville this small group of teachers who were locally judged incompatible with the district program.[68] The local board felt that a failure to grant this request would indicate that the local community had no meaningful control over its schools. Some time before, 14 assistant principals in the district had been transferred elsewhere in one day at their own request and 16 teachers from one Ocean Hill school had been allowed to transfer out voluntarily just as the system was to reopen following the summer. Consequently, it could be assumed that transferring teachers was a rather routine administrative matter. The local board and its supporters, according to Ward, felt that the central powers regularly supported the teachers federation and were determined not to grant meaningful powers to the local community.[69]

On September 9, 1968, the opening of school, the UFT ordered a city-wide walkout to reinstate the ten remaining involuntarily transferred teachers since the others involved had accepted transfers. It also demanded the return of the colleagues who had supported these teachers by refusing to teach. Community residents prevented the ten unwanted teachers from reentering the schools and on September 13, UFT struck again, closing all the schools in New York City except those in I.S. 201 and Ocean Hill-Brownsville. There the majority of the teachers remained loyal to the community-elected governing board and classes proceeded as usual.[70]

On September 30, the disputed teachers were readmitted under the surveillance of union observers. The governing board, which had been suspended by New York State Commissioner of Education James Allen, was reinstated. The schools reopened throughout the city. But, on October 7, the Ocean Hill-Brownsville Unit Administrator declared he could not assign the teachers. He and seven of the school principals were again suspended. On October 11, they were reinstated and on October 14, UFT struck again throughout the city, saying that it would not reopen schools again until the governing board, the unit administrators, and all of the principals were removed.[71] On October 18, the custodians union struck in support and on November 15, the Appellate Division of New York State ruled in favor of a suit brought by the

68 Ibid.

69 Ibid., p. 5.

70 Rosalie Stutz. "Chronology of the UFT-Community Confrontation 1967-68." In: Annette T. Rubinstein, editor. Schools Against Children. New York: Monthly Review Press, 1970. pp. 267-70.

71 Ibid. The remaining text about Ocean Hill-Brownsville is based on this chronology.

Council of Supervisors and Administrators against the appointment of special demonstration principals in Ocean Hill-Brownsville. These principals won their appeal and were reinstated and finally, on November 19, schools reopened throughout the city after agreement was reached with UFT.

The Ocean Hill-Brownsville case demonstrates the problems of unmobilized power in the A/B reality. The local board was continually hamstrung in its efforts to operate, direct, and implement the programs necessary for educating the youth entrusted to its responsibility. The professional bureaucracy presented unordinary obstacles and, once the matter was thrown before the electorate, the black community lost. Decentralization programs which destroyed all opportunities for community control were then implemented.

The hidden issue for UFT was job protection. Should local governing boards gain the right to hire and fire teachers, UFT would lose its value to its members. Consequently, the union declared due process to be the issue. The majority of the evidence indicates, however, that transfers were largely routine matters which were usually made by the professional bureaucracy as predicted by Iannaccone. By declaring that the local board had violated due process, UFT created an extraordinary issue out of a largely routine matter, and other political actors were forced into the situation.

This movement for community control in New York City was an issue-oriented movement. Parents wanted to make the schools responsive to them, and they mobilized their power to address the educational system. In that particular community, this may have been viewed as a symbolic goal since other problems were certainly more welfare oriented. The main obstacle to sustaining the movement, however, was the fact that there was no ideology.

Ideologies generate group solidarity, and this kind of cohesion is necessary for maintenance and strength. In fact, according to Wilson, "until that ideology emerges and is understood by many of those who claim to support the notion of community control, the movement will be as vulnerable to its friends as it now is vulnerable to its avowed enemies." [72] Once this ideology develops, minority communities can continue the use of community control in order to make the routine decisions which affect the service delivery systems necessary for the achievement of welfare goals.

[72] Charles E. Wilson. "201 First Steps Toward Community Control." In: Annette T. Rubinstein, editor. *Schools Against Children.* New York: Monthly Review Press, 1970. p. 226.

Community Control in Education: The Minority Community

Ocean Hill-Brownsville was but one of the so-called "experiments" in decentralization. Others were: I.S. 201 and Two Bridges in New York City, Morgan-Adams and Anacostia in Washington, D.C., Rough Rock in Arizona, and The Woodlawn Experimental Schools Project (WESP) in Chicago, Illinois.

The WESP situation differed from others in that a community organization, The Woodlawn Organization (TWO), collaborated with two other institutions, the University of Chicago and the Chicago Board of Education, and supposedly negotiated from a position of parity. The project was a Title III, ESEA government-funded operation under Public Law 89-10. WESP consisted of four components: (a) administration, (b) community, (c) in-school, in-service, and (d) research and evaluation. By an unwritten agreement the University of Chicago controlled administration and research and evaluation, TWO controlled the community component, and the Chicago Public Schools controlled the in-school component. By control is meant the right to choose and appoint the personnel in that component. Technically and theoretically, all institutions were to agree on the personnel, and the Woodlawn Community Board Personnel Committee was to act as their agent. This process never fully materialized in this way during the life of the project from July 1, 1968, through June 30, 1971.

The objectives of the project emanated from the need to improve the quality of education in three all-black public schools—Wadsworth Elementary, Wadsworth Upper Grade Center, and Hyde Park High School in East Woodlawn—and to restructure these schools as a social system in terms of the community through mutuality of effort by subsequent interventions having two foci: (a) roles and relationships of persons acting within the schools, and (b) roles and relationships of persons acting in the home and community. WESP considered changes in terms of *how* people worked together, as well as *who* worked together.

The local governing board was called the Woodlawn Community Board (WCB). Its purposes were (among other things) to review, discuss, initiate, and recommend policies and projects in urban education that would directly affect the children, adults, community, and community organizations of the Woodlawn area and to provide a channel for communication with the institutions represented on the board. The WCB consisted of seven representatives each from the Chicago Public Schools, TWO, and the University. It was later reconstituted so that TWO had ten representatives; the Chicago Public Schools, seven, two of whom were teachers from the district schools and one a high school student; and four representatives from the University. It was hoped that this change would offer the opportunity for maximum citizen participation at the policy-making level.

TWO had a reputation for militancy and protest. TWO discovered that 80 percent of the children in Chicago on double shifts were black and that there were over 300 empty classrooms [73] in other parts of the city. The Board of Education was picketed and a public charge of segregation was made. The response from the bureaucracy was the purchase of millions of dollars of mobile classrooms promptly dubbed "Willis Wagons" (with reference to the then superintendent of schools Benjamin C. Willis) by TWO.

Consequently, when the project opened in July 1968, there were great fears that the community would threaten the positions of teachers and principals since the organization's belief in community participation in the selection of professionals was well known. Additionally, TWO representatives visited schools often on behalf of parent members, and professionals had often complained about these unannounced visitors in their schools and classrooms.

The first sessions at restructuring the social system revealed great differences between the parents and the teachers. Parents were recruited by 25 community agents hired by TWO and employed by WESP to organize and maintain parent councils in every block in East Woodlawn, where the schools' children lived. In addition, approximately 60 teacher aides were hired to assist teachers with the many new programs anticipated by the survey conducted before the project was funded.[74] One of the first conflicts was over the retention or removal of the Jewish upper grade center principal and some black upper grade center teachers who were in opposition to community leadership. The WCB made it clear that any teacher who did not want to participate in the project was free to request a transfer with no penalties for that teacher. Additionally, wanting to avoid another Ocean Hill-Brownsville at all costs, TWO moved very cautiously at all times to provide due process even in a later case involving a white high school teacher.

The Chicago Board of Education provided a private hearing for

---

[73] Brazier, op. cit., pp. 46-47.

[74] Willard Congreve. Institutional Collaboration To Improve Urban Public Education with Special Reference to the City of Chicago. Urban Education Development Project. Final Report, Project No. 7-0346, Contract No. DEC 3-7-070346-2881. Washington, D.C.: U.S. Department of Health, Education, and Welfare, Office of Education, Bureau of Research, March 15, 1968.

these black teachers, who are reported to have testified that TWO was hiring "Black Power" advocates to man the professional posts in WESP and that many of the people who were participating as parents had no children in their schools. Several of the teachers were moved to other schools and the upper grade center principal was transferred. The two schools were consolidated under the leadership of the elementary school principal who also happened to be Jewish.

The greatest problem which arose from WESP was not, however, with the Chicago Teachers Union. It was with TWO itself. For the principal of the high school, TWO had selected a very aggressive and militant black woman with a long history of struggle against the previous superintendent. Her appointment had been disapproved by the area superintendent and by many people in the community itself. For the second project director, TWO selected another black woman well known in the profession for her ability as an innovative administrator and for her success in elevating student achievement and in curtailing behavior problems.*

From the onset, the principal of the high school had trouble with her staff and her students. She blamed her problems the first year on the project director, who was white. During the second year she blamed her white teachers. She was accused by black and white teachers of being too rigid to share power, too vindictive to forgive mistakes, and too conservative to understand creativity. Under the second project director, she was faced with a great deal of student unrest. Suspension was the principal's solution. TWO had always been against suspensions, or the "pushout program," but this time it opted to criticize the teachers instead, in order to create a controversy between parents and teachers as an issue.

Community agents were instructed by TWO to tell the parents that the teachers at Hyde Park High School would not cooperate with the black principal. When the agents were questioned about this dishonesty, they said that great efforts had been made to convince the parents that they should select this person for the high school principalship and that a reversal in this decision would cause the organization to lose face with these parents.

The necessity for creating issues and the fear of losing face kept TWO from dealing with this administrator throughout the project. The WCB meetings were filled with student and teacher grievances about her noncompliance with WCB policy and the goals of the project. Staff

* Editor's Note: This second project director is the author of this chapter, Barbara A. Sizemore.

meetings were stalemated and relations between community agents and the high school teachers grew worse.

In May 1970, the Hyde Park High School teachers who had been having a running battle with the principal for the entire school year submitted to the WCB a proposal for their evaluation, involving not only the principal, but community and students. Their proposal requested a superior rating for all the teachers for the 1969-70 school year as the price for this involvement. The project director recommended this to the WCB for approval since it would give the community the opportunity to rate teachers. Teacher rating determines promotion and tenure within the system in Chicago and would have given the community real power. The WCB approved the proposal and advised the principal to rate the teachers. She refused to do so. At a closed meeting of the WCB she accused the project director of working against her and at cross purposes. She said that the project director refused to involve her in decisions about the high school and that at times she did not know what was going on. When the project director produced correspondence indicating otherwise, the principal said that she had never received it.

TWO was in an embarrassing dilemma. The WCB had ordered the high school principal to do something and she had refused. At the next board meeting, she produced a letter from the Director of Teacher Personnel advising her that the principal was the person responsible for rating teachers by board rules and she could not delegate that responsibility to anyone else. She told the WCB that she was employed by the Chicago Board of Education and also responsible to it.

Finally, the TWO president convinced her that she should sign the superior ratings for the teachers but, by that time, the teachers had become so disillusioned that they did not believe her when she said that she had done so. The teachers protested. TWO sent in teams of parents and community agents to watch the Hyde Park High School teachers, which made a bad scene much worse. Later, the teachers asked the union to file grievances against the principal, charging harassment by her, failure to discipline students identified as throwing firecrackers which injured two students, failure to use security guards assigned to the school to enforce order in the hall, and failure to meet with the faculty to discuss school problems.

Students began to organize in collaboration with the teachers but their movement was intercepted by TWO's community agents, who warned the seniors that they might not graduate if they continued to be involved. The student leadership abandoned the project and the students stayed out of the controversy. School finally closed, but the problem continued into the next year.

The 1970-71 school year began with a marked hostility between the project director and the high school principal. The latter refused to attend any meetings called by the former. Angry letters and memos were circulated back and forth during most of the school year. Then the time came for the implementation of the teacher proposal for community involvement in teacher evaluation. In April 1971, the students, incensed by the principal's refusal to hold a Black Culture Assembly, conducted a walkout. Because the students would not permit the principal to talk to them in the assembly, TWO sent community agents and organizers into the high school to control the students.

But this time the students had changed their strategy. During the summer the Associate Director of the Community Component had taught the students about community organizing and thus the students were using what they had learned. Instead of senior leaders, the students selected freshmen, sophomores, and "pushouts." In the negotiation which ensued the students indicated discontent with the failure of the principal to comply with the rules dictated by the high school senate, which was to be the governing body. The principal indicated that she could not abide by this structure since she was the sole person responsible for decisions.

The teachers submitted the timetable for their evaluation, but before the WCB could act on the proposal, the high school principal issued unsatisfactory ratings to the five teachers who had done the most to further project programs. The teachers struck and this time they were accompanied by the students. At the televised public hearings which were held on April 15, 1971, the students who had assembled proved to be very learned in community organization and protest. They expressed themselves well and stated their case. Only two of the five parents who testified actually had students in the high school. The others were employees of WESP and TWO. The students and the teachers asked for the principal's removal. At the suggestion of the president of TWO, the project director was ordered by the area superintendent to stay out of the high school. Moreover, the president of TWO requested that the project director make her charges against the high school principal at the public hearing. This the project director refused to do for ethical reasons. The next day the press reported that TWO felt the whole thing was a power struggle between the black militant project director and the beseiged but competent high school principal.

From that day forward, with one exception, the press projected and emphasized this analysis. Under cover and with its face saved, TWO persecuted the teachers, five of whom were removed from Hyde Park High School. Many students were arrested. In his letter to the high school students enlisting their aid to stop the chaos, TWO's president said the following:

> In a close athletic event, a referee or umpire makes a decision which we believe is wrong. We shout, jump up and down and even curse, but his decision stands and if we are going to eventually win the contest we must go on. A racist cop stops you at 63rd and Harper and accuses you of being the one who snatched somebody's purse, and in the process he violates your civil rights, by searching you on the street and maybe even placing a stick of "pot" in your pocket. You are taken before a judge, who seemingly hears the story, but eventually finds you guilty and gives you two years probation. We accept this because two years is not life and one must keep on living.[75]

Students rejected this position and called TWO a sell-out. Disturbances continued until the end of the school year. The student leaders were dropped from the school and placed elsewhere.

Like Ocean Hill-Brownsville, the project was designed for failure because of the following limitations: (a) authority was not clearly defined; (b) the entire constituency was not represented by TWO; (c) the power of the WCB derived from preexisting bases which preserved institutional loyalties; (d) the WCB lacked approval-veto powers; and (e) the WCB had no control over money.[76] TWO collaborated with the administration and supported unilateral decision making excluding students and teachers, thereby contradicting the goals of the project. This support affirmed the existing bureaucratic order and all the other external offices higher than the school. The community organization, allegedly fighting for local control, actually supported more bureaucratic and less aggregate grassroots decision making.[77] In the end it lost the chance to evaluate teachers. No other project had had that opportunity.

The demand for community control is derived from an ideology taken on by a group because of specific theoretical elements conducive to its interests and needed by every group in social conflict to generate solidarity. Without it, "B" groups fall constant prey to "A" group tactics.[78] Without an ideology, TWO supported the very power which

[75] E. Duke McNeil. "An Open Letter to Hyde Park High Students." *The Chicago Defender*, June 7, 1971. p. 8.

[76] This evaluation is taken from the "End of the Project Report," Woodlawn Experimental Schools Project, ESEA, Title III, Chicago Board of Education, June 1972.

[77] See: Barbara A. Sizemore. "Education for Liberation." *School Review* 81 (3): 401; May 1973. Also: Barbara A. Sizemore. "Is There a Case for Separate Schools?" *op. cit.*, p. 281.

[78] *Ibid.*

destroyed its community. The inadequacy of the issue approach is clear. With no union to fight, TWO had to create the issue of teacher opposition. Consequently, it failed to recognize the fruits of power when teachers extended them. Having no ideology to guide it, in the end, it was pushed into the untenable position of advocating police action against its own youth. TWO had become a part of the problem.

The Use of Power

Cruse argues that the concept of "Black Power" is open to as many interpretations as is freedom. Originated by Adam Clayton Powell in May 1965 at a Chicago rally and picked up by Stokely Carmichael in the summer of 1966, this concept, Cruse charges, represents a concerted shift from radical-protest integrationism to a position between separatism and racial integration.[79] One point in this chapter has been to show that black power is necessary to accomplish any goal for the masses . . . integration *or* separatism.

Most blacks in this country want to stay here and want to participate in the social order as equals with full preservation of their ethnic differences. Thus black power is a means to an end—*inclusion*. If black power represents nothing more than a strategic retreat for a purpose, then it has no praxis [80] and no use. But if it can reform the black world inside culturally, politically, and economically through ideology (religion and nationalism) so that a praxis for inclusion emerges for the masses, maybe a strategy pertinent to the broader struggle can be developed. The power to deal with this struggle resides in the masses.[81] It needs mobilization.

More study is necessary to develop a dynamic for synthesizing integrationist and nationalist strategies. Cruse's advice is as follows:

Black Power slogans reveal the depth of unpreparedness and the lack of knowledge that go along with the eagerness of the new black generation of spokesmen. The farther the Negro gets from his historical antecedents in time, the more tenuous become his conceptual ties, the emptier his social conceptions, the more superficial his visions. His one great and present hope is to know and understand his Afro-American history in the United States more profoundly. Failing that, and failing to create a new synthesis and a

[79] Harold Cruse. *The Crisis of the Negro Intellectual*. New York: William Morrow & Company, 1967.

[80] Word + reflection + action = praxis, according to Paulo Freire.

[81] Paulo Freire. *Pedagogy of the Oppressed*. New York: Herder & Herder, 1970.

social theory of action, he will suffer the historical fate described by the philosopher who warned that "Those who cannot remember the past are condemned to repeat it." [82]

TWO forgot the lessons Marcus Garvey taught. It failed to listen to W. E. B. DuBois. It never looked at the Nation of Islam.

So black power was as dysfunctional for this community as it was for its originator in whom more black power was invested than in any other person at that time. The black community has yet to learn how to use black power to gain community control.

[82] Harold Cruse, *op. cit.*, p. 565.

CHAPTER 9: STUDENT POWER

LEON MET

WHAT IF THEY gave students power and nobody came? The question may not be quite as facetious as it sounds. At this writing American schools are again experiencing peace or quiet. Stokely Carmichael has emigrated. Jerry Rubin has made the best-seller lists. Bobby Seale has run for public office. Dennis Shaul has become Commerce Director for the State of Ohio. The student power people of the sixties are finishing graduate work, teaching, governing, and otherwise taking care of business in the early seventies. All of them have crossed over the generation gap and are now on the other side of what used to be called the "trust" threshold. The war (Vietnam) is now largely out of our consciousness. The Great Society has been deactivated. The urgency of "We Shall Overcome!" has been muted, transmuted to "We shall come over—by and by."

Changes in the Quality of Student Power

Educators today again are worrying about apathy and quietism, about "freaks" and "crazies" of various pursuits and persuasions, who are off on trips characterized by self-gratification, privatism, social withdrawal, and alienation. The demands for education to be politically and socially relevant have faded. Students, faculty, and administrators are much less visible in the common media. Professional meetings, journals, and books are no longer focusing attention on students' power movements, their causes, implications, and cures. In fact, it almost seems as if the sense of movement among students is no longer a condition of our time. Clark Kerr's prediction in 1967 that student activism, protest, and violence had crested seems much more appropriate today. Students are not taking powers or buildings much any more.

On the face of it, the dramatic change from protest to peacefulness

would seem to give credence to Lewis Feuer's thesis that student movements are a historically repeating phenomenon, a generational conflict
born of emotional causes that is characterized by high ideals but that
results in self-defeating and socially destructive ends.[1] His analysis finds
that because the movements are youthful, they are transitory and result
in no lasting relationships with the more established agents of social
change in any given period. The latest period of student activism in the
United States seems to fit the criteria Feuer set in his analysis in 1968.
If we accept his thesis, we can look at student movements as inevitable
symptoms of youth, study them in a psychosocial historical context,
and be prepared to react to them with patience and understanding. That
view allows us to relax temporarily and enjoy the calm while it lasts.
Of course, we also have to live with the uneasy feeling that it will not
last long.

The counter to Feuer has two major themes. First, the most recent
activism was qualitatively different from previous adolescent movements
and cannot legitimately be classified with them. The character of the
times in which it occurred was also unlike any that came before. Thus,
although there may be similarities in conditions, the similarities are not
sufficient to warrant direct historical comparisons. Second, this adolescent generation is genuinely different from its precursors. As Erik Erikson
noted, "more than any young generation before, and with less reliance
on a meaningful choice of traditional world images, the youth of today
is forced to ask what is universally relevant in human life in this
technological age at this juncture of history."[2] Keniston, Meade, and
other thoughtful scholars have pointed out that today's youths are
better informed, educated, and nurtured than previous generations.
Their efforts to adapt to a radically different world and society with
calls for radical reform of institutions and relationships are rooted in
a higher social consciousness than was true with previous generations.

If we accept this latter line of reasoning, then our concern with
students and their movements, peaceful or otherwise, goes beyond
specific behaviors. It extends more deeply to the causes and potentials
of student involvement with the larger society. And, if we accept this
line of reasoning, we must look at what has been happening with all
students to try to understand where they are coming from and where
they want to go. In this context, student power is more than a matter of

[1] Lewis Feuer. *The Conflict of Generations.* New York: Basic Books, 1969.
[2] Erik H. Erikson. "Memorandum on Youth." *Daedalus* 96 (3): 860-70;
Summer 1967.

specific rights and authorities. It is a matter of the power of students to help shape the course of things to come.

Which is it? Do we look at the most recent upheavals as another episode in a continuing historical pattern to be repeated after another ground swell of apathy and quiet? Or do we look for the qualitative aspects of student power and the ways they may help condition the future of our educational and social communities?

Certainly things have changed over the past five to ten years, changed in such a way that they will never be the same again. In spite of parallels with past events, it is clear that students' relationships with adult institutions are not and will not be the same as before. Reference to the past is important to help us understand the future, but it must not limit our vision of what the future may become. It is almost like Casey Stengel's insight into baseball, "The game ain't what it used to be—and it probably never was."

With that proposition in mind, the question of student power is vitally important today as an educational question. It is a question that affects both young and old because it concerns the relationship that is established between us, between the institutions that connect us. It boils down to what we can and should be able to do with, for, and to each other. The question involves all of us at all times and can best be answered by all of us together. It includes the concerns raised by militants, but should not be limited to, or by, them. If we limit our concern to specific groups or to specific social dramas, then we deal only with symptoms that disrupt "normalcy." The relative absence of crisis should be used as an opportunity to respond constructively to the basic need for a definition of a relationship between students and educators.

Changes in Students' Legal Rights

What are the powers that students have? A cursory review of the status of their relationship to educational institutions shows that they have become quite different beings from what they were before 1960. Today's children and young adults enjoy rights, privileges, and advantages unknown to previous generations. The range and quality of experience that is routinely available to them are unprecedented. The scope and complexity of decisions that are theirs to make are staggering. In addition, we have seen the doctrine of *in loco parentis* slowly fade away, not just in colleges and universities but in secondary and even in elementary schools. Parental responsibilities and powers that used to belong to educators are being withdrawn from them and given to students, returned to parents, or assumed by the courts. Students are not so much coming as children to our schools as they are becoming clients and citizens.

This new client/citizen role has profound implications for student power in relation to institutional power. The change makes obsolete the absolute authority formerly vested in school people to control their charges. The client can hold the professional accountable for his professional performance. The citizen can hold him accountable for performance in his interest. The suit of a San Francisco student now pending against that city's public school system for its failure to teach him to read is one startling example of the former. The award of damages to a student against an administrator as a result of unreasonable action is another example. Many professional organizations are now offering malpractice insurance to their members. The presence of students on boards and committees and in elective offices is a very concrete example of the use of citizens' rights. "I'll sue" and "Wait till the next election" are no longer idle threats. The old order is changing.

The most easily visible changes have been in the area of students' legal rights. The U.S. Supreme Court 1967 *Gault* decision is probably the landmark. It affirmed that neither the Bill of Rights nor the 14th Amendment to the Constitution is for adults alone. That and other federal and state court decisions have extended to minors the protections afforded all citizens by our Constitution. In fact, the tendency has been to extend more protections to minors precisely because they are deemed to be more vulnerable to abuse and mistreatment than adults. Specifically, courts have extended to students the rights of due process, freedom of inquiry, expression, association, peaceful assembly, equal educational opportunity, and freedom from discrimination. Parietals, dress codes, censorship of publications, restriction of political activity, arbitrary administrative codes and actions, all have been denied in various legal actions.[3] The changes spelled out here are not necessarily common in educational practice—yet. Nevertheless, the handwriting is clearly on the wall.

[3] Good summaries of the changing legal status of students are available from a number of sources. The *Code of Student Rights and Responsibilities* developed by the NEA Task Force on Student Involvement in 1971 and the *Reasonable Exercise of Authority* developed by the National Association of Secondary School Principals in 1969 are good ones to start with. Most local chapters of the American Civil Liberties Union have documents available on student civil rights and liberties. These are especially helpful because they often detail local conditions and developments. Other good sources for thought and fact are: The Center for the Study of Student Citizenship, Rights, and Responsibilities, Dayton, Ohio; The National Juvenile Law Center, St. Louis University, St. Louis, Missouri; and the Harvard Center for Law and Education, Cambridge, Massachusetts.

The traditionally oppressed or ignored of our system's schools have assumed a new status also. Blacks, Spanish-speaking Americans, Indians, and women are certainly no longer ignored. Although the goal of equal educational opportunity has not been fully achieved, it is much more actively and imaginatively being pursued in all of its aspects. The numbers of school systems that are being desegregated, the concern for equal opportunity and for affirmative action are examples of that. The agreement in Atlanta to integrate administrative personnel in lieu of school desegregation is an especially interesting example. There is also evidence of a search to alleviate the inequities in collection and distribution of educational revenues. Within the educational profession and the industry that serves it, an active examination of curricula, textbooks, and materials for bias has begun.

The powerlessness of minorities has been even more significantly alleviated by an ongoing change in minority peoples' views of themselves. If a slave is one who waits for someone to free him, there are many fewer slaves in our schools. More blacks feel beautiful, more Spanish-speaking Americans and Indians prize their cultural heritage, more women want liberation. More and more this new positive self-consciousness is bringing institutional change. If students as a group are to be added to the list of those treated as minorities, then we must acknowledge that they too have a new perspective of themselves. The student activism of the sixties has contributed to this.

Even in the current context of quiet, it is not easy to ignore the powers that students have used. The primaries of 1968 and 1972 testify to that, as do the disruptions of the same period. Students have proven that they can participate as effectively in elections as they can bring down institutions. And more of them are acting as if they know it. Even though students have not become the masters of their educational communities, they are not quite the "niggers" that Farber talked about.[4] Members of minorities, students, and educators all have a new awareness of the positive and negative roles that can be played by young people. That awareness has brought with it a new respect for individuals and for groups within our schools.

Changes in the Schools

Accompanying and a part of the foregoing changes have been alterations in schools as institutions that have expanded students' powers

---

[4] Jerry Farber. *The Student as Nigger.* North Hollywood, California: Contact Books, 1969.

of choice and abilities to learn. Perhaps the best indicator of that change is a look at contemporary educational parlance. Accountability, alternative schools, computer-assisted instruction, personalized instruction, mod-flex scheduling, criterion-referenced assessment—all of these are indicative of a new concern for the effect of education on the individual student and for the potential of individuals to become more self-fulfilling in their growth as people. The Parkway School, Freedom Annex, and Street Academies have been joined by less well-known alternative schools in most major cities of the nation. Within schools there has been fairly widespread experimentation with new methods, curricula, and structures. Preservice and in-service teacher education have added new dimensions. The expanded role of the federal government in education through the 1965 Elementary and Secondary Education Act, especially through Title III of that act, has been the catalyst for many of these changes by providing the wherewithal and often the motivation for experimentation. It is interesting to note that the legislation provides for community and student participation in the development and operation of federally funded programs.

Students and the Open Society

All of these changes in students, laws, society, and schools have enhanced the power of students to be clients and citizens of our schools. They are, however, part of a larger context of change which has brought us closer to the ideal of an open society. Other chapters in this Yearbook deal with other elements of these changes and with their interconnections. This chapter has been concerned with their implications for student power, rights, and influence. The question now becomes: what are the implications of the emerging role of students as clients and citizens for education in an open society?

Student power is an important element of the power relationships in an open society. It is a power that is built from within to contribute to the development of the whole. Student power (or anybody else's, for that matter) becomes destructive if used as an end unto itself without relationship to the purposes of the community of which it is a part and to the powers of others in that community. By the same token, when student power is repressed or ignored, it may become destructive or the value of its potential to contribute to the community may be lost. In an open society, student power is not defined through an enumeration of specific rights and authorities, although such an enumeration is important in establishing expectations. Nor is it something that comes at the expense of, or is subtracted from, the powers of others (although that too may be necessary). The power orientation of an open society is to the potential of people to create and build together for the betterment of all. In that sense, power may be unlimited.

The open society is not, however, an anarchy. It is not a return to Hobbes' or Locke's State of Nature. It represents a new social contract, one that both offers more and expects more of its members. The open society affords access to information and democratic decision making to all of its citizens. It acknowledges their dignity and worth, values their diversity, and promotes their self-fulfillment. It represents an order that minimizes restraint as it maximizes responsibility. It leaves itself open to the influence of all its citizens, promotes their individuality, and risks their power to share in what they and the society become. The open society is open to change, conscious of the need for values to serve as the bases for action. Its politics, economics, education, and psychology are based on a positive faith in the potential of man.

Education in an open society regards students, above all, as people in their own right in the here and now. It is willing to risk their participation as citizens in the educational enterprise because it values them as human beings, and because that participation is most congruent with its educational purpose of allowing students to develop as citizens in a democratic society. It accepts them as clients in the educational enterprise because it offers them a professional service that is effective only when it satisfies both individual needs and interests and socially valued goals and standards. This dual obligation to serve client and society is analogous to the lawyer's responsibility to the individual who retains him and to the community which establishes him as an officer of the court. Thomas Jefferson foreshadowed the importance of both the client and citizen roles when he called upon Virginia educators to devise a system of school governance founded in "reason and comity" that would "be more likely to nourish in the minds of our youth the combined spirit of order and self-respect, so congenial with our political institutions, and so important to be woven into the American character." [5]

Earl Kelley in his article, "Another Look at Individualism," adds to that reasoning. He said:

Many school teachers and administrators are afraid to take a chance on consulting their young, for fear that they will not come up with the right answers. They fear that unless they sit tight on the lid which contains explosive human energy in great quantity the whole institution of the school will blow up. . . . The schools, however, are most important if we are to have

[5] Gordon C. Lee, editor. *Crusade Against Ignorance: Thomas Jefferson on Education.* New York: Teachers College Press, 1961. p. 128.

freedom. They affect the lives of almost everyone who lives in this country. The basic objection which I have concerning our schools is that they do not provide for choices required by free people. The young person . . . cannot explore or initiate, but only follow orders. This produces a society composed of people who are unaccustomed to making choices, and unskilled in it. The schools, for example, have tried since the beginning of formal education to produce people who all knew the same things and had the same ignorances. They have never succeeded in this, even though they are still trying. The reason that it has not been possible to standardize everybody is that people have uniqueness built in from the very moment of conception.[6]

We cannot really control the amount or kind of power students have. Their ability to influence and shape us is not derived from our will. As long as we share time and space with students our powers are interactive. Whether legitimated or not, authorized or not, actively or passively expressed, students and adults joined in education condition each other's behavior and effectiveness. In education for an open society we abandon the myth that students are "preparatory adults" only and, as such, incapable of decision, choice, reason—and thus unqualified for real participation. In the real world of our schools they are very real people, very much capable of owning their present and future and of participating in ours.

Framework for Student Power

The structure and uses of power in education for an open society must be consistent with the functions of students and schools. This means that:

1. *Students must be regarded as real people, here and now, living real lives, in and out of school.* Their being and becoming must be accepted in that way, not as something simply in apprenticeship or in preparation. Students will be future citizens, parents, workers, etc. But our concern for future must not artificially limit our acceptance of them as people in the present. If it does, we just may mortgage their future and ours.

2. *Adults must free themselves to be real people too.* Being an educator does not require any one model or role. We sell ourselves short by overplaying adult status or by underplaying maturity either to force

[6] Earl C. Kelley. "Another Look at Individualism." In: Donald L. Avila *et al.*, editors. *The Helping Relationships Sourcebook.* Boston: Allyn and Bacon, Inc., 1972. pp. 325-27.

responsiveness or to win favor. Neither adults nor students can be free if their humanity and spontaneity are constrained by artificially contrived roles.

3. *Structures for student-educator relationships must permit open, honest, and reasonable interaction and confrontation on current realities.* The forms of governance in this interaction must follow the functions of school government. Student councils, especially, should not be used simply as gaming devices or as simulations at the expense of real citizen participation by students in schools. Delayed participation in real authority and responsibility too easily prepares a docile, reactive citizenry. Playing games just accustoms us to playing.

4. *All students must be considered.* The services of the school and the structures of governance must be genuinely open to any student and efforts made to enlist participation from all. The vocal, the eager pleasers, the super-achievers, and the disruptive are not all of the students in a school community. Special efforts must be made to serve and to involve the silent and the average as well.

5. *Students must be able to make real choices for themselves and for their schools.* This requires access to the information necessary to set goals, structures adequate for real communication and interaction with decision makers, and feedback from them on the results of their participation. This room for choice includes the content and method of instruction, the policies and procedures of school operations, and the definition of values that direct the school program.

6. *Double standards, usually used to condone a weakness in adults while condemning it in young people, must be eliminated.* It is morally and ethically wrong to allow ourselves behaviors that we will not extend to students as a privilege of age or of status. Beyond that, the behaviors we model condition the learnings and attitudes of youngsters. Like the father who beats his child to teach him not to beat on others, the teacher who smokes where students may not, or disrespectfully compels showings of respect, teaches unintended but lasting lessons.

7. *The exercise of authority by students and adults must be accountable to those from whom it is derived and justifiable to those with whom it is employed.* If power is used without this kind of dual responsibility, the power itself becomes corrupt and the people become its victims.

8. *The uses of power in schools must be consistent with the values and purposes of the educational community and the society at large.*

This requires that all involved share in the development of a philosophy that defines the ends to be sought in any school community and that these ends be the criteria for evaluating the activities, programs, and relationships in that community. Although individual schools will and should vary in the value system that is developed, common components for all should be the valuing of people, truth, and reason.

9. *Students' civil rights and liberties must be protected.* The protections of the Bill of Rights and of the 14th Amendment do not stop at the schoolhouse door. Students have a right to participate in the development and administration of codes of conduct and to be fully informed of such codes. Students and school authorities need not enter into adversary relationships if rights and responsibilities are jointly and constructively defined and administered by both.

10. *Students' human and educational rights must be protected and enhanced.* The dignity and worth of each student must be affirmed in all of our interactions with students. Their individuality and personhood must be accepted and respected, even if all of their behaviors cannot be approved. The opportunity of each student to achieve the maximum of his potential must be established. The need to be adequately prepared for meaningful participation in the world of work and in the society of man is a student's right and our professional responsibility.

What if they gave students power and nobody came? That is really an academic question. Students have powers, rights, and influence. The operational question for us and for them is how ready we are to recognize those powers and to help students be able to use them openly and constructively. The answer really depends on how much courage and intelligence we can muster.

References

Joseph Axelrod *et al. Search for Relevance.* San Francisco: Jossey-Bass, Inc., 1969.

Daniel Bell and Irving Kristol, editors. *Confrontation: The Student Rebellion and the Universities.* New York: Basic Books, Inc., 1968.

Arthur W. Chickering. *Education and Identity.* San Francisco: Jossey-Bass, Inc., 1969.

Erik H. Erikson. "Memorandum on Youth." *Daedalus* 96 (3): 860-70; Summer 1967.

Jerry Farber. *The Student as Nigger.* North Hollywood, California: Contact Books, 1969.

Lewis Feuer. *The Conflict of Generations.* New York: Basic Books, Inc., 1969.

Richard Flacks. "Student Activists: Result not Revolt." *Psychology Today* 1 (6): 18-25; October 1967.

Mary Harrington Hall. "Mary Harrington Hall Interviews Clark Kerr." *Psychology Today* 1 (6): 25-31; October 1967.

Richard Hart and J. Galen Saylor, editors. *Student Unrest: Threat or Promise?* Washington, D.C.: Association for Supervision and Curriculum Development, 1970.

Earl C. Kelley. "Another Look at Individualism." In: Donald L. Avila *et al.*, editors. *The Helping Relationships Sourcebook.* Boston: Allyn and Bacon, 1972. pp. 300-29.

George F. Kennan, editor. *Democracy and the Student Left.* New York: Bantam Books, 1968.

Edward T. Ladd. "Regulating Student Behavior Without Ending Up in Court." *Phi Delta Kappan* 54 (5): 304-309; January 1973.

Gordon C. Lee, editor. *Crusade Against Ignorance: Thomas Jefferson on Education.* New York: Teachers College Press, 1961.

Charles H. Monson, editor. *Education for What?* Boston: Houghton Mifflin Company, 1970.

NEA Task Force on Student Involvement. *Code of Student Rights and Responsibilities.* Washington, D.C.: National Education Association, 1971.

Vito Perrone. *Open Education: Promise and Problems.* Bloomington, Indiana: Phi Delta Kappa, 1972.

Gary Saretsky and James Mecklenburger. "See You in Court?" *Saturday Review of Education* 55 (42): 50-56; November 1972.

Harold G. Shane. "Looking to the Future: Reassessment of the Educational Issues of the '70s." *Phi Delta Kappan* 54 (5): 326-31; January 1973.

Carol Towarnicky, editor. *What We Study in School and Why.* Dayton, Ohio: Center for the Study of Student Citizenship, Rights, and Responsibilities, 1972.

CHAPTER 10: THE MYTH AND THE HOPE OF TEACHER POWER

DAVID SELDEN

PEOPLE INTERESTED IN the future of American education—to say nothing of the future of American society—have been speculating for some time about the significance of the recent rise in teacher power. Since most of the crystal-ball gazers are representatives of groups other than teachers—school administrators, school board members, militant community groups, and researchers—the future is usually seen fraught with fear and trouble. To these educational commentators, teacher power is a mysterious lemming-like urge arising from God knows where, but sure to result in the destruction of us all.

Actually, the rise of teacher power is a response to deteriorating conditions in the schools, and in society at large. Following World War II, the real wages of teachers steadily declined while conditions in the schools became ever more turbulent and difficult. The old-line teachers associations proved themselves utterly inadequate to cope with the situation. All this social tinderbox needed was a spark to set it aflame. That spark was the development of collective bargaining in New York City in the early 1960's.

Teacher Power Still Undeveloped

Teachers in most school districts across the nation still have surprisingly little power in spite of all the scare talk. Even where teachers have achieved a measure of power through collective bargaining, success at the bargaining table rests primarily on willingness to refuse to work unless the terms and conditions of employment are satisfactory. Apart from some big-city school districts and a few other atypical localities where strikes are considered a normal result when negotiations fail, it requires a superhuman effort for teachers to screw up their courage to the point where they are willing to stop work. Even then the results are limited because it is terribly difficult to produce the kind of money needed to solve today's educational problems.

During the early weeks of 1973 there were four major teacher strikes going on at the same time. One was in Philadelphia where after 53 days a good four-year settlement was achieved, but the funds for the first year came from savings resulting from the school shutdown. In St. Louis teachers were out more than a month in order to win a $1,000 salary increase for the next year, a rudimentary health plan, and the right to vote in a collective bargaining election. In Chicago teachers were forced to strike two weeks, essentially to protect conditions negotiated a year before. In Warwick, Rhode Island, teachers were out a little more than a week and went back with a fair salary increase but meager benefits.

The failure of these strikes to generate enough added funds to permit significant improvement in school programs was due primarily to the decentralized nature of educational finance. No agency or level of government is charged with seeing to it that the schools have enough money. Local school districts, except in a few large cities, receive funds from the local property tax, state aid, and federal aid. Local property taxes in most districts are near the saturation point; therefore, the big money must come from state and federal sources.

Getting money out of the state is a more complex operation than getting it from local sources. There is a well-developed education lobby in most states, but there are many cross currents which make it difficult to generate teacher power. Upstate/downstate rivalries, big city/small city conflicts, partisan politics, teacher/administrator conflicts, and the personal ambitions of politicians, all must be taken into account. The power realities in a lobbying operation are rooted in the help or harm the organization can do for or to legislators. In a few states teachers have a great deal of "clout"; but compared with the directness of collective bargaining, state lobbying is a tenuous process, and the results often fall far short of needs, let alone expectations.

Development of teacher power at the state level is further limited by the nature of teacher organizations. The American Federation of Teachers is basically a collection of local unions spottily distributed throughout the Northeast, Midwest, and the Pacific Coast region. The AFT includes a majority of the teachers in only two states—New York and Rhode Island. As for the associations, most of them try to be all things to all people in the educational establishment and end up incapable of forthright action on behalf of teachers.

There have been a few statewide work stoppages by teachers. All have been called by the associations, and all except the Florida teachers' strike of 1967 have been for limited objectives and of short duration. Many, if not most, have been aided and abetted by superintendents and other administrators, thus making questionable their authenticity as demonstrations of teacher power.

The Florida strike, however, was a genuine attempt by teachers (led by state and national staff members, to be sure) to confront the power of the state government and to negotiate a settlement. It failed for a number of reasons, none of which was indicative of a fundamental flaw in the theory of the statewide strike. Nevertheless, the National Education Association has frowned on such confrontations ever since.

If teacher power is limited at the state level, it is even more diffused at the national level. Both the NEA and the AFT maintain active lobbies in Washington, the latter strongly assisted by the AFL-CIO, generally conceded to be the most potent noncommercial lobby on Capitol Hill. In recent years all educational groups have joined together in a loose coalition called the "Full Funding Committee." The group concerns itself mainly with appropriations for federal aid programs. Its mode of operation is by consensus, and since it includes administrator organizations and other special interest groups, the committee hardly qualifies as an instrument of teacher power.

Impact Within the Establishment

So far this discussion has dealt only with the impact of the growth of teacher power on school boards, legislatures, and the Congress. While there certainly has been a noticeable increase in external teacher power since World War II, this is more a comment on teacher powerlessness prior to that time than an indication that teachers are about to take over the schools. Nevertheless, within the establishment where collective bargaining has been recognized, teachers have made substantial gains vis-à-vis principals, superintendents, and other administrators.

A review of the kinds of teacher tenure cases which were once commonplace gives an idea of how far we have come. During the twenties, thirties, and forties women teachers were being dismissed because their skirts were too short, because they did not live in town, or because they refused to truckle to impossible orders from male administrators. Men teachers were dismissed if they wore beards (mustaches were okay), refused to collect tickets at Saturday athletic events, refused to attend PTA meetings in the evening, refused to change grades on the order of the principal, or refused to hand in detailed plan books to principals who had no knowledge of the teacher's specialty.

In Boston during World War II, Mary Cadigan, a wispy but determined high school teacher, refused to give her time free of charge during spring vacation for the purpose of rationing coffee. She was dismissed, but a year later she was rehired at the insistence of the labor movement in Boston. In fact, all teachers (except Miss Cadigan) gave free time to the government for the purpose of issuing rationing booklets while workers in defense plants were on overtime, and the owners of the plants went "on strike" by refusing to bid on government contracts until they were guaranteed "cost plus." All of this seems incredible now, although a large amount of petty oppression and injustice continues in nonbargaining districts.

All teacher bargaining contracts now include grievance procedures, and teacher negotiators have become sophisticated about time limits, forfeit clauses, arbitration clauses, quickee arbitration, and other provisions which keep administrators wary of overstepping their bounds.

Other contract clauses have enlarged the scope of teacher power in other directions. Class size limitations force principals to open up new classes in order to stay within contract limits. Many contracts require monthly consultations between principals and union committees in their schools. These consultation sessions often become full-fledged negotiations, although, since they occur within a contract period, the union cannot properly resort to a strike to enforce its demands. Many contracts incorporate personnel practice booklets, which spell out the duties teachers may be asked to perform.

There is no gainsaying the fact that much of the growth of teacher power has been at the expense of administrators—but the powers wrested from the principals and superintendents are powers these officials never should have had in the first place.

The effect of collective bargaining on morale, it must be confessed, has occasionally not been positive because of the constant friction generated by an adversary situation. Also, in secondary schools, hard bargaining on class size limits can squeeze out some curriculum offerings when money is scarce. For example, analytical geometry may have to be offered every two years instead of every year because the school cannot afford to operate a class which often falls so far below the maximum allowable limit. None of these negative effects is inherent in the system, however, and it would not be an improvement in school functioning to go backward to the days when a principal was like the captain of a ship and could do anything he wanted to do—except perform marriages, perhaps.

School and Society

Some critics of the thrust of teachers for more power have argued that more power for teachers means less for local communities and society at large.

However much schools may resemble mass production enterprises in all too many respects, they do differ from corporations in their purpose. In our society, as Milton Friedman has put it, the duty of company management is to make profit for the owners. Thus the social responsibility of private industry is considered by the general public to be very limited indeed. It is only lately that we have even come to believe that auto manufacturers, for instance, have a responsibility to produce safe, pollution-free vehicles. Beyond that rather limited standard the auto makers are free to do anything they wish in their efforts to sell their products at the maximum margin of profit.

Schools, of course, are social enterprises. Their purposes are primarily the achieving of goals mandated by society: to foster a body politic knowledgeable enough so that democracy can function; to teach marketable skills so that everyone "pulls his weight"; to equip individuals with the basic tools for improving life, liberty, and the pursuit of happiness. The case for increased teacher power, therefore, must rise or fall on the effect such a change would have upon the quality of education.

The autocratic/bureaucratic traditional organization of American schools served us well from a cost effectiveness standpoint when it was morally and socially acceptable to neglect the education of a third to a half of our children. Such an elimination system is no longer acceptable, however, and schools must be more flexible—more humanistic—if they are to educate the atypical children who are squeezed out by the old system.

The old school reformers—Conant, Counts, and the others—expressed the need for school reform in terms of the needs of society as a whole, but many of the new school reformers are concerned because underprivileged local communities are not being properly served by their school systems. Teacher power in the long run must take into account the needs of such communities, as well as the goals of society as a whole.

The need for changes in American education has been recognized by many people ever since the mid-fifties. During the 1960's, in fact, large amounts of money from federal sources and the foundations were devoted to programs designed to "bring about 'change' "— a phrase which many teachers find annoying. The word "change," when used by the reformers, is pronounced with a reverent air as though it possesses a compelling mystique. Teachers are looking for new ideas which will help them do a better job; to achieve more success in the classroom. But they are not in favor of change merely for the sake of change.

More than a decade of "change," effort, and innovation has had very little effect upon the hard core of American education. There are two basic reasons that so much time, money, and effort have produced so little:

1. The would-be changers have largely been alienated from the school system, and their lack of credibility has created resistance, and

2. Funds for innovations have come from outside sources and have rarely been a part of the regular school budgets; when the funds dry up, the programs wither and blow away.

The Uses of Teacher Power

Teacher power up to now has been as much a defensive measure as it has been a weapon of offense. Teachers have wanted protection against actions of supervisors, administrators, school boards, and legislatures which appear to be contrary to teacher interests. Consequently, teacher publications tend to take on a complaining, truculent, carping aspect. Part of this, of course, is merely the response to the journalistic imperative that good news is usually bad news or no news. But more than that, teachers have felt a resentfulness about their lack of power, and it is hard to be both positive and resentful at the same time. As teachers achieve a greater measure of power within the educational enterprise, it can be hoped that their greater sense of security will generate a more positive approach to the use of power.

The British, the Danes, the Belgians, Austrians, Germans, and other social democratic nations have concluded that teachers as an occupational group must be given responsibility for reshaping their school systems to the needs of the latter quarter of the 20th century. Can American teachers do it, too? Perhaps it will take decades to accomplish the changeover, but it will never be done if we do not start, and it will never be done unless teachers do it for themselves.

CHAPTER 11:
POLITICAL EDUCATION AND THE CONCEPT
OF BLACK POWERLESSNESS

CHARLES E. BILLINGS

WHITE SOCIAL SCIENCE analysts have labored under several assumptions for almost three decades. Among these assumptions are the following:

1. Because black politicians and community leaders operate within majoritarian structures, black leadership exists largely by the grace of white institutions.

2. Black political separatism on a local scale is doomed to failure because the separate ethnic institutions necessary for the mobilization of blacks as a power bloc do not exist.

3. The major predictive variable in American political analysis will continue to be area, albeit the axis will no longer be North vs. South, but urban vs. suburban.

4. Black power means mobilizing black people and their sympathizers within rather traditional structures. The game is still numbers and minimum winning coalitions rather than philosophies and ideologies.

Each of these assumptions is based upon analysis of black-white politics over several years. There are good reasons that they have come to stand at the center of contemporary political dialog. They are not, however, valid. Their use shows a yearning for the simple truths of a bygone age, an age when black politicians were well advised to "listen much and to talk little." That was an age when the black voter could be counted upon to pay more attention to the politician who promised to leave him alone than to one who promised "pie in the sky," like equal pay for equal work. It must be remembered that when the phrase "Black Power" was first shouted from the parched throats of black activists on the dusty road to Selma, black people had already given

155

up the "low profile" that had been their social and political *modus operandi* since the dark days of the Racist Reformation that followed the aborted enlightenment of the Reconstruction period.

Again black people were *demanding* their right to justice. They were not only seeking redress for oppressions past but they were also charting a new course for the future. It is perhaps the myopia of the social science fraternity that prevented them from seeing that blacks had once again become not only the moral heart of America but its political brains as well. Black people around the country, in a curious unanimity of thought for those without the "institutional wherewithal" for collective action, began to stand before (and in some cases *upon*) those vested with the public trust to demand change, reform, and reparations. The lesson was not lost upon the other groups in our society that had long contented themselves to remain powerless and impotent, comforted only by their designation as "nonblack."

James Forman's demand that the temples be cleansed of past sins by paying reparations to the progeny of the church's former property led to an examination of the role of society's sacred institutions in the support of racism, repression, and war. Could Catholic nuns prostrate themselves in the aisles of St. Patrick's Cathedral during mass as a protest to the Church's attitude toward the Southeast Asian war without Forman's example years earlier on Riverside Drive? Perhaps . . . but it is unlikely. Were there White Panthers before there were Black Panthers? Is it only coincidence that Students for a Democratic Society grew out of a group of University of Michigan students whose first activities were in support of Southern black students protesting racism? Is not the 1963 Freedom March the sire of almost a decade of similar descents on the Capitol? If the issue in support of which the pilgrims come is different, what of the organization and logistics of the crusade? Who was the first to trust in the leadership capacity and organizational ability of the poor and of youth . . . of women and of Native Americans, of Chicanos and of the rank and file . . . McCarthy? McGovern? Billy Graham? It is my contention that the Black Power movement and more specifically the civil rights movement of the sixties educated a new generation of political actors. The fruit of that education is only now beginning to ripen. For some it is a sweet harvest, for others its flesh has the taste of gall.

It is the purpose of this chapter to offer an analysis of this process of political education in the light of the assumptions about black politics mentioned earlier and the effects of the process upon black people as political actors. Although an equally important subject, the effects of the reeducation of other "out-groups" in American society cannot be considered within the scope of the present effort. My principal contention is that the impact of the civil rights struggle of the sixties has been not only the genesis of a "new politics," but also the emergence of a legitimate black "presence" in American political life.

A Taxonomy of Black Political Foci

In order to understand the importance to American politics of the emergence of a legitimate black presence, it is necessary to outline the principal foci of black political activity. Before taking up this analysis, I would ask the reader to consider and to retain the following definition of the concept of "political presence." Political presence can be defined as a set of activities through which a group makes it known to the public and to political activists that it has entered the arena of politics. The evidence of a group's having achieved acceptance in the political arena may come in several ways . . . and these acceptances herald the group's legitimacy. In some cases acceptance may take the form of changes in the symbols and rhetoric of political discourse. Witness the popularity over the years of the phrase, "Judeo-Christian ethic." The phrase has come to stand not only for the commonly held values of American citizens but also as an acknowledgment that Jews are a legitimate and accepted group within the body politic. One does not yet hear the phrase, "Islamic-Judeo-Christian ethic," although Muslims are a not insignificant minority in America. The point is that Jews and Jewish values must now be considered in the process of the adjudication and allocation of values in the society—the very definition of the political process.

Legitimacy can also be evidenced in concrete as well as in symbolic terms. The notion of a Jewish "chair" on the Supreme Court and the historic and oft-abused practice of "ticket balancing" are examples of the concrete rewards that come from the achievement of a legitimate "presence" in the political arena. It is perhaps worth mentioning, as Chuck Stone has pointed out, that black people have often been denied the concrete fruits of their potential political power (Stone, 1968). In short, the evidence of symbolic legitimacy is easier to come by than that of concrete legitimacy. Stone reasons that the lack of black political cohesion, the presence of white political cohesion (in specific elections), and the tendency toward partisan loyalty on the part of black voters have prevented blacks from gaining their just deserts from the political process. ". . . owing to the absence of all three factors, *ceteris paribus*, in national, state, and local elections of the past 20 years, the Negro vote has been considered more a loyal ally than a neutral balance of power by white party bosses. This is the principal reason that Negro political power has not been accorded its share of the political spoils." To Stone's analysis, I would add the factor of the quality of black political presence at the times of the election. Do politicians seeking the black vote make known that they recognize the difference between doing something about the "Negro Problem" and accepting black concerns as a legitimate plank of their platform? It seems rather odd that one could even run for office without considering the values and predilections of an important segment of our society. But such has often been the case while blacks were maintaining a "low profile" in political affairs (Stone, 1968, pp. 42-57).

Against this background, then, let us set out the principal foci of black political activity. It should become apparent that the concept of visibility, or presence, is useful in explaining the movement of black politics from one focus to the next. The manner in which black people have protested their condition and the methods they have used to improve their lot are directly related to the way in which they conceptualize their condition. The philosophic bases of black protest can be divided into four main headings: Christian Egalitarianism, Restitution Orientation, Legal-Rational Orientation, and Anti-Imperialist/Anti-White Orientation. It would, of course, take much more than a single chapter to elucidate all the ramifications of these divergent philosophic positions; therefore, the present discussion will only sketch their bare outlines.

Christian Egalitarianism

A close reading of black spirituals and folk tales reveals that blacks never really accepted the deferment of full equality as a goal. Though the slaves were urged to accept Christianity, principally to assuage the conscience of the planters and to make blacks regard their suffering as a positive good, they did not accept heaven as a viable alternative to emancipation. Black spirituals with lines like "Go down Moses, way down in Egypt land, tell old Pharaoh to let my people go," or "Oh Mary, don't ya weep, don't ya moan; Pharaoh's army got drowned, Oh, Mary, don't ya weep," gave eloquent testimony to the slaves' awareness of, and loathing for, their condition here on earth. Later, the freed slaves would sing of the "captain" or "Bossman" in the most derisive and defiant manner:

"If I'd a had my weight in line
I'd a whopped dat captain
Till he went stone blind."
(Chain gang song.)

The power and appeal of Christianity were not potent enough to overcome the day-to-day horror of slavery. A parody of the Lord's Prayer composed by an unknown slave survives:

"Our Father who is in heaven
White men owe me eleven, and pay me seven,
Thy kingdom come, thy will be done,
And if I hadn't took that, I wouldn't have none."

The god of the slaves was not the God who commanded: "Servants be obedient to them that are your masters . . ." (Ephesians 6:5) but God who delivered the Israelites from bondage, the God who delivered Daniel from the lion's den:

"Little David blow on your horn
Hallelujah! Hallelujah!"
(Black spiritual.)

As the slaves had seen the essential contradiction in the white man's profession of Christianity and the treatment of his fellow human beings ("Everybody talking 'bout heaven ain't going there . . ." [black spiritual]), blacks would in later years appeal to Christian morality in an effort to secure justice and freedom. Both the Abolitionist movement and Martin Luther King's passive resistance techniques were aimed at the supposed Christian character of the American public. The suggestions at the Southern Christian Leadership Conference for conduct in newly integrated (Montgomery, Alabama) buses are illustrative of this theme. Rule eight states:

"Be loving enough to absorb evil and understanding enough to turn an enemy into a friend."

The Christian precept that "love turneth away evil" was put to the test on a massive scale by Dr. King and his followers. King, following Gandhi, believed that incurring suffering was redemptive, that to suffer injury for no cause would ultimately prove the essential rightness of one's cause and the victim would emerge the victor. Other blacks held that if the nonviolent movement were to be successful, whites as well as blacks must adhere to the rules. Charles Sims, President of the Bogalusa Chapter, Deacons for Defense and Justice, enunciated this feeling in an interview held in August of 1965:

Q: Mr. Sims, why do you feel that there is a need for the Deacons in the civil rights movement and in Bogalusa?

A: First of all, the reason why we had to organize the Deacons in the city of Bogalusa was the Negro people and civil rights workers didn't have no adequate police protection.

Q: Can you tell us what difference it may have made in Bogalusa to have Deacons here?

A: Well, when the white power structure found out that they had mens, Negro mens that had made up their minds to stand up for their people and to give no ground, would not tolerate with no more police brutality, it had a tendency to keep the night-riders out of the neighborhood (Grant, 1968, p. 357).

Mr. Sims' reference to "Negro mens that had made up their minds to stand up for their people and to give no ground" is reminiscent of the "new Negro" who began to emerge as the hero in numerous folk tales.

The black person who stands up for his rights, in reality, is only "new" to those unfamiliar with the history of America's black citizens. The term "new Negro" can only be understood in the light of the "chameleon-like" character of black protest. Blacks have known since they arrived in America that in order to survive they must, at times, hide their true feelings. The image of the shuffling, grinning Negro is the image of a human being fighting as best he can for his life. It is important to understand this image in order to make sense out of Dr. King's nonviolent movement. Afro-Americans consciously chose passive resistance as a method of protest because that method suggested tactics that would effectively use the country's Christian ethic and, at the same time, avoid confrontation with forces of massive repression. King's followers believed that civil authorities would be forced to protect them from the hooligans they expected to meet in lunch counters and on the streets. They felt that the tenets of Christianity and the U.S. Constitution were deeply enough ingrained in the minds of Southerners to affect their antipathy for mingling with blacks. Passive resistance, as a technique, was suggested by King as a possible solution to the problem of finding a method of protest that would be effective in securing the rights of blacks while protecting them from annihilation.

For Afro-Americans, the dilemma has another dimension. To preserve some sense of self-worth, blacks have had to reject methods that would serve to accommodate them to their oppressed condition.

From a logical standpoint, of course, there can be only two basic responses to arbitrary imposed power: open revolt or accommodation. The Negro resistance movement has moved within the confines of two contradictory imperatives: (a) the need to reject open revolt, and (b) the need to reject acceptance. This is a cruel and grinding dilemma. If the Negro revolts, in other words, he loses all. But if he refuses to revolt, he also loses all. For acceptance, on whatever level, is violation (Bennett, 1966, p. 30).

King's movement, then, attempted to bridge the gap. Bennett, writing in 1966, thought that King had been successful: "Martin Luther King, Jr., and the sit-in students, as we shall see, solved the technical problems by clothing a resistance movement in the comforting garb of love and forgiveness." As blacks were beaten, hosed, and bitten by dogs, however, it became difficult for blacks to retain their self-respect. Groups like the Deacons rose in opposition to the flowering image of the "new Negro" as a passive object that sought physical abuse and met it with prayers and hymns. Blacks did not desire the promulgation of this new image. They still recalled the forceful resistance of their forefathers to slavery during the Civil War. "All business was suspended and those (slaves) that did not go on with the enemy, remained at home to do much worse" (Bennett, 1966, p. 441). They understood, too, that behind each slave who raised a rifle to the Confederates were hundreds of others who supported their actions. "The conclusion is inescapable that behind each of the numerous instances of disloyalty to the Confederacy must have existed a folk opinion among the slaves that the acts were in behalf of freedom."

Neither the slaves nor the blacks of the civil rights movement were able to translate Christian dogma into an effective means of protest. Christian love, like nonviolence, only works as an offensive tactic if one's antagonist is also Christian or nonviolent. The blacks of the 1960's reaffirmed the discovery of their slave forebears, that so long as they were docile they were mistreated, but when they struck back changes occurred. The civil rights movement became a Black Power movement as the black man's faith in the existence of white America's professed Christian "heart" faded. The feeling that America ought to compensate the black man for his losses has permeated all of the phases of black protest. If the aforementioned Christian egalitarian basis can be labeled, one would call it an ethical, moral, or religious basis for protest.

Restitution Orientation

This demand for restitution, while certainly a question of ethics as well, can perhaps best be understood as a social demand. More than legal rights were involved in the freedom struggle; there is, and has always been, a strong economic component. Black Americans feel that the country owes them compensation for their labor. One of the current jokes circulating among blacks is that if whites ever gave the country back to the Indians, blacks would have a lien on it!

An attempt was made following the Civil War to make up for the lack of educational and economic opportunities afforded blacks during the antebellum period. The Freedmen's Bureau, whose work has been blamed for many of the innumerable ills of the Reconstruction period, attempted to compensate blacks for their enforced labor. The work of the Bureau was summarized by DuBois in this way: "For some fifteen million dollars, beside the sums spent before 1865, and the dole of benevolent societies, this Bureau set going a system of free labor, established a beginning of peasant proprietorship, secured the recognition of black freedmen before courts of law, and founded the free, common school in the South" (Grant, 1968, p. 144). The government, however, failed to provide blacks any permanent economic base through the aegis of the Bureau. The slaves quickly discovered that while white immigrants were being given free land in the West, they were not going to get their promised 40 acres and a mule. Furthermore, no attempt was made to establish a new social order through an attack upon the attitudes of Southern white landowners.

On the other hand, it (The Freedmen's Bureau) failed to begin the establishment of good will between ex-masters and freedmen, to guard its work wholly from paternalistic methods which discouraged self-reliance, and to carry out, to any considerable extent, its implied promises to furnish the freedmen with land (Grant, 1968, p. 144).

The Freedmen's Bureau, rather than becoming a permanent fixture of American institutions, died or was murdered before its work could bear much fruit. The economic gains that were made were quickly erased by white Southern legislatures that seemed bent on reducing the freedman again to slavery. "Almost every law and method ingenuity could devise was employed by the legislatures to reduce the Negroes to serfdom, to make them slaves of the state, if not of individual owners" (Grant, 1968, p. 144).

One hundred years later, black Americans were still struggling for an end to economic exploitation. The recruitment literature of the Mississippi Freedom Labor Union (organized in January 1965) is indicative:

Wake up and think. We as Negroes should want to be equal and get high wages. For over two hundred years we have been working for nothing. Please join the union because if you are not in a union, you just aren't anywhere.

One recognizes a subtle shift in reasoning. In 1868 blacks were still hopeful of being compensated for past unpaid labor. In 1965 they wanted merely to be paid a decent wage for their present labors. The idea of compensation through the warding of land remains, however, in the writings of Malcolm X and in the works of his followers. The separationists from Garvey to Imari have all started from the premise that America is indebted to the children of the slaves. It is only when one becomes embroiled in the content or form of the restitution that one fails to see the generalizing thread of compensation.

Bayard Rustin, in an article that described the "Black Power Movement" as calculated to provide only "momentary satisfaction" and the ultimate demise of the organizations associated with it, spoke of a vast compensatory scheme for all the poor in America. "For the truth is that it need only take ten years to eliminate poverty . . . ten years and the $100 billion Freedom Budget recently proposed by A. Philip Randolph." Rustin declares that the precedent for such an outlay on the part of the nation was set by the Marshall Plan. The idea of compensation emerges clearly in the following statement covering the Freedom Budget:

> If we were to allocate a similar proportion of our G.N.P. to destroy the economic and social consequences of racism and poverty at home today, it might mean spending more than 20 billion dollars a year. . . . It would be intolerable, however, if our plan for domestic social reform were less audacious and less far-reaching than our international programs of a generation ago (Grant, 1968, p. 471).

Rustin, Brother Imari, and others then have not given up the idea of some payment for the years in which black Americans have been held in physical and/or economic bondage. The suggested methods by which such compensation should be made differ from group to group and from individual to individual, but the basic idea remains a principal base of black protest.

Legal-Rational, Anti-Imperialist/Anti-White Foundations

Only a few words need be said about the remaining philosophic bases of black protest . . . the legal-rational and the anti-imperalist/anti-white foundations. The wealth of court actions familiar to all reveals an abiding faith in the judicial process on the part of black Americans. This faith is based upon three basic assumptions regarding the legal system of the United States: first, that the constitutional guarantees enunciated principally in the Bill of Rights and the 13th, 14th, and 15th Amendments apply to Afro-Americans as well as to white Americans; second, that the state, local, and national governments have a duty and an obligation to protect their citizens and to secure them restitution when their rights are denied or abridged; last, that ignorance of color on the part of jurists is a prerequisite to justice.

The attitudes and beliefs underlying the anti-imperialist/anti-white foundation can be described as having two dimensions: first, that capitalistic systems are necessarily racial and imperialistic; second, that white people are by "nature" given to exploitation. The latter position has been widely promulgated by the Muslims associated with Elijah Mohammed, who routinely refer to whites as "blue-eyed devils." These attitudes most often emerge during times of slow progress in race relations, and are perhaps exacerbated by "backlash" behavior among the white population. It should be noted that the quality of the black presence is determined by the philosophical orientation of the movement. I should add that this orientation is tempered and, in many cases, dictated by the view that blacks have of their political position at a given point in time. For several decades blacks have maintained the view that they are virtual pawns in the game of politics. This conception of blacks as powerless and impotent political actors had for many years been supported by social scientists.

One of the first analyses to review the concept of black political powerlessness was the seminal work of Henry Lee Moon, *Balance of Power: The Negro Vote*. Published in 1948, the book analyzed the impact of the role of black Americans on the national elections to that date and concluded that the black vote represented the balance of power in presidential elections when the non-Negro vote is about evenly divided (Moon, 1948).

Another view is that the class structure of Negro society and the character of urban political life made for Negro political weakness (Banfield and Wilson, 1963). This analysis of black politics was done at a time when the politics of protest and dissension was not as yet fully understood. It was also completed before blacks had absorbed and inculcated the reeducation that was instituted by the civil rights movement. Since 1963 blacks have begun to move from the streets and into city hall and Congress in increasing numbers.

Although one cannot dismiss the shift of population as a prime factor in the success of blacks at capturing political office, especially in Northern urban cities, it should be apparent that it cannot account completely for this phenomenon. Senator Brooke certainly could not depend upon the black vote as much as his predecessor Senator Revels. Of the six American cities that now boast black majorities, four of them now have black mayors. And most important, many smaller American cities without black majorities have also elected black mayors.

One can only conclude that it is becoming increasingly acceptable for blacks to hold positions of authority over both blacks and whites. It is no longer true that blacks must only concern themselves with issues salient to the black community in order to be elected. Rep. Ronald Dellums has probably gotten more publicity for his actions in Congress in opposition to the war than for purely black causes. His priorities for legislative activity reflect his stewardship of his constituency, a goodly proportion of which is white, liberal, and vehemently anti-war. The point has been passed at which the black politician could represent only blacks; it is necessary now to reflect upon this change, as it has profound implications for American politics. Whether the condition is permanent or not, it is necessary to see how blacks have passed from a powerless minority to a powerful and legitimate presence in American political life.

White Attitudes and the Black Political Presence

If we would believe Hyman's familiar dictum "interaction leads to liking," then we would be compelled to believe that the possibilities of amiability between the races have increased. The perception of contact between the races in all but one of three major locales where political socialization takes place is growing stronger. At work, in the schools and other public places, whites and blacks are experiencing, or at least reporting, more contact between the two groups. Only in the family (the third principal locale for political socialization) has there not been an increase in interracial contact (Campbell, 1971, p. 159). Furthermore, it has been observed that "the apprehension (on the part of whites presumably) about closer contact and social relations will diminish as *perception* (my emphasis) of the rising education and class position of American Negroes grows among whites" (Hyman, 1969, p. 15).

Finally, it should be added that the college educated white population is the group that shows most clearly the progress in racial attitudes (Campbell, 1971, p. 57). As Campbell concludes from the Institute for Social Research's three-wave study of 15 American cities, although there is a modest difference in racial attitudes associated with age, the major difference in racial attitudes observed among age cohorts can most parsimoniously be accounted for by the presence in the samples of the college educated. He also reports that those most active politically —those who have taken more than a spectator role in the political process—are also more likely than others to exhibit positive attitudes toward blacks and black concerns. Most significant, these data show that on many questions of principle and policy, white and black attitudes have moved closer together.

One might summarize these findings by stating that over the years, whites have come to perceive increasing black presence, and whites have found the college experience to be a liberalizing influence on their racial attitudes (or at least the population that goes to college has shown itself to be more pro-black than their less well-educated fellows). Whites and blacks have begun to share positions on public policy questions and finally to hold that the trend should continue especially as more blacks move into the middle class.

Before offering an explanation for these occurrences we should point out that Campbell's data also show that suburban whites are no more or less racist than are their city brothers. The reader will recall that one of the assumptions previously mentioned referred to the predicted "gap" in the perceptions and political attitudes of white urbanites and suburbanites. It was suggested that urban policy could not be formulated that would satisfy both increasingly powerful urban black voters and white suburbanites. On the three basic measures of racial attitudes used by Campbell, "attitude toward racial contact," "perception of discrimination," and "sympathy with black protest," he found little difference in the racial attitudes held by white people whether they lived in the suburbs or in the city. Only on the last measure, "sympathy with black protest," is there a suggestion of a less positive reaction. And here, white suburbanites were found to be slightly more sympathetic to black protest than were white city dwellers. The image of the suburbanite as an avowed racist who seeks suburbia as an escape from the black presence seems to be greatly exaggerated. One can only conclude that as more white and black youngsters go to college, the trend toward a liberalization of racial attitudes will continue . . . all other things being equal.

The New Black Politician

It cannot have escaped notice that the "high water mark" of violent black protest at least in the urban areas seems to have passed. Blacks are now using the ballot, perhaps for the first time, as the principal weapon in their struggle for civil and political rights. What has been the effect on black politics and the black politician of this new power? Is he still exhibiting the characteristics of one who "serves at the sufferance of white institutions"? Little data exist on the "new black politics" but, sparse as they are, they contain an interesting counterpoint to that assumption concerning the black political leader.

Although there is evidence that new leaders often emerge from the characteristic crisis nature of black politics, it should be remembered that it has been the oppression of blacks that has provided the chief impetus to black political solidarity (Killian and Smith, 1960, pp. 253-57). New leaders emerge because of the need to develop new solutions to essentially old problems. As we have seen, black politics may change in its tactics and in the philosophical rationalizations that support the new stratagems, but it rarely changes its primary goal, the civil and social liberation of black people.

It is for this reason that crisis periods in the black community often lead to a drawing together of black leaders of differing political and philosophical persuasions. Periods of crisis provide the opportunity for the merging of political factions rather than an occasion for fragmentalization (Clarke, 1961, pp. 318-28). These periods of crisis in the black community come often. They need not be created. As we have seen over the years, the black masses as well as the political elite can be, and are, organized readily around crisis issues. It is important, then, to recall that black leaders, in order to remain leaders, must have the resources necessary to confront (if not to alleviate) the root causes of the problems within the community. Their main resource is the support and admiration of the black community. Remember that black people have learned that their leaders can be removed from office (Powell), shot (King, Evers), hounded from the country (Robeson), defeated at the polls by former allies (Stokes), jailed for long periods (Davis), or simply ignored (Chisholm).

Often, blacks simply want a leader who will "stand up" for their interests whether he is successful in bringing about change or not. Shabazz (Malcolm X), for example, did not accomplish anything if one looks at his career through the eyes of the practical politician. Yet he was one of the most effective black political leaders in recent history. He was effective for two reasons. First, he recognized that the leader of blacks must be free from the control of white institutions. Second, he recognized that his chief resource was the support and admiration of the black constituency, *not* his ability to manipulate them or to "get things done." He was principally and most importantly a political educator who held at a just angle the mirror of his blackness so that both black and white Americans could see themselves.

The "fall-out" from Shabazz's life has affected many Americans, whose numbers are now swelling the ranks of black elected officials. There are probably only a handful of black political leaders who now reject the notion of Black Power. Indeed the phrase has now been stretched with various prefixes, to cover a variety of causes from "Gays" to "Greys" (homosexuals to the elderly). Black elected officials in the South, surveyed recently on their attitude toward the phrase, overwhelmingly accepted it as a legitimate characterization of their political posture. The officials, of course, remain committed to nonviolence and traditional politics. They most often described the meaning of "Black Power" in terms of economic, social, and/or political power for Afro-Americans (Feagin, 1970, pp. 107-22). The point is that black people and their elected officials have come to regard the generation and wielding of power, in all its forms, to be a legitimate and justifiable pursuit. The phrase also carries with it the suggestion that black people already have power—one needs only to direct it at the appropriate target.

This feeling, this new conceptualization of the black political condition, has now allowed black officials in the South to report that their feelings of efficacy are based not upon a change of heart in the white community, as they might have been earlier, but because "white citizens and officials were being forced to cooperate with black elected officials because of the growing strength of the black vote" (Feagin, 1970). The political support of black voters is for these men their principal strength, not their connections within the white community. Even though the white citizens governed by both Charles Evers and Richard Hatcher attempted to sabotage their new administrations, the black voters returned these men to office. In the case of Hatcher, even his own party (Regular Democrats) failed to support his candidacy, and like Evers he received his share of death threats. The prior white administrations of Newark, Gary, and Fayette all left the public coffers bone dry and did what they could to ensure the failure of the new black administrations. Although Stokes has turned his forensic skill to other directions and his choice for mayor of Cleveland (black) was defeated, the other regimes persist. What is most important: they persist in spite of white institutions rather than at their sufferance.

Although it is still correct to assume that black elected officials need the support of white institutions, it is probably wrong to insist that black elected officials exist "largely by the grace" of white institutions. It should also be clear that the notion that black political organization is predicated on the existence of the same kind of institutional structures presumed necessary for white ethnic groups is inaccurate, or at least obsolete. As has been pointed out, it is the posture of crisis and danger that provides the wellsprings for black political organization. Were these crises to be short-lived and ephemeral, were blacks able to escape the problems of racism and oppression through education or personal affluence, the main vehicle for their organization would evaporate. This is not, however, the reality of the black experience in

America. Oppression still is the mother of organization. Furthermore, the civil rights years provided black people with the experience necessary to create and to sustain a host of politico-civic organizations.

The Congress of Racial Equality spawned the Student Nonviolent Coordinating Committee, which in turn spawned the Northern Student Movement. King's Montgomery campaign (built around crisis) produced the Southern Christian Leadership Conference that later organized Chicago's Operation Breadbasket. King is dead, SCLC is weakened, SNCC no longer dominates the student movement, CORE has moved to a physical separationist posture, and Operation Breadbasket now has a new name and has split from SCLC. But the lessons learned by the persons involved in those organizations have changed the politics of America. Witness—the man who celebrated, with clenched fist, the denial of a delegate's seat at the 1972 Democratic Party Convention to Mayor Richard Daley of Chicago was the same man who had been told to "see his precinct captain" by Daley when he had offered his organizational abilities to the Democratic Party years earlier. The Rev. Jesse Jackson, who was schooled in the methods of political organization during his years with SCLC, was able to show that the "organization" needed lessons in organization. But the political education that has tutored Jackson has not been limited to lessons in tactics and strategies. A much more profound pedagogy has also been in evidence.

Education for the New Politics

"I close as I began with the statement that what an immense majority of the loyal millions of your countrymen require of you is a frank, declared, unqualified, ungrudging execution of the laws of the land. . . ."

These words, written over a century ago, capture the spirit and the content of the political lesson that has now been taught by blacks if not completely absorbed by all Americans. What was pounded into the heads of Americans throughout the recent past was that public officials were being allowed to scoff at the laws of the land. Civil rights marchers, in most cases, were seeking to overturn laws that were in contradiction to the Supreme Law of the land. All those observing the events through the intimate medium of television must have felt vague stirrings of uneasiness at scenes in which law-abiding citizens (albeit black, noisy, and in droves) were set upon by dogs and hoses. But it is not simply that Americans were moved to sympathize with blacks during this period that is important. Many Americans, no doubt, applauded the actions of the Bull Connors of the nation. Further, the lesson taught by the civil rights movement was not that humility and nonviolence ought to be the path of all public leaders. The lesson was simply this: that the citizen is not the government.

Americans have always been a bit cynical toward government, as evidenced not only by the constitutional restraints on the power of our leaders but also by the periodic catharses of "reform." The schools of the nation, however, stressed the role of the "good citizen" whose main attribute was obedience. White Americans, though perhaps harboring a latent cynicism, could report that all in all they trusted the government to do what is right. They identified with the government. The civil rights movement, through its chief spokesmen, began systematically to alter that image, at least as it was held by a segment of the population. Malcolm X could ask white college students why the Senate has never approved the United Nations protocol on Human Rights and add that our ally in Indochina against Japanese colonialism is now our enemy. White students, as Vista volunteers, could find themselves hounded out of cities because they helped to organize the poor and to offer them legal aid. The War on Poverty, whose genesis was rooted in the goals of the civil rights movement, could find itself beset with problems because of its statutory demand for "maximum feasible participation" of its poor clientele in all phases of planning and operations. Slowly, the message, the lesson, began to sink in. Young people who had witnessed the "success" of blacks at achieving change through mass demonstrations found themselves in the Capital, thousands strong, only to discover that the war went on . . . and on.

It is not fair to say that Americans, and more specifically, American youth, distrust their government more than they did before the "Negro Revolution." One awaits that analysis. It is obvious from recent events that they no longer feel that the government is accurately representative of the people. The Democratic Party's recent convention reforms were aimed not simply at assuring a "voice" to youth, blacks, minorities, and women, but at structuring the convention to fit better the realities of the voting constituency. Through these reforms the largest and oldest political party in the country gave evidence that one of the major lessons of the civil rights movement had been learned . . . that the government is not of the people. The party also acknowledged by its actions that all phases of political activity must be governed by the rule of law—Richard Daley notwithstanding. Only by the careful and deliberate application of the rules could government be truly responsive to the people.

One need not, however, be overawed and unduly optimistic about these so-recent events. Whether the Democratic Party returns to business as usual in order to capture the White House is yet to be seen and in some ways is irrevelant. What is crucial is that a new generation of Americans have been reeducated toward an interpretation of the citizen's role in American democracy. The audaciousness of the Black Power movement's assertion that people have the right, the duty, and the power to alter the course of governmental policy by their own actions has captured the thinking of hosts of Americans. Societal groups heretofore content to let policy be made by their "betters" have begun to question the assumptions upon which their former attitudes rested.

The arrival of a legitimate black presence in American politics heralds a reawakening of political visibility for America's "out groups." Many social commentators predicted that the phrase "Black Power" would "do no service to the Negro." They rightly saw in it a rejection of the myth of white supremacy. What they did not see at that time was that there were other groups in society who also needed to throw off the psychological fetters forged by the acceptance of an inferior role. The majority of persons in positions of power in this country are not only white, but they are also well-to-do, Anglo-Saxon, middle-aged, and male. When blacks declared their right to stand in the midst of the decision makers, as *blacks*, they gave support and encouragement to other groups as well. The assumption that Black Power means only the mobilization of black people and their sympathizers within rather traditional structures misses the point of the civil rights struggle. Black politics, based as it is on the reinstitution of the equality of all citizens that stems from the role of law, has broad implications for all American citizens.

As I have already stated, one of the principal assumptions underlying the legal-rational orientation of black protest and politics is that the state, local, and national governments have a duty and an obligation to protect their citizens and to secure them restitution when their rights are denied or abridged. These rights are guaranteed by the Constitution to all citizens regardless of class, sex, or race, and governmental officers of whatever rank have no recourse but to protect them. That is why the political behavior of blacks during and after the civil rights movement could so alter the character of American politics. Citizens once again learned that they could not only petition their government for a redress of grievances but that they could demand their rights under the Constitution. It is axiomatic that one without power submits requests and performs supplications. One with power makes demands. The very character and rhetoric of the act presuppose a posture of strength.

In summary, I began with the contention that the impact of the civil rights struggle of the sixties had been not only the genesis of a "new politics," but also the emergence of a legitimate black presence in American political life. The two phenomena, as I trust should now be apparent, are both complementary and interdependent. Because of the history of ethnic relations in this country, any social movement can be altered by the addition of a black presence. Not only are the goals and strategies of movements augmented by the recognition of the black experience, but the very language of the collective discourse must take on new modulations.

I do not mean here that provision has to be made in the new politics for the "special condition" of black people. If this were the case, the black presence would not be the powerful catalyst for reexamination and reflection that it is. The potency of the black presence lies in its universality, not in its exclusivity. It is because the black experience can be used as an analogy for the experience of so many other citizens in the Republic that its examination and broadcasting have had the effect that they have.

When black leaders have described their struggles for dignity and liberation, they have found that they have struck responsive chords in other, nonblack people. When they have insisted upon their right to have these experiences noted and acted upon by those holding the public trust, they have found others with similar experiences following their example. I have described al-Shabazz as a great political educator. I could as well describe the civil rights movement as a curriculum in political education.

Finally, I believe that what has begun here is a reexamination of the assumptions upon which has rested the analysis of black politics. We have seen that there are black politicians who hold power in spite of "white" institutions. We have seen that independent black political organizations are not only viable but mundane. Black caucuses now exist at every level of government. We have also noted that the differences between the attitudes toward blacks of urban and suburban whites are not nearly so sharp as one might suppose; that, indeed, factors other than metropolitan location might more readily account for the differences that do exist. Last, it must now be recognized that the emergence of a black political presence has heralded a new attitude toward government and the citizen's role within government. One can no longer consider political education to be confined only to the schools and to the civic curriculum. A new cohort of Americans have been led to a reexamination of our Republic. Their classrooms were their living rooms, and their teachers were black.

References

Edward C. Banfield and James Q. Wilson. *City Politics.* New York: Vintage Books, Random House, Inc., 1963.

Lerone Bennett, Jr. *Before the Mayflower . . . A History of the Negro in America, 1619-1964.* Baltimore: Penguin Books, Inc., 1966.

Angus Campbell. *White Attitudes Toward Black People.* Ann Arbor, Michigan: Institute for Social Research, 1971.

Jacquelyn J. Clarke. "Standard Operating Procedures in Tragic Situations." *Phylon* 22: 318-28; Winter 1961.

Joe R. Feagin. "Black Elected Officials in the South: An Exploratory Analysis." In: Jack R. Van Der Silk, editor. *Black Elected Officials in the South: A Reader in Social and Political Analysis.* Columbus, Ohio: Charles E. Merrill Publishing Company, 1970. pp. 107-22.

Joanne Grant, editor. *Black Protest: History, Documents, and Analyses 1619 to the Present.* New York: Fawcett Publications, Inc., 1968. Reprinted by permission of Fawcett Publications, Inc.

Herbert H. Hyman. "Social Psychology and Race Relations." In: I. Katz and Patricia Gurin, editors. *Race and the Social Sciences.* New York: Basic Books, Inc., 1969.

Lewis Killian and Charles Smith. "Negro Protest Leaders in a Southern Community." *Social Forces* 38: 253-57; March 1960.

Henry Lee Moon. *Balance of Power: The Negro Vote.* New York: Doubleday and Company, Inc., 1948.

Chuck Stone. *Black Political Power in America.* Indianapolis: Bobbs-Merrill Publishing Co., 1968.

CHAPTER 12: WOMAN POWER AND EDUCATION

DEBORAH PARTRIDGE WOLFE

DID YOU KNOW that nine out of ten women will work at some time in their lives, or that the average woman worker is as well educated as her male counterpart? These and other background facts summarized in "Twenty Facts on Women Workers," published in April 1973 by the Women's Bureau, Employment Standards Administration, of the U.S. Department of Labor, called to our attention the tremendous woman power in America. In effect the 1970 census reminds us that there are more women than men in America at this time. What would happen if the woman power of America were truly organized? What would happen if this organized woman power were concentrated on the improvement of education in America?

The well-being of all citizens should be our primary goal as a nation. Our aim is to look squarely at some of the fundamentals pertaining to the existence of women in our society and to ask what challenges are on the calendar for tomorrow as we look at woman power and education. Woman's progress has been gradual, becoming more marked as both men and women learned that one could not advance far without the other. Most uncivilized peoples have held women inferior to men, but as civilization has progressed it has recognized that all the people, men and women alike, must be fitted to share in the world's support and betterment. Hence, the basic documents of American life say without delineation "all . . . are created equal." The civil rights legislation, feeling the need for spelling out this equality, has added the word "sex" in discussing elimination of discrimination, and the current struggle for the ratification of the Equal Rights Amendment calls to our attention the importance of careful enunciation regarding the treatment of women in a democracy pledged to equal rights for all.

Under certain systems of ancient law, traces of which have survived even into modern times, a woman, no matter how old, was theoretically a perpetual minor—always subject to control by husband, father, or some male guardian. So old-fashioned propriety usually shook its head in protest when women gained new privileges—higher or professional education, the privilege of earning their own living outside the home, of competing in business or the professions on an equal basis with men, and the right to control their own property. But most important of all was a voice gained in making the laws which control the well-being of women and men alike and the homes and children of this land. This was the strong voice of suffrage.

Through the years, women the world over have followed the progress of the American woman. They have been and are interested in the jobs held by the American woman, in the pay she receives, and in her efforts to improve the schools and the communities. The picture presented to the world has not always been a balanced or an impressive one.

The struggle for suffrage is a prime example of the lessons our nation has had to learn in giving each individual the opportunity to achieve maximum fulfillment. In the early history of the women's rights movement, the struggle was for education opportunities and the right to enter business and the professions. Then women turned to the fight for suffrage. This achieved, they attacked other inequalities, using the ballot in the desire for an improved legal status and for advanced social legislation.

Margaret Brent, heir and executrix of Governor Leonard Calvert of Maryland—brother of Lord Baltimore—is believed to have been the first taxpaying woman in America to ask for political representation. She demanded "place and voice" in the Maryland legislature in 1647, and her plea was refused only after hot debate. Taxpaying widows and unmarried women voted later in some of the colonies. For example, in New Jersey women voted and in New England women attended town meetings on occasion.

A brief résumé of the dark days when women were striving to attain suffrage is not out of place. We recall how women became targets of discrimination. We recall how the attitude of an entire nation had to be reversed.

History of Women's Rights

The organized women's rights movement began in the United States in 1848 as a direct outgrowth of the anti-slavery struggle. In 1840 several women delegates, among whom was the Quakeress Lucretia Mott, were sent to a world anti-slavery convention in London, but were not allowed to take their seats. Lucretia Mott and Elizabeth Cady Stanton thereupon resolved to hold a women's rights convention on their return to America. Eight years later it was held at Seneca Falls, New York. Although the movement received aid from broad-minded men like William Lloyd Garrison, Wendell Phillips, Henry Ward Beecher, and Ralph Waldo Emerson, the women pioneers, prominent among whom were Susan B. Anthony, Lucy Stone, and Julia Ward Howe, faced ridicule for many years.

In 1869 women from 19 states met in New York and formed a National Woman Suffrage Association, headed by Elizabeth Cady Stanton and Susan B. Anthony. The Association worked for an amendment to the federal Constitution which would give women the right to vote. Later in the same year was formed the American Women's Suffrage Association, headed by Henry Ward Beecher and Lucy Stone. They worked to obtain suffrage chiefly through amendment to the state constitutions. The two bodies united in 1890 to form a National American Woman Suffrage Association, which thereafter pursued both methods.

For 50 years representatives of the National Association had hearings before the committees of every Congress. But the campaign in the states was the first to show results. The first territorial legislature of Wyoming—in 1869—gave women the vote. The territory of Utah did the same the next year, and both states came into the Union with women's suffrage clauses in their constitutions.

Colorado had granted women's suffrage in 1893, Idaho in 1896. One by one other states fell in line, until by the end of 1919 the women of 15 states had equal suffrage with men, and in 12 others they had the right to vote for presidential electors.

As previously stated, a women's suffrage amendment to the federal Constitution had been presented to every Congress since 1878, but it was not until August 26, 1920, that, at the passage of the amendment by the Congress, ratifications were obtained from the necessary three-quarters of the states. It was then that the 19th Amendment to the Constitution was proclaimed law of the land. Women citizens throughout the United States were enabled to vote at the presidential elections in November of 1920. That is a relatively recent attainment.

Time does not permit us to recount the numerous women—individually, and collectively in organizations—whose labors through those years finally brought the right to vote. Yet we cannot pass on to more current problems without noting that women's organizations have had a great influence on politics—both in obtaining the vote for women and in attempting to obtain more and better education not only for women but for all people, and urging their membership to use their franchise wisely in behalf of good government.

And so, the Women's Liberation Movement which we hail as an innovation and creation of the 1970's actually might be said to date back to Deborah Gannett, a New Yorker who served as a private soldier in the American Revolution, thereafter entitling her widower to a "widow's pension," which his heirs collected. She had enlisted under an assumed name and successfully hid her gender until she became wounded by a musket ball and was mustered out of the service. Modern day Deborahs are found in the Congress of the United States, where today there are only 11 women in the 535-member U.S. Congress. There are no women in the President's Cabinet. Since the death of Alabama's Lurleen Wallace—whose tenure was a holding action for her husband, George—there have been no female governors. Few women have been high court judges or served in state legislatures or as large-city mayors. No woman has gone to the moon, and so in 1973 there is new effort made to have the states of the United States ratify the Equal Rights Amendment to the federal Constitution which was finally passed by both houses.

In the mid-1960's Betty Friedan wrote a best-seller, *The Feminine Mystique*, decrying the loss to the nation of intellectual talent because educated women were dominated by males who kept them "barefoot, pregnant, and in the kitchen." Mrs. Friedan organized a militant activist group, the National Organization for Women (NOW). The organization has lobbied strenuously for the enactment of the Equal Rights Amendment to the Constitution and has entered court suits as an *amicus curiae* (friend of the court) in behalf of women who suffered discrimination in employment and deprivation of judicial rights. This energetic group allied itself with the National Women's Party (NWP), which was organized in 1920 to gain equal civil rights for females. Together the two organizations, buttressed by many other women's groups and individual women demonstrating the real woman power of America, succeeded in getting the Equal Rights Amendment passed.

As the presidential election year of 1972 approached, women's rights advocates organized a new group, the National Women's Political Caucus. With as many as 11 million 18-, 19-, and 20-year-olds newly eligible to vote, it was important that the women's issue be clearly presented so that all Americans would recognize that women's rights are an integral part of and necessary to the freedom of all Americans. The women's caucus is led by national figures, including Representatives Shirley Chisholm and Bella Abzug of New York, who both claim they were elected to office because of, not despite, being women. Others include Betty Friedan, Fanny Lou Hamer, and Gloria Steinem.

Utilizing existing state party structures, the caucus plans to work for equal female representation in relationship to the national parties, and to have a woman with legal experience appointed to the Supreme Court. It also plans to provide the President of the United States with the list of qualified women for national appointments in every area of our government.

For some time there has been a feeling that women were already covered by the federal Constitution in the 14th Amendment, which was originally designed to guarantee legal equality for former slaves. Senator Birch Bayh of Indiana has entered two suits before the U.S. Supreme Court that test women's coverage under the equal protection clause of the Constitution's 14th Amendment. One suit before the high court tests an Idaho law that gives a male executor preference over a female executor with equal qualifications for administering an estate. The other tests a Louisiana jury service rule that discriminates against women. All in all, then, four cases or suits before the Supreme Court call to the attention of the American public the importance of recognizing women as equal partners with men before the law.

Women continued in 1973 to constitute a majority of the total population (51 percent) and only a few, according to public opinion sampling, considered themselves to be a social minority. Yet again there has been need through legislation to reiterate fair treatment of women along with black and other minorities in employment promotion policies. Thus the Civil Rights Act has been amended with the heading "Prohibition of Sex Discrimination," and Section 901 reads: "no person in the United States shall, on the basis of *sex*, be excluded from participation in, be denied the benefits of, or be subjected to discrimination under any education program or activity receiving federal financial assistance." (Emphasis added.) Likewise, in implementing this legislation the Presidential Executive Order originally signed by President Johnson on September 24, 1965, as Executive Order 11246, later amended on October 13, 1967, as Executive Order 11375, and still later amended by President Nixon on August 8, 1969, as Executive Order 11478 reads:

Under and by virtue of the authority vested in me as President of the United States by the Constitution and Statutes of the United States, it is ordered as follows: Part 1—Nondiscrimination in government, employment . . .

The contractor will not discriminate against any employee or applicant for employment because of race, color, religion, *sex*, or national origin. The contractor will take affirmative action to ensure that applicants are employed, and that employees are treated during employment without regard to their race, color, religion, sex, or national origin. Such action shall include, but not be limited to the following: employment, upgrading, demotion, or transfer; recruitment as advertising; layoff or termination; rates of pay or other forms of compensation; and selection for training, including apprenticeship. The contractor agrees to post in conspicuous places, available to employees and applicants for employment, notices to be provided by the contracting officer setting forth the provisions of this nondiscrimination clause. (Emphasis added.)

Thus the 1970's have not only recognized woman power, but have dictated affirmative action in providing for the full utilization of the skills and talents of all women.

Women in the Labor Force

Working women represent 43 percent of the full-time labor force, and three-fourths of them are employed because they have no support or help support their family. Thus women are playing an increasingly major role outside the home and are demanding rights long denied or overlooked. Let us look at the statistics from the U.S. Labor Department as of April 1973 that the number of women workers jumped 8 million between 1964 and 1972, from 25.4 million to 33.3 million, and is expected to take another leap to 39.2 million by 1980. Seventy percent of the 1964-1972 rise was among women under 35. This tremendous gain is a recognition of the fact that Americans, both men and women, have learned that the talent and skills of women are needed by the American economy. The development of new industries and expansion of other industries have opened new doors for women in business, the professions, and the production of goods and services.

Decisions of individual women to seek employment outside the home are usually based on economic reasons. However, more and more women are realizing that work is also a psychological factor in the fulfillment of the needs and ambitions of the woman as a person. Most women in the labor force work because their families need the money they can earn—some work to raise family living standards above the level of poverty or deprivation; others, to help meet rising costs of food, education for their children, medical care, and the like. Only a few women have the option of working solely for personal fulfillment.

Millions of the women who were in the labor force in the spring of 1973 work to support themselves or others. This was true of the majority of the single women workers. Nearly all the women workers who were widowed, divorced, or separated from their husbands—particularly the women who were also raising children—were working for compelling economic reasons. In addition, the millions of married women workers whose husbands had income above the poverty level continued to work due to rise in the cost of living. Unfortunately, however, as recently as June 1973, there was evidence of discrimination against these women in the higher income brackets. The marital status of women workers in America in 1973 has changed considerably, and as of April 1973 there were 12.7 million working mothers in the labor force; 4.4 million of these mothers had 5.6 million children under six years of age, and another 3.9 million had children under 18 years of age. The number of men and women between the ages of 25 and 34 in the work force has been roughly equal in the recent past and will continue to be in the future. Hence, woman power is a reality.

Even though women constitute such a high percentage of the labor force, regrettably there is great discrimination in the salaries paid to these women. The comparison of the median wage or salary incomes of women and men who work at fulltime jobs the year round reveals that, while those of women are considerably less than those of men, the difference was less in 1973 than it had been in recent years. However, the median earning of women represents approximately 60 percent of the salary received by men. For example, median salaries of women scientists were from $1,700 to $4,500 less than those of all scientists in their respective fields. The greatest gap was in the field of chemistry, where the median annual salary of women was $4,500 less than that received by men. In the other fields of science we see similar discrepancies. For example, in earth and marine sciences the differential was $3,000, in atmospheric and space sciences $2,000, in physics $4,000, in mathematics $3,400, in computer sciences $2,000, in biological sciences $2,000, in psychology $2,000, in statistics $2,900, in economics $3,000, in sociology $2,000, in anthropology $1,300, in political science $3,000, in linguistics $2,000.* Similar discrepancies were noted in other fields. For example, the average monthly salary of an accountant is $100 more for men than women. In engineering the differential is not as great and I am glad to say that in education there has been greater tendency toward equalization of salaries than is typically true in most fields.

Yet, as we regret to note, there are other problems to which we will give our full attention at this time. Before this happens, though, I feel it is exceedingly important to note that colleges and universities need to

---

* See: *Fact Sheet on the Earnings Gap.* U.S. Department of Labor, Wage and Standards Administration, Women's Bureau. pp. 4-5.

emphasize, much more than in the past, the availability of a wide variety of opportunities for women in all fields so that there is not the continual feeling, as has long been the case, that there are certain "women's occupations." Statistics reveal that even though women are increasing in numbers in the colleges and universities of our land, they are perpetuating the trend of occupational segregation in certain areas. For example, the figures indicating the percentage of those majoring in selected subjects were: teacher education—39 percent, humanities— 22 percent, social sciences—15 percent, health professions—4 percent, natural sciences—4 percent. Analysis of additional data by majors supports a conclusion that distribution of women's college majors changed to only a limited degree in the past 20 years. It was heartening to note that the Texas Women's University published a brochure entitled "Careers for Women" in which they called attention to the wide variety of opportunities for women in all areas of human endeavor. This brochure encouraged women to participate fully and to major in biology, business and economics, chemistry, English, foreign languages, history and government, journalism, mathematics and physics, sociology and social work, speech, education (including all of its special areas of counseling education, curriculum instruction, educational foundation, psychology, and philosophy), as well as special education, fine arts, health and physical education, household arts and sciences, library science, and health services (including nursing, health care, occupational therapy, and physical therapy). Such openness must become a continuing trend so that we can capitalize on and utilize to the fullest extent resources found in the woman power of America.

Women in Education

How do women fare in the field of education? Everyone knows that women make up the majority of the public school teaching force. Yet what about the upper echelon positions in education? As one would guess, even though women far outnumber men in the public schools as teachers, they are a very, very small minority when it comes to the administrative and supervisory roles and positions. This likewise is manifest on boards of education, whether they be local or state boards of education. Sexism permeates every level of education, both in terms of the job and in terms of the curriculum. An examination by the New Jersey chapter of the National Organization for Women completed a study of 150 reading texts collected from the state's public schools. Not surprisingly, it revealed that, whereas nearly 1,500 stories featured males, less than 500 featured females. Significantly, an overwhelming majority of the stories showed boys involved in adventures and girls either watching or playing subordinate roles. Such sex stereotyping is prevalent in all aspects of the curriculum, reading, language arts, social studies, geography, and science; and all of the materials tend to perpetuate the concept of a female role which is long outdated and inconsistent with a basic philosophy of utilization of all of America's citizens. Thus in job and in curriculum the elementary and secondary schools of our country continue discrimination against women and misutilization of the tremendous woman power possible.

And what about higher education? The problem here is even more blatant. In a study by the National Education Association in its research report 1972-R5: "Salaries Paid and Salary-Related Practices in Higher Education, 1971-72," we read that the median salary of women is 82.5 percent of the median salary of men faculty. This is a very, very minimum difference from the differential experienced six years earlier and far from the regulation imposed by the Civil Rights Act and the Executive Order 11246. Let us look more specifically and in detail at this problem of the status of women faculty members and administrators in higher education institutions. Perhaps the most startling fact is that women faculty members constitute only 19 percent of the total faculty in all four-year institutions in the United States. Among all universities the percentage is even smaller—16.8 percent. The largest proportion of faculty members who are women occurs in groupings of institutions and classifications of faculty in which salaries of all faculty members are lower. The existence of both of these situations contributing to the differences in median salaries of men and women faculty members is shown in a comparison between the proportion of faculty in universities and in colleges at each rank who are women, as follows:

	Percent of Faculty Who Are Women	
Faculty Rank	Universities	Colleges
All ranks	16.8	23.5
Professor	6.9	13.4
Associate Professor	12.6	19.1
Assistant Professor	18.5	24.8
Instructor	39.3	39.6
Lecturer	36.7	38.7

Table 1. Percent of Women Faculty in Universities and Colleges 1971-72 by Rank *

* NEA Research Report 1972-R5: "Salaries Paid and Salary-Related Practices in Higher Education, 1971-72."

Analysis of the salary differential is even more startling. Looking at all four-year institutions, the median salary for men faculty in 1971-72 was $13,359 as against $11,026 for women faculty. Analyzing that by rank, we find:

Faculty Rank	Median Salary Men	Women	Percent of Faculty Who Are Women
Professor	$18,185	$16,423	8.6
Associate Professor	14,026	13,219	14.6
Assistant Professor	11,619	10,969	20.7
Instructor	9,408	8,898	39.4
Lecturer	12,112	11,469	37.2

Table 2. Median Salary of Women and Men by Rank in Four-Year Institutions of Higher Learning 1971-72 *

Thus it is clear that women are paid less on the same rank and that more women appear on the lower ranks. This is true of both four-year institutions and two-year institutions. For as we look at the comparative figures by sex for two-year institutions, we find that the median salary for the male faculty is $12,337 as against $11,118 for the female faculty, and that women compose only 31.2 percent even in two-year institutions.

The problem of tenure status by sex is even more alarming. According to the NEA report the number of tenured faculty members in 1971-72 was reported by sex by 821 four-year institutions and by 330 two-year institutions. The report noted that the percentage of women faculty members having tenure is highest in the public institutions, particularly the medium and small public universities, where almost half of the women have tenure. The percentage of women having tenure is lowest in the small nonpublic universities and in the medium-sized nonpublic colleges where less than one-third have tenure. The percentage of men faculty members having tenure is more than five percentage points greater than the percentage of women with tenure in each classification of institution, except public colleges, the smallest nonpublic colleges, and the nonpublic two-year colleges.

The greatest disparity is found, as one would expect, when one examines the salaries of administrators in institutions of higher learning. Of the 2,550 administrative positions in four-year institutions reported in the NEA study, only 159 of them were held by women. Most of

* NEA Research Report 1972-R5: "Salaries Paid and Salary-Related Practices in Higher Education, 1971-72."

these positions were as: dean of the School of Nursing—85, dean of the School of Home Economics—37, or dean of the School of Education—7. Hence, the very small percentage of women administrators recorded tended again to be in those areas which have usually been considered "women's occupations."

Only 32 of the 953 presidents recorded were women. The median annual salary of these women was 84.2 percent of that of their male counterparts. Such percentages of salary paid women as compared with that paid men were consistent. As executive vice president, the woman was paid only 57.6 percent of that paid her male counterpart; as assistant to the president she was paid only 72.1 percent of the salary extended to the male. As vice president for student personnel services the 80 women reported out of a total 754 persons received only 76.6 percent as much as their male counterparts. As director of student placement a woman received 69.2 percent; as controller, only 63.1 percent of the salary paid the male.

And so it goes in each category. Women, few in number among those who receive administrative positions, likewise fall short when it comes to the salaries paid to them. The level of faculty and administrative salaries tends to be lower in small than in large institutions, but throughout the study it was obvious that women serve fewer institutions of higher learning as administrators, just as fewer women serve as administrators in the elementary and secondary schools. What of the future?

Woman Power and the Future

Records of the ages tell us that every group that has wanted political recognition, educational opportunity, and economic security has had to fight for them, organize for them, work for them, pay for them—whether the group be blacks, farmers, labor unionists, military men, businessmen, or any other kind. History insists that if the women of this nation are to demonstrate and utilize and capitalize upon the tremendous power which rests with them, they will have to obtain it in the same way. They must recognize that if they benefit from politics, if they improve the nation as well as themselves through better education and better employment opportunities, they must be willing to organize and work for these benefits. It is also important to note, however, that they cannot work alone. For if we are truly to utilize woman power all Americans must change their concept of the image of the woman.

Just as we have spent years helping blacks in their reorientation of the self-concept, so must little girls begin to see themselves as potentially powerful American citizens without the hindrances of being female. We must not have the situation of which Matina Horner writes in *Psychology Today* (November 1969): "A bright woman is caught in a double bind. In achievement-oriented situations she worries not only about failure but also about success." Women as well as men, girls as well as boys must realize that they must capitalize upon all of the resources with which God has endowed them.

We must so bolster the ego and sensitivity of boys and men that they are not threatened by the changing role which must occur if we are to use woman power to the fullest extent. We must change the curriculum of our schools on all levels so that there is full understanding of the potential force of the intellectual potential of women. Not only must there be concern for women's studies in higher education, but the books and materials used in all areas of human study must reflect an honest picture of women. As we plan for continuing higher education we must provide for differences in our present occupational and vocational and career guidance.

We must be cognizant of the growing changes in our complex technological society which reflect differences and potential and aspirations for women. Teachers on all levels must become aware of the tremendous opportunity and responsibility that they have in helping not only girls, but also boys to appreciate females as contributing citizens in every area of human life. Historians must begin to write the history, including women and their contributions to the total development, not only of America, but of the total civilization. Greater stress must be placed upon aptitude testing to determine who is best fitted for administrative responsibilities whether male or female so that the traditional concept of a male boss will be removed.

Education has a unique responsibility in this change of image, since in our society we believe that the public school is the means by which and through which we perpetuate the American dream. The American dream must recapitulate the commitment that our founding fathers had to the value and dignity of each individual and his or her worth. As we move ahead in the 1970's toward an open society, we must remove every possible trace of discrimination in any form whether it be against blacks, Puerto Ricans, Mexican Americans, native Americans, or women. Only then can we truly achieve for all America the potential power which rests in women.

PART 4

WHERE DO WE GO FROM HERE?

SINCE THIS YEARBOOK was started in 1971, this final chapter attempts to update some of the data and other information mentioned in the previous chapters. This chapter also affords the Yearbook Committee a chance to recommend plans of action for ASCD members who are desirous of developing and enhancing an open society. This does not imply that all of the answers are here; it merely gives a place to start. Yearbook Committee members present their personal viewpoints for your consideration, in some cases sharing common viewpoints but, for the most part, presenting unique personal perceptions.

The whole thrust of this volume has been that every child, regardless of where he lives, is entitled to the best education that we can provide. This can best be achieved by opening the communications network. Everyone who is affected by an educational decision must be able to make choices, but, more important, he or she must be given greater access in determining what the choices are to be. Race and ethnic origin should not be a factor in deciding who should participate in these crucial decisions. There is still hope that the American dream of a meaningful and personalized education can be provided for those who desire it. Each of us who wants an open society has the responsibility to work toward increased acceptance of the concept.

CHAPTER 13: CAN EDUCATORS HELP CREATE AN OPEN SOCIETY?

JAMES A. BANKS
M. LUCIA JAMES
CLARE A. BROADHEAD
DELMO DELLA-DORA
JAMES E. HOUSE

IF WE USE the year of *Brown* v. *Topeka* (1954) as a bench mark, the American society has become more open in some ways—and much more closed in others. However, prospects for the next several years are rather clouded and uncertain: the *facts* seem to indicate a more authoritarian society will come into being soon. The *hope* is that forces for a more open society will prevail.

Since 1954 polarization of the races has become more evident. The hatred, fear, hostility, and antagonism engendered by racism are now out in the open more than ever before. By itself, that could be a healthy phenomenon—because solution of problems requires that people recognize that there *is* a problem. Balanced against this is the fact that most indices of its nature show that racism is becoming worse. For example, the gap between blacks and whites has been growing steadily in jobs (unemployment, underemployment) and in education. In addition, more black and white children attend predominantly segregated schools and classes today than in 1954. The U.S. Supreme Court decisions in 1973 in Denver and Richmond give us an unclear picture of which way the Court will rule in other major test cases. As of this writing the metropolitan Detroit plan has been upheld in the U.S. Circuit Court of Appeals but has not been ruled on by the Supreme Court. Housing patterns remain tightly segregated, with the abandonment of the big cities by whites as a major by-product. It is true that more black, Chicano, and other minority faces appear in movies, on television, and in sports; but even this is becoming segregated in its pattern, as witness the black exploitation films for showing in areas where black people live.

Not all evidence is negative, however. This is where hope grasps at all straws. Honesty of expression in print (books, magazines, newspapers) has been allowed in a way heretofore unheard of in our country. Yet we know that current planned increases in postal rates have already killed or will soon eliminate a greater number of such publications and also that the executive branch of government is moving to curb that freedom of expression. We also do not know what the specific effects of the July 1973 Supreme Court decision on obscenity will be. The degree of freedom of expression is still at an all-time high. We have it now, however brief the moment.

The movies and television are also exploring new ground in providing a showcase for alternative ways of living, particularly those related to sex and marriage. Alternative schools and alternative school programs still evoke interest. Keep your fingers crossed, friends. May it be so for a long, long time to come.

These are only a few illustrative examples of some of the positive and negative factors which make up the current movements toward an open society. The one pervasive syndrome of the closed society is still very much with us, however, and it is hard to tell whether or not it has been touched. The notion that there is one way (or more) of establishing a hierarchy of human worth and that some people are better human beings than others because of their race, or ethnicity, or sex, or education, or income still predominates as a way of thinking for most people in all avenues of life. This notion is manifested in obvious ways, such as in different salaries paid; how people are hired, fired, and promoted; or how people are depicted in textbooks, movies, and television.

The Watergate situation tells us, as we have been told countless times before, that power corrupts individuals and can cause them to consider themselves as superior to those with less power and that no man or woman is immune—particularly when power can be used in dark and closed ways. This also happens in more subtle ways, even more often, such as in how we say "hello" (or *don't* say "hello"), choice of friends, who comes to dinner at our house, and where we choose to live. Is it not "natural" for all this to be true: don't people who are alike want to be together in all parts of the world? Not so, in our opinion. These existing behaviors are all "carefully learned" in our society and others. The challenge to American education is to help its clients "carefully learn" to love and to cherish differences and variety among people. As we said earlier, it looks as if that will not happen but we are hoping, desperately hoping, that we are wrong.

What can members of ASCD, and other readers, do to promote

their aspirations for an open society? Several members of the Yearbook Committee offer the following suggestions.

James A. Banks: To help create an open society, the school must help students to learn to respect and appreciate cultures which differ from their own. Most Americans grow up in communities which may be called "ethnic enclaves," because within them they learn the values, behavior patterns, and beliefs which are unique to their ethnic cultures. White Anglo-Saxon Protestants, as well as nonwhite ethnic minorities, grow up in ethnic communities which provide the individual with a restricted way of viewing the world and of behaving. Because most Americans grow up in ethnic enclaves, they are *culturally encapsulated.* Ethnic minorities, in order to attain social and economic mobility, are usually forced out of their ethnic encapsulation. However, dominant groups, who control entry to most social, economic, and political institutions, usually spend their entire lives within their ethnic communities. The cultures of other groups usually seem foreign, nonhuman, and exotic to them.

The school must help students—from both dominant and minority groups—to break out of their ethnic encapsulations, and to learn that there are other ways of living and being, and that to be different does not necessarily mean that one is inferior or superior. Students should learn that different ethnic groups have devised a wide variety of means to meet common survival needs. We will not have an open society—one in which different cultures are equally valid—until students learn that their own values and life styles are not the only ones, and until they learn to respect cultural differences and to regard people who are ethnically and racially different from themselves as *humans.*

Many Americans, especially members of the dominant ethnic group, tend to regard nonwhite people as *nonhuman.* Because dominant group Americans, like other Americans, grow up in ethnic enclaves, they are unaware of other ways of being human. They assume that their cultures and values are synonymous with *humanness.* The school must help dominant group students to become familiar with human cultures which are different from their own, and to see that individuals within our society have cultural options. It is not the school's role to try to force students to opt for other life styles. However, the school which fails to help students to become aware of and sensitive to cultural differences is irresponsible and detrimental because it is not preparing children and youth to live in an increasingly small and diverse world.

Ethnic minority young people, too, grow up within ethnic enclaves. However, to attain economic and social mobility, they must acquire the dominant cultural traits. During this process of cultural assimilation and upward mobility, these individuals must reject and violate their own cultures in order to succeed. A person's sense of "identity" and "people-hood" is essential for his psychological health. Thus, when minority groups reject their own cultures to attain social and economic mobility, they become marginal men, develop confused identities, and have ambivalent attitudes toward self and others.

To create an open society, the schools must help ease the trauma which students experience in the process of becoming culturally as-similated, and help make it possible for them to maintain their ethnic identities while acquiring dominant culture traits. It is not necessary for them to reject one culture to attain the other because man is highly capable of functioning *within* and *between* cultures or of being *bi-cultural*. Historically, the school has intensified, rather than helped to mitigate, the cultural conflicts which ethnic minority groups experience.

The school must also help ethnic minority children and youth to learn that there is nothing "wrong" with the way that they eat, talk, or act, and that each culture must be evaluated within a situational context. No life style is functional for all times, situations, and pur-poses. Rather, a life style is functional if it helps the individual to acquire his survival needs. Thus, students should learn different life styles and how to determine when each is most appropriate or functional.

The school must help ethnic minorities to develop a belief in their own *humanity*, learn ways to bring about social change, and know how to function *within* and between two worlds. Dominant group students must be helped to develop feelings of "pan-humanism" and "ethnic literacy," so that they will realize that they are not the only *humans* on earth, and become aware of the strength which diversity gives to human societies.

Although many factors are necessary for a curriculum which is designed to liberate culturally encapsulated students, the classroom teacher is the most important. The teacher should help students to explore cultural alternatives and to view cultures from within rather than from outside. He should also help shatter the melting pot myth so that students may both understand and appreciate the cogent impact which ethnic diversity has on American life.

The severity of our current racial and ethnic problems has rarely been exceeded in human history. The decaying cities, anti-busing move-ments, escalating poverty, and increasing racial polarization are alarming manifestations of the ethnic hostility which is widespread throughout America. Our very existence may ultimately depend upon our creative abilities to solve our urgent racial problems. Immediate action is imperative if we are to prevent racial wars and chaos and the complete dehumanization of the American man or woman.

M. Lucia James: Any curriculum that will lead toward an open society should be one that involves, draws from, extends into, and has an impact on the *entire* community, not just its dominant or established cultural group. Cognizant of this, instructional leaders should work toward developing a curriculum that reflects an open society, rather than one which merely states that it will educate students for one. Students should not be educated for an open society; they should live it, help create it, and participate in it. Their school is their life, or their society; hence, all aspects of their curriculum should endeavor to implement the concept of an open society.

The concerns or priorities which curriculum leaders should consider in planning a curriculum that will lead toward an open society are numerous, but none can be considered as a panacea. Each must be chosen to respond to a particular problem or situation. Likewise, the alternatives or suggestions will often not conform to prevailing practices and "community conscience," but if curriculum leaders are to develop curricula that will lead toward an open society, it may be necessary to spearhead major social changes.

With a commitment to create the learning environment that will lead toward an open society, curriculum leaders may consider the following actions:

1. Minimize, if not completely eradicate, those barriers that prevent students from knowing, understanding, and appreciating each other.

These barriers, often perpetuated by tradition, mores, and myths within a given community, limit the degree to which students communicate freely and candidly, or work harmoniously together. Involvement of students of all economic, racial, and religious groups in cooperatively-sponsored community projects may help to allay the fears and apprehensions created by the barriers.

2. Include the history, life styles, values, and other pertinent information about mankind as an integral part of the curriculum, not as a separate or isolated body of knowledge.

All races, nationalities, and religious groups should be presented as a part of the continuous stream of our nation and of our civilization. The commonalities and the diversities of all cultural groups, as well as the contributions which all have made because of their differences or similarities, should be recognized, emphasized, and utilized.

3. Utilize the world or community in which students live as the framework to develop a "relevant" or "open society" curriculum.

The child's real humanistic and physical world, with its complex human and technological problems, should be the learning environment, rather than a contrived situation within a highly structured facility. This approach should permit the students to deal more realistically with all peoples of the community. It should also provide an opportunity for students to become more aware of the social consciousness of their nation, state, and community, enlightening them as to the relationship to, or the effect each has upon, the development of an open society.

4. Identify and work to achieve realistic skills or proficiencies that, purportedly, are basic to one's ability to function in an open society.

Skills in decision making, problem solving, analyzing, etc., as well as skills in human relations, are as important as the three R's, and should be a significant facet of the entire educational experience of all children and youth. This is not to suggest, however, that less attention should be given to the latter skills. In fact, basic skills in communication should remain of primary concern and may incorporate the previously mentioned skills. There should be no substitute in skills and communications because of racial differences.

5. Create opportunities or in-service programs for administrators, teachers, and staff members to develop intergroup or human relations skills, techniques, and strategies necessary to provide opportunities for educational experiences for all cultural, racial, or economic groups.

The leadership needs to learn how to interact with all groups and cultures. There is a need to understand and relate more effectively with the total community, and to deal with such forces as the culture of poverty, power, verbal and nonverbal communication, subcultures, and values. More often than not the college or university training has been painfully inadequate, and the teachers and administrators are not prepared to deal effectively with problems involved in creating a curriculum for an open society.

Curriculum leaders who work for the development of a curriculum that will lead toward an open society should be less concerned with gadgets and buildings, and more concerned with people and their involvement. They are committed totally to understanding and working with each child as a human being, and to creating situations in which the personnel of the school and the community will respond likewise.

Intellectualizing racial and cultural differences and confrontation is one thing, but living them is an entirely different experience.

Clare A. Broadhead: The central question to which this volume addresses itself is: How can schools lead us toward an open society? This question assumes that schools are one of the decisive social institutions in our society, one in which change can be generated in ways which will ultimately lead to the realization of the American dream. To be sure, as curriculum leaders we apply our energies and talents where we are, in the daily life of the schools. Yet the perspectives within which we work at these tasks determine the degree of our effectiveness as leaders in the processes of change. It is not always easy to know what our own perspectives are.

One way to know about this is to examine one's own position or commitment to open schools for an open society. This requires an assessment of behavior which is difficult to achieve alone. I can tell myself what I believe and I can even proclaim my commitments publicly. But when I can work with friends or colleagues in assessing what I *do*, and what I fail to do, then I can change myself and can influence others to change. So the first step is knowing one's own commitment and what actions spring from it.

If we view ourselves as persons responsible for preserving an institution in which established values can be passed on from generation to generation so that survival and stability of these values can be assured, then we are essentially conservators of the present social system. We may try to help young people seek ways to improve existing social institutions so that they support the status quo functions more effectively. In that case, we are avowed conservatives, and if that is our commitment it should be clearly enunciated and supported in what we do.

If, on the other hand, we accept the idea of deliberate social change, "reform," we candidly propose to change existing institutions, including schools, in order to achieve goals which society professes to aspire to but which the actual performance of institutions negates or thwarts. For example, the elimination of racism has become a generally accepted goal in business, government, law, schools, etc. We who work in schools can strive to understand, act, teach to eliminate racist behavior in ourselves and racism in education. Can we assume that with this perspective, which involves desegregation of schools, experiencing the strengths inherent in diversity, clarifying values toward cooperation rather than competition—that in trying to achieve these kinds of things we can help teachers and students know and understand the social realities which pervade all our institutions? What is the impact of educational reform, or what can we assume that impact to be, on the broad social problems of discrimination in housing and jobs, sexism, corruption in high places in government and law, hunger in the midst of plenty, massive bombing in an era of proclaimed "peace with honor"?

What I am suggesting here is that schools and school leaders cannot lead us toward an open society if we limit our perspectives, or the arena within which we see our responsibilities as educational reformers, to pedagogy and methods. The education of children and youth is our area of expertise and we have an obligation to continually expand and improve in this area. But schools for an open society will not be achieved unless or until we understand and act on the concept that the problems of our closed society are based in the social conditions which prevail generally and not in the schools alone. Racism, poverty, poor physical and mental health, social class discrimination, and elitism are manifested in the schools but are not created there and cannot be solved solely in the schools.

So an essential function of *all* persons in leadership positions in schools is knowing, and helping colleagues and students to know, the social forces that shape the schools—knowing what facilitates and what restricts change toward an open society. What uses do teachers make of the fact that while the income of blacks reached an all-time high in 1972, the gap between black median income and that of white families continues to widen? Do we have and use this kind of data about other minorities? Is this important? Teachers and school people generally resist the search for and uses of this kind of knowledge until or unless the freedom to teach is threatened. Then we act from a defensive position. A more productive approach to the study and uses of the social forces which influence change springs from a recognition of two major opposing segments of opinion and action which are increasingly clear in school communities and in the larger society. Support for positive change in schools and society is increasing, and at the same time pressures to maintain the status quo are mounting. There are parents who want their children to know and understand both the positive and the negative impact of the social institutions that influence their lives, with the hope that future generations will create a better world. There are other parents who fear this change-agent role of the school. Curriculum leaders must help teachers and students identify and understand these countervailing forces and incorporate the serious study of them into the life of the school. Whenever the ostrich posture is assumed, the change resisters prevail.

I do not propose that school leaders attack social problems on all fronts. We are educators by choice and our institutional base is the school. The context within which we have to work for social change is the school as the reflection of the society. The quality of life in the school cannot be viewed as wholly separate from the quality of life in the community outside of the school. If we deny the truth of this concept, or if our behavior as educators conveys a different message, we are the gatekeepers of traditional social values and systems. Not that these are all "bad," but they need constant reexamination. How long will parents continue to assume that while children are in school, they are under the "control" of teachers and safe from the harsh realities of the drug scene, street crimes, the ugliness of war, the pollution of air and water, etc., diligently learning the Three R's and getting ready to compete for the highest paying jobs in the adult world? And how long will parents feel that if this is not what is happening in schools, we are not performing our proper function? The answer is, as long as we accept these roles and judgments either by our performance or by our silence.

Creating a school in which adults and children are free and encouraged to think, to ask, to choose, and to act about the real world is an essential social and political and educational responsibility. We cannot do this in the narrow perspective of reforming the curriculum and the methodology of the school as a closed, isolated institution where children will be "trained" for effective citizenship in a democracy when they become adults. To the extent that teachers and all adults in school model their thinking, asking, choosing, and acting about the whole society and quality of life in it in ways that children and young people find inspiring and exciting will we be educating them—and ourselves—for an open society.

Delmo Della-Dora: Every teacher, student, and administrator in our country has a great deal of power *as an individual* and yet few use it. This is also true of all those who work with the schools or who care about education—including parents, paraprofessionals in the schools, and volunteer aides. Each person who reads this can make a significant difference in his/her school, school district, college, or university in promoting an open society. The issue is not so much whether each of us *can* "do something," it is more a matter of knowing *what* we want to see happen and deciding *whether* we are willing to take the personal consequences of specific actions toward our goals.

There are two fundamental values which, if held and acted upon consistently by individuals, could produce rapid changes wherever we are. The first of these is to believe that *all people affected by decisions have an inherent right to participate in making them.* I am not saying that it would be "nice," or "democratic," or "good management practice" to involve affected people in decision making, although all those words may be appropriate. What I do say is that it is the *right* of those affected to be involved in a real way. To use available power in any other way is to deny basic human rights. That means how boards of education relate to administration, teachers, other staff members, young people, and parents at one end of the spectrum of legal power. *However, the basic principle applies at every level, beginning—and most importantly—with each teacher and the students in that classroom.* You simply cannot believe in and respect the work of all human beings if you have any kind of power and do not share it fully with the people you personally and directly affect. This is the touchstone of an open society and every one of us can act on it: teachers with children and their parents; principals with teachers, students, and parents; central office staff with building staff, students, and parents, and so on.

A corollary, and complementary, value basic to an open society is for each of us to act in open, honest ways in all human interactions. Lack of candor, deliberate dishonesty, secretiveness, withholding of facts and opinions, and unwillingness to share thoughts and reactions are the hallmarks of a closed society. Access to all avenues of full participation in the society is dependent upon reducing (or completely eliminating) the sham and hypocrisy that characterize all bureaucracies in this country, including the education establishment. We have to level with each other as educators, with our clients, and with the public at large if we are to have any hope of producing an open society.

The foregoing may seem like a simplistic formula approach to attaining the goals we seek. However, I honestly believe that each person who wants to do so has a great reservoir of untapped power to produce desired changes—*without* waiting for groups to mobilize, *without* waiting for new laws to be passed or old ones to be enforced, *without* more favorable rulings of the U.S. Supreme Court, and even *without* the President of your choice to be selected for the office. I believe that the teachers of this country *are* the curriculum of the school and that teachers are *the* major potential force for achieving the goals we cite. *Teachers are the real curriculum leaders of this nation,* and every supervisor, principal, consultant, assistant superintendent, superintendent, and professor knows it. All the rest must also make the commitments necessary and take the actions which are consistent with the two values expressed.

We must do what we can on our own, but we must also provide the direct support, the conditions, and the encouragement needed by each teacher with whom we come in contact. They are the ones who work directly with students. If teachers act on those values and model such behavior in their daily contacts with their students, and if all administrators, supervisors, and college personnel work to support such behavior in their contacts with teachers, an open society will come to fruition—and soon.

James E. House: The mood of Americans during the early stages of this decade appears to be one of self-preservation. There seems to be a concerted effort to carve out a square of turf for one's self and protect it. The pressures of an inflationary society, imaginary fears about busing, the money crisis, racism, and a loss of faith in the political structure only add to the dilemma. Most professional educators agree that developing a society in which people care for and respect each other deserves prime attention. Since pupils forget most of the factual information that they learn, this suggests that the quality of pupil relationships and the development of decision-making skills may be our most important products in schools. This notion further supports the development of a spirit of cooperation rather than competition. A cooperative environment produces patience and a sense of responsibility within human beings. An open society would nurture the cooperative spirit as an option to be treasured and valued by those who favor this life style.

In responding to the question, "What can curriculum leaders do to enhance an open society?" I decided to seek the advice of two friends in the education community. Dr. William C. Miller, Deputy Superintendent, Wayne County Schools, suggested that curriculum leaders have a natural role for enhancing an open society. They have process skills that are invaluable. He further states that curriculum people can help by modeling the behavior they want in parents, teachers, and pupils. This can be done professionally and personally. Curriculum leaders can help in clarifying values, goal setting, and priority identification as we move toward an open society. Curriculum leaders should seek involvement by a wide range of people in their community. They can create a climate whereby those who are interested in working toward an open society can do so.

Dr. Alvin Loving, Past President of ASCD, believes that curriculum leaders must focus their attention on the plight of education in large urban centers. As the flight to the suburbs continues, the cities have been left to fade away gradually. If curriculum leaders are to enhance an open society, they cannot join this flight from the cities. They must make a strong commitment to improve education in large cities and rededicate their efforts to give those who remain in large cities the same option for an education that exists in other school districts.

I believe that all curriculum leaders must exercise skill and influence in seeing that the truth is taught to all pupils relative to the major institutions in our society. Let pupils know that some individuals, in whom we place the public's trust, do not always act responsively to that public. Let the pupils know about the racist nature of our society and the talents that never emerge because of it. Let them know that our economic power is concentrated into the hands of a few Americans who make crucial decisions for the masses of people. Let the pupils know that in spite of the shortcomings, a large number of Americans share in the dream, but that number must be increased. Let the pupils know that *their* talents and skills are needed if we are to achieve an open society. In short, curriculum leaders must "tell it like it is."

Curriculum leaders can, indeed, enhance a movement toward an open society. They can start by looking at themselves and how they presently operate in the education arena. In some instances this may involve some risk, because many of the decisions they make would not be popular. However, if they are to make effective contributions toward an open society, one that gives people choices, curriculum leaders cannot afford to do less.

NOTES ABOUT THE AUTHORS

BANKS   BILLINGS   BOSMA

James A. Banks is Professor of Education, University of Washington, Seattle. He is Chairman of the Racism and Social Justice Committee, National Council for the Social Studies; a member of the National Advisory Board, ERIC Clearinghouse for Social Studies–Social Science Education; and a member of the U.S. Office of Education's Leadership Training Institute on Teacher Education.

Charles E. Billings is Assistant Professor of Politics, New York University. Dr. Billings is also Co-chairman of the Political Socialization Discussion, Ford Foundation National Invitational Conference on the Status of Research in Black Politics, 1973.

Boyd Bosma is Specialist in Civil Liberties and Intergroup Relations, National Education Association, Washington, D.C. Formerly a member of the NEA Board of Directors from Michigan, he was also a classroom teacher in the Redford Union school system near Detroit for 12 years. Dr. Bosma counsels and assists educators with problems resulting from abridgment of civil and human rights, and serves as a consultant to state and local teacher associations on such problems as school desegregation, personnel policies, fair dismissal procedures, minority involvement, and student rights.

BROADHEAD   DELLA-DORA   DODSON

Clare A. Broadhead, Principal of Old Mill Elementary School, Mill Valley, California, formerly served as Director of the Desegregation Advisory Project of the Wayne County Intermediate School District in Michigan. She taught at Wayne State University and Central Michigan University. Since moving to California, she has worked as a consultant in human and intergroup relations in school systems in the Midwest and on the West Coast.

Delmo Della-Dora, Co-chairperson of the 1974 Yearbook Committee, is Chairman of the Department of Teacher Education, California State University, Hayward. He served as an educator in Michigan for 22 years as teacher, principal, curriculum consultant, and associate superintendent for instruction. He was also Director of Planning for the Michigan-Ohio Regional Educational Laboratory and Holder of the Chair of Educational Innovation for Wayne County, Michigan.

Dan W. Dodson, Professor Emeritus, New York University, is currently Professor of Sociology, Southwestern University, Georgetown, Texas. He has served as consultant to the Human Rights Commission of Pennsylvania as a specialist in *de facto* segregation in Northern communities. His expert testimony has been offered in six federal and two state trials involving desegregation. He is widely known as an authority on desegregation and other problems of intergroup relations.

ETHRIDGE   HOUSE   IRONS

Samuel B. Ethridge is Director of the Teacher Rights Program, National Education Association, Washington, D.C. He was formerly Assistant Executive Secretary and Director of the NEA's Center for Human Relations and Assistant Secretary of the Professional Rights and Responsibilities Commission. His career began in Mobile, Alabama, as an English and journalism teacher. He was also a principal and supervisor of secondary schools in Mobile County. He has been Assistant Chief of Intergroup Relations with the National Foundation–March of Dimes headquarters in New York.

James E. House, Co-chairperson of the 1974 Yearbook Committee, is Deputy Director, Education Task Force, Detroit, Michigan. Dr. House is on leave as Education Consultant, Wayne County Intermediate School District, Detroit. He has served as a teacher, assistant principal, and curriculum consultant for 22 years. He is Past President of Michigan ASCD and presently a member of ASCD's Executive Council.

R. Bruce Irons is Assistant Professor, College of Human Development and Learning, University of North Carolina at Charlotte. Dr. Irons has been a high school teacher in California, where he developed public high school courses designed to promote the emotional growth and psychological development of students. He chaired a curriculum development writing project for such courses at the Humanistic Education Center of the University of Massachusetts at Amherst.

JAMES　　　　　　　MET　　　　　　　MILLER

M. Lucia James, Professor of Library Science Education at the University of Maryland, College Park, has been a speaker and consultant for numerous education workshops and institutes. She has also been a member of the Maryland state committee which developed guidelines for the selection and evaluation of instructional materials treating ethnic and cultural minorities.

Leon Met is Project Coordinator, Student Leadership Center, Cincinnati Public Schools. In addition to teaching a course in Educational Psychology, he headed experimental programs in student governed and managed residence halls and in decentralized counseling at Indiana University. He has been a counselor and instructor for Upward Bound, and is currently working with the ASCD project on the curricular implications of the National Assessment of Educational Progress.

LaMar P. Miller is Professor of Education, and Education and Research Director, Institute of Afro-American Affairs, New York University. He has also taught at Eastern Michigan University. He served on a number of committees of national organizations, including responsibility as Secretary, Division G, American Educational Research Association, and as a member of ASCD's Working Group on Ethnic Bias in the Preparation and Use of Instructional Materials.

SELDEN   SIZEMORE   WOLFE

David Selden, President of the 280,000-member American Federation of Teachers, AFL-CIO, is currently serving his third two-year term of office. Selden has been a leader in the teacher union movement since he joined the Dearborn, Michigan, Federation of Teachers in 1940. In addition to teaching social studies in Dearborn, he has taught school in Florida and New York, and has always been a strong supporter of teacher militancy to gain improved conditions, benefits, and treatment of educational workers.

Barbara A. Sizemore, formerly Associate Secretary of the American Association of School Administrators, is now Superintendent of the Washington, D.C., school system. In Chicago, where she spent 26 years as a teacher and school administrator, she was a member of the team heading The Woodlawn Organization (TWO), a school decentralization project.

Deborah Partridge Wolfe is Professor of Education, Queens College of the City University of New York. Dr. Wolfe has been Education Chief, U.S. Congress, as well as a classroom teacher, principal, department chairman, and director of a community center for migratory laborers. She is currently a member of ASCD's Review Council and has been a member of the ASCD Board of Directors.

ASCD 1974 YEARBOOK COMMITTEE MEMBERS

DELMO DELLA-DORA, *Co-chairperson and Co-editor*
Chairman, Department of Teacher Education
California State University, Hayward

JAMES E. HOUSE, *Co-chairperson and Co-editor*
Deputy Director
Education Task Force
Detroit, Michigan

JAMES A. BANKS
Professor of Education
University of Washington, Seattle

CLARE A. BROADHEAD
Principal
Old Mill Elementary School
Mill Valley, California

DAN W. DODSON
Professor of Sociology
Southwestern University
Georgetown, Texas

M. LUCIA JAMES
Professor of Library Science Education
University of Maryland, College Park

ELIZABETH S. RANDOLPH, Administrative Assistant for School Operations, Charlotte–Mecklenburg Schools, Charlotte, North Carolina

JEFF WEST, District Superintendent, North Central District, Miami Springs, Florida

BOARD MEMBERS ELECTED AT LARGE

Mitsuo Adachi, University of Hawaii, Honolulu (1974)

Louise M. Berman, University of Maryland, College Park (1974)

Leslee J. Bishop, University of Georgia, Athens, (1976)

Julianna Boudreaux, New Orleans Public Schools, Louisiana (1977)

John E. Codwell, Houston Public Schools, Texas (1975)

Joseph W. Crenshaw, State Department of Education, Tallahassee, Florida (1977)

Grace S. Epps, Robeson County Schools, Lumberton, North Carolina (1975)

Marie Fielder, University of California, Berkeley (1974)

Richard L. Foster, Berkeley Unified School District, California (1974)

Robert S. Fox, ERIC Clearinghouse for Social Studies Education, Boulder, Colorado (1975)

C. Glen Hass, University of Florida, Gainesville (1976)

Milton Kimpson, Greater Columbia Chamber of Commerce, Columbia, South Carolina (1977)

Wilma S. Longstreet, University of Michigan, Flint (1975)

James B. Macdonald, University of North Carolina, Greensboro (1974)

Barbara T. Mason, Queens College, City University of New York, Flushing (1976)

John E. McGill, University of Illinois, Urbana (1975)

Raquel H. Montenegro, California State College, Los Angeles (1977)

James A. Phillips, Jr., Kent State University, Kent, Ohio (1977)

Vincent R. Rogers, University of Connecticut, Storrs (1976)

Bette Treadwell, New York, New York (1976)

UNIT REPRESENTATIVES TO THE BOARD

(Unit Presidents are listed first; others follow in alphabetical order.)

Alabama: Robert F. Bumpus, Decatur City Schools, Decatur; Mildred Ellisor, Auburn University, Auburn; Grace Rockarts, University of Alabama, University.

Arizona: Phyllis McMennamy, Cartwright School District, Phoenix; James J. Jelinek, Arizona State University, Tempe; Dorothy G. Talbert, Tucson.

Arkansas: Herbert H. Lawrence, KETS-TV, Conway; Calvin G. Patterson, Fort Smith Public Schools, Fort Smith.

California: Jon Slezak, Donlon School, Pleasanton; Lewie Burnett, California State University, Hayward; Arthur L. Costa, Sacramento State University, Sacramento; A. Renee LeRoy, Pasadena Unified School District, Pasadena.

Colorado: Robert C. McKean, University of Colorado, Boulder; William Liddle, Colorado Springs Public Schools, Colorado Springs; Doris Molbert, University of Denver, Denver.

Delaware: Catherine Y. Bonney, Newark Public Schools, Newark; Melville F. Warren, Capital School District, Dover.

District of Columbia: Inez Wood, Clark Elementary School; Bessie D. Etheridge, Spingarn Instructional Unit; Lorraine H. Whitlock, Spingarn Instructional Unit.

Florida: Joseph Bondi, Jr., University of South Florida, Tampa; Aquilina C. Howell, Leon County Public Schools, Tallahassee; Harry F. McComb, Broward County Schools, Ft. Lauderdale; Patrick F. Mooney, North Miami; Evelyn W. Sharp, Bethune-Cookman College, Daytona Beach.

Georgia: Tom Sills, West Georgia College, Carrollton; Harold T. Johnson, Georgia Southwestern College, Americus; John H. Lounsbury, Georgia State College for Women, Milledgeville; Susie W. Wheeler, Bartow County Schools, Cartersville.

Hawaii: Leon H. Burton, University of Hawaii, Honolulu; James R. Brough, The Kamehameha Schools, Honolulu; Sigfried Ramler, Punahou School, Honolulu.

Idaho: David A. Carroll, Boise; Gerald Wallace, Boise State College, Boise.

Illinois: Donald R. Frost, Leyden High School, Northlake; Marlin Baxter, Moline Public Schools, Moline; Margaret L. Carroll, Northern Illinois University, DeKalb; Reuben M. Conrad, Township High School District #214, Mt. Prospect; Earl Dieken, Glen Ellyn School District #41, Glen Ellyn; Raymond Hendee, Park Ridge Elementary Schools, Park Ridge; Mildred Hindman, Collinsville.

Indiana: Donna Delph, Purdue University, Calumet Campus, Hammond; J. Earl Hefner, Portage Public Schools, Portage; Charles E. Kline, Purdue University, West Lafayette; Sister S. Elaine Kohn, State Department of Public Instruction, Salem.

Iowa: Claude R. Snell, West Des Moines Community School District, West Des Moines; Horace S. Hoover, Community School District, Dubuque; Fay Layne, Webster City.

Kansas: Nelson A. Bryant, Jr., Newton Public Schools, Newton; Eunice Bradley, Manhattan U.S.D. #383, Manhattan; Walter L. Davies, Kansas City Public Schools, Kansas City.

Kentucky: Billie Jean Cawood, Harlan County Schools, Harlan; J. R. Ogletree, University of Kentucky, Lexington; Pat W. Wear, Berea College, Berea.

Louisiana: Darryl W. Boudreaux, St. Mary Parish Schools, Morgan City; Edwin H. Friedrich, Orleans Parish School Board, New Orleans; Katye Lee Posey, Caddo Parish Schools, Shreveport; Emelie M. Willkomm, Orleans Parish School Board, New Orleans.

Maryland: Mary R. Hovet, Howard County Board of Education, Clarksville; L. Morris McClure, University of Maryland, College Park; Elizabeth McMahon, Board of Education of Prince Georges County, Upper Marlboro; Richard F. Neville, University of Maryland, College Park.

Massachusetts: Arthur F. Baker, Bridgewater State College, Bridgewater; Gilbert W. Berry, Maria Hastings School, Lexington; Gilbert F. Bulley, Lynnfield; C. Louis Cedrone, Westwood Public Schools, Westwood; Paul V. Congdon, Springfield College, Springfield.

Michigan: William B. Cansfield, Mt. Clemens Community Schools, Mt. Clemens; Morrel J. Clute, Wayne State University, Detroit; Ruby King, Michigan Education Association, East Lansing; Stuart C. Rankin, Detroit Public Schools, Detroit; Virginia Sorenson, Western Michigan University, Kalamazoo.

Minnesota: Stanley Gilbertson, Bloomington; Floyd E. Keller, State Department of Education, St. Paul; Richard D. Kimpston, University of Minnesota, Minneapolis.

Mississippi: Linfield Miller, Yazoo City Public Schools, Yazoo City; R. B. Layton, Jackson Public Schools, Jackson.

Missouri: Doris Stumpe, Ferguson-Florissant Reorganized School District, Ferguson; Richard King, State Department of Education, Jefferson City; Patricia Rocklage, Normandy School District, St. Louis; Louise Young, Public Schools, Kansas City.

Montana: Charles Frank, Billings Public Schools, Billings; Lloyd B. Ellingsen, Billings.

Nebraska: Ron Brandt, Lincoln Public Schools, Lincoln; Gerald Bryant, Grand Island Public Schools, Grand Island; Dale D. Rathe, Lincoln Public Schools, Lincoln.

Nevada: Robert Dunsheath, Clark County Public Schools, Las Vegas; William K. Moore, Las Vegas.

New England: Lyman C. Hunt, Jr., University of Vermont, Burlington; Edward G. Hunt, Warwick School Department, Warwick, Rhode Island; Leora E. Richardson, East Brewster, Massachusetts.

New Jersey: Thomas Lane, Buckshutem Road School, Bridgeton; Kathryn M. Cooper, Public Schools Ridgewood; Mary Jane Diehl, Monmouth College, Witong Branch; Alma Flagg, Public Schools, Newark; Donald J. Gudaitis, Ringwood; Gabriel A. Massaro, Huntington.

New Mexico: Everett Miller, Chelwood Elementary School, Albuquerque; Patricia Christman, Sandia High School, Albuquerque; Royce B. Martin, East Area Career Education, Albuquerque.

New York: Conrad Toepfer, Jr., State University of New York, Buffalo; Dianne Gess, Hillcrest School, Suffern; Peter Incalcaterra, Bailey Junior High School, Kingston; Helen F. Rice, Rochester; Thomas A. Schottman, Lincoln School, Scotia; Robert E. Sudlow, Spencerport; Walter R. Suess, Wantagh Public Schools, Wantagh; Gordon E. VanHooft, State Education Department, Albany.

North Carolina: Betty L. Bowman, Marvin B. Smith Elementary School, Burlington; Jack Blackburn, University of North Carolina, Chapel Hill; Robert C. Hanes, Chapel Hill–Carrboro City Schools, Chapel Hill.

Ohio: James A. Phillips, Jr., Kent State University, Kent; Robert J. Alfonso, Kent State University, Kent; Gary H. Deutschlander, Berea High School, Berea; Alice W. Holt, Wood County Schools, Bowling Green; Hugh S. Morrison, Miami University, Oxford; Maxwell Werner, Lockland Board of Education, Lockland.

Oklahoma: Helen R. Carter, Oklahoma City University, Oklahoma City; Gene D. Shepherd, University of Oklahoma, Norman.

Oregon: Margaret L. Hiatt, Oregon College of Education, Monmouth; Harry Boyd, Ontario Public Schools, Ontario; William B. Brewster, Central Point Public Schools, Central Point; Charles R. Gengler, Oregon College of Education, Monmouth.

Pennsylvania: Hughes Brininger, Millcreek School District, Erie; Kenneth R. Chuska, Peters Township School District, McMurray; Fred Haas, Public Schools, Lester; Margaret McFeaters, Slippery Rock State College, Slippery Rock; Henry W. Ray, Bucks County Schools, Warminster; Claude P. Swartzbaugh, Jr., Derry Township School District, Hershey.

Puerto Rico: Gladys Davila de Fuente, University of Puerto Rico, Rio Piedras; Ilia Del Toro, University of Puerto Rico, Rio Piedras.

South Carolina: Ceicle I. Heizer, School District of Greenville County, Greenville; Ben Carson, School District of Greenville County, Greenville; Fred Splittgerber, University of South Carolina, Columbia.

South Dakota: Orville J. Pederson, Mitchell Public Schools, Mitchell; Signie A. Johnson, Sioux Falls Public Schools, Sioux Falls.

Tennessee: Mattie R. Crossley, Memphis City Schools, Memphis; Jerry C. McGee, Middle Tennessee State University, Murfreesboro; Perle C. McNabb, Newport.

Texas: James L. Williamson, Pan American University, Edinburg; Dorothy Davidson, Texas Education Agency, Austin; Donald McDonald, Texas Technological College, Lubbock; Dwane Russell, Stephen F. Austin State College, Nacogdoches.

Utah: Jean Pugmire, Utah State University, Logan; Nellie T. Higbee, Murray Public Schools, Murray.

Virginia: Floyd L. Gravitt, Arlington Public Schools, Arlington; Larry Bowen, University of Virginia, Charlottesville; William J. Hopkins, Sussex County Schools, Sussex; Gennette Nygard, Arlington County Public Schools, Arlington.

Washington: William Gaskell, Central Washington State College, Ellensburg; Donald Hair, State Office of Public Instruction, Olympia; Clifton Hussey, Inter School District 101, Spokane.

West Virginia: Wilhelmina Ashworth, Fayette County Schools, Fayetteville; Lucille Heflebower, Jefferson County Schools, Charles Town; Betty Livengood, Mineral County Schools, Keyser.

Wisconsin: Robert D. Krey, University of Wisconsin, Superior; Harold Anderson, Individualized Instruction Project, Madison; James E. Claude, Black River Falls Public Schools, Black River Falls; William Ernst, State Department of Public Instruction, Madison.

Wyoming: Bruce Pryde, Sheridan; Laurence A. Walker, University of Wyoming, Laramie.

ASCD REVIEW COUNCIL, 1973-74

ASCD HEADQUARTERS STAFF
as of November 1, 1973

Executive Secretary: Gordon Cawelti
Associate Secretary; Editor, ASCD Publications: Robert R. Leeper
Associate Secretary: Clark Dobson
Business Manager: John H. Bralove
Administrative Assistant: Virginia O. Berthy

Staff Assistants:

Elsa Angell
Sarah Arlington
Elizabeth A. Brooks
Martha M. Broomhall
Barbara Collins
Teola T. Jones
Judith B. Merriman
Carvangeline B. Miller
Frances Mindel

Nancy Olson
Mary Albert O'Neill
Julita C. Pearce
Lana Pipes
Alice H. Powell
Carolyn M. Shell
Barbara J. Sims
Enid Wilsker